JAMESTOWN LITERATURE PROGRAM
Growth in Comprehension & Appreciation

# Reading & Understanding
# *Plays*

## LEVEL I

## About the Cover and the Artist

*The design on the cover of this book is a quilt called* High Tech Tucks V,
*created by quilt artist Caryl Bryer Fallert of Oswego, Illinois.
In addition to quilts, Caryl makes "wearable art"—clothing that is pieced together as
quilts are. Her work is included in many private collections as well as in the
collections of The Museum of American Quilts in Paducah, Kentucky, and
The National Air and Space Museum in Washington, D.C.*

## Books in the Program

| | | | |
|---|---|---|---|
| Short Stories, Level I | *Cat. No. 861* | Short Stories, Level II | *Cat. No. 881* |
| Hardcover Edition | *Cat. No. 861H* | Hardcover Edition | *Cat. No. 881H* |
| Teacher's Guide | *Cat. No. 871* | Teacher's Guide | *Cat. No. 891* |
| | | | |
| Nonfiction, Level I | *Cat. No. 862* | Nonfiction, Level II | *Cat. No. 882* |
| Hardcover Edition | *Cat. No. 862H* | Hardcover Edition | *Cat. No. 882H* |
| Teacher's Guide | *Cat. No. 872* | Teacher's Guide | *Cat. No. 892* |
| | | | |
| Plays, Level I | *Cat. No. 863* | Plays, Level II | *Cat. No. 883* |
| Hardcover Edition | *Cat. No. 863H* | Hardcover Edition | *Cat. No. 883H* |
| Teacher's Guide | *Cat. No. 873* | Teacher's Guide | *Cat. No. 893* |
| | | | |
| Poems, Level I | *Cat. No. 864* | Poems, Level II | *Cat. No. 884* |
| Hardcover Edition | *Cat. No. 864H* | Hardcover Edition | *Cat. No. 884H* |
| Teacher's Guide | *Cat. No. 874* | Teacher's Guide | *Cat. No. 894* |

JAMESTOWN LITERATURE PROGRAM
Growth in Comprehension & Appreciation

# Reading & Understanding
# Plays

## LEVEL I

Jamestown Publishers
Providence, Rhode Island

# JAMESTOWN LITERATURE PROGRAM
## Growth in Comprehension & Appreciation

### *Reading & Understanding Plays*
#### LEVEL I

Catalog No. 863
Catalog No. 863H, Hardcover Edition

Developed by
Jamestown Editorial Group
and
Helena Frost Associates, Gaynor Ellis, Editor

Cover and Text Design: Deborah Hulsey Christie
Photo Research: Helena Frost Associates

Illustrations:
Chapter 5, T. Sperling
Chapter 6, R. Bishop

Photographs:
Chapters 1, 2, 3, 9, MOMA/Film Stills Archive
Chapters 4, 7, 8, The New York Public Library
Chapter 10, Culver Pictures, Inc.

Printed in the United States   HA

89  90  91  92  93  94  95  96  9 8 7 6 5 4 3 2 1

ISBN 0-89061-488-1
ISBN 0-89061-691-4, Hardcover Edition

# Acknowledgments

Acknowledgment is gratefully made to the following individuals and publishers for permission to reprint the plays in this book.

*The Devil and Daniel Webster* by Stephen Vincent Benét. Copyright © 1938, 1939 by Stephen Vincent Benét. Copyrights © renewed 1966 by Thomas C. Benét, Rachel Benét Lewis, Stephanie Benét Mahin. *The Devil and Daniel Webster* is reprinted by permission of the copyright owners and the Dramatists Play Service, Inc. The use of the play in present form must be confined to study and reference. Attention in particular is called to the fact that this play, being duly copyrighted, may not be publicly read or performed or otherwise used without permission of the author's representative. All inquiries should be addressed to the Dramatists Play Service, Inc., 440 Park Avenue South, New York, NY 10016.

*The Ugly Duckling* by A. A. Milne. Copyright © 1941 by A. A. Milne. Reprinted by permission of Curtis Brown, Ltd., London.

*The Master Thief* by Paul Sills. Adapted by Paul Sills from *Grimms' Fairy Tales*. Reprinted by permission of Samuel French, Inc.

*A Marriage Proposal* by Anton Chekhov. Copyright © 1967 by Joachim Neugroschel, translator. Reprinted by permission of the translator.

Excerpt from the radio broadcast of *War of the Worlds* by Howard Koch (based on the novel by H. G. Wells). Copyright © 1940 by Princeton University Press; copyright © 1968 by Howard Koch. Reprinted by permission of International Creative Management.

# Contents

# *To the Student*

When was the last time you saw a play? If you have watched television or gone to the movies, you have seen a play. You may usually think of plays as live theater. Plays, however, can also take many other forms.

Plays are the kind of literature in which actors take the roles of characters, perform the indicated action, and speak the written words. Plays are one of the oldest types of literature. Nearly every culture, from ancient Greece to modern Japan, has produced plays. Early plays were often simple stories. But plays have changed over the centuries into rich, complex forms of expression.

The plays in this book will teach you about some of the many aspects of drama. Unit One introduces you to a full-length play, Shakespeare's *Julius Caesar*. In that unit you will study elements that contribute to the basic framework of every play.

Unit Two contains four short plays. As you will learn, each play contains the basic elements common to a full-length play. But those elements are more compact in short plays. In the lessons you will study aspects of staging, analyze the tensions in a play, and identify some methods of creating humor.

Unit Three introduces you to some twentieth-century innovations in plays. You will read excerpts from a radio play, a television play, and a screenplay. The lessons will examine some of the differences between traditional stage plays and newer kinds of plays.

Information is provided at the beginning of each selection to introduce you to the play and the playwright. The lesson that follows each chapter teaches skills that will help you understand the play. The last feature of the book is a glossary that includes all the literary terms introduced in the book. As you read, you will find several literary terms underlined in each chapter. The first time a term appears in the text, it is underlined and defined. In the glossary, a page reference following each term indicates where the term first appears.

# The Full-Length Play

## Julius Caesar, Act 1
WILLIAM SHAKESPEARE

*Character and Plot*


## Julius Caesar, Acts 2 & 3
WILLIAM SHAKESPEARE

*Dialogue, Monologue, and Soliloquy*


## Julius Caesar, Acts 4 & 5
WILLIAM SHAKESPEARE

*Tragedy and Theme*

*E*arly Greek plays were performed in connection with religious festivals. They were presented in huge outdoor amphitheaters carved into the hillsides. Instead of sitting below the stage and looking up at the actors, the audiences in ancient Greece looked down from great heights onto the actors below.

Greek plays told of heroes, myths, and legends that all the people had heard about from childhood. The same plays were performed from year to year so that both the actors and the audiences were familiar with the plays.

Plays are sometimes called dramas. <u>Drama</u> is the kind of literature designed for the theater. Actors take the roles of the characters, perform the assigned actions, and speak the written words. The term *drama* comes from the Greek word *dran,* meaning "to do" or "to act."

The plays that you will study in this book are meant to be seen in a theater, where actors can play their parts in front of an audience. As written works, however, they are literature: they are meant to be read. The two elements—literature and theater—are closely connected. Even though you are *reading* the plays, keep in mind that they were also intended to be *performed.*

In Unit One you will study *Julius Caesar,* a full-length play consisting of five acts. An <u>act</u> is a major section of a play. Within each act are several scenes, or smaller sections. Because the play is long, you will study it in three chapters of this book. In Chapter 1, you will read Act 1; in Chapter 2 you will read Acts 2 and 3; and in Chapter 3 you will read Acts 4 and 5.

When you start to read the play, you will notice that before the beginning of each scene there is a brief summary in colored type of the action. The summaries are not part of the original text. They have been added to help you understand the major developments in each scene.

*Julius Caesar* was written by William Shakespeare, one of the greatest dramatists and poets in English history. The play is based on the historic event of the murder of the famous Roman statesman and general, Julius Caesar.

| Selection | ***Julius Caesar, Act 1*** |
| --- | --- |
| | WILLIAM SHAKESPEARE |
| **Lesson** | *Character and Plot* |

## About the Selection

The Roman statesman and general Julius Caesar has fascinated historians and biographers ever since his murder in 44 B.C. His name has been given to July, the seventh month of the year. His family name, Caesar, became the title for the Roman emperors. The name was even used in other languages. The word *czar* in Russian and the word *kaiser* in German mean emperor.

Julius Caesar has always been a figure of controversy. Some people have viewed him as the defender of the rights of the common people of Rome. Others have regarded him as an ambitious and power-hungry ruler. One fact is certain: he was a successful and determined leader.

Caesar was both a politician and a general. As a politician, he favored reforms that would help the common people. He wanted to create laws that would help landless farmers and provide housing for the poor. He supported public entertainment and free food for the poor. Among his most important reforms was introducing the Julian calendar, the most accurate calendar of his time.

As a general, Caesar won many victories. At the head of the Roman legions, or army, he conquered most of Gaul (the present-day countries of France and Belgium). He led his legions into Britain and later into Egypt. His successes in battle made many Romans fearful that he would seize power. Therefore in 50 B.C. the Senate, the ruling body of Rome, ordered him to disband his army.

Caesar disobeyed the order. With his soldiers, he crossed the Rubicon River from Gaul into Italy. That action set off a civil war between those who supported Caesar and those who opposed his rise to power. Caesar was eventually victorious, defeating his rival and former friend Pompey.

As Caesar's popularity with the people of Rome grew, his power increased. In 44 B.C. he was made dictator for life. Past Roman leaders had been made dictators for only short periods of time. Now even some of Caesar's friends and followers worried that he would destroy the republic, Rome's traditional form of government. In the Roman Republic the senators and other elected officials directed government affairs. Many of them, as well as other Roman citizens, feared that Caesar would declare himself emperor and rule without consulting the elected officials.

Some members of the Senate believed that the only way to stop Caesar was to assassinate him. They murdered him on March 15, 44 B.C. The events surrounding Caesar's assassination are the subject of William Shakespeare's play *Julius Caesar*.

Like many other writers, Shakespeare was fascinated by Caesar. He wrote *Julius Caesar* in 1598 or 1599. The play was first performed in London in 1599—more than sixteen hundred years after the murder of Caesar. The play is Shakespeare's own interpretation of the plot to murder Julius Caesar.

Shakespeare is considered by many to be one of the greatest poets and playwrights in the English language. He wrote during the Elizabethan period (1558–1603), the years when Queen Elizabeth I ruled England. Despite Shakespeare's fame, scholars know little about his life. They do know that he was born in a small town called Stratford-upon-Avon in 1564. In 1582 he married Anne Hathaway, and they had three children.

Shakespeare eventually moved to London, where he became an actor and a playwright. Between 1590 and 1613, Shakespeare wrote at least thirty-seven plays. Among the most famous are *Hamlet, King Lear,* and *Macbeth,* which are considered to be his masterpieces. Shakespeare's plays have been translated into many languages and performed all over the world.

In 1599 Shakespeare became part owner of the Globe, a theater in

London. He may have performed some lesser roles in his own plays. In 1613 he retired to Stratford, where he died three years later.

Although little is known about Shakespeare, his work has had a great impact on the English language. Shakespeare invented words and expressions for his characters to use. Over the years, many of those words became part of the English language. Shakespeare's many plays are filled with memorable phrases and ideas. For almost four hundred years, people have been quoting Shakespeare's lines. As you read *Julius Caesar*, you will come across several well-known phrases and speeches.

## Lesson Preview

As you learned in the unit introduction, you will study *Julius Caesar* in three chapters. The first chapter includes Act 1, the second chapter, Acts 2 and 3, and the third chapter, Acts 4 and 5.

The lesson that follows Act 1 of *Julius Caesar* focuses on character and plot. Just as in stories, the <u>characters</u> in a play are the people who act and speak. The <u>plot</u> is the sequence of events in a piece of writing. In the first act of a play, the author usually introduces the main characters and gives some background information about the plot.

Reading a play is different from reading a short story or a novel. A play depends on the conversation between people. Some information, however, is given at the beginning of each scene, or when a person enters or leaves the stage. In colored type at the beginning of each scene, brief summaries outline the major developments in that scene. When reading a play, pay attention to which character is speaking to whom. Also pay attention to the information about when characters enter or leave, so that you will know which characters are hearing the conversation.

Because people reveal a lot about themselves through their words, you should always notice what the characters are saying. Shakespeare is a master at developing his characters through their conversations. In addition, he often uses words to make jokes.

The questions that follow will help you to identify the characters and recognize the elements of the plot in Act 1. As you read, think about how you would answer these questions.

**1** In Act 1 which characters appear to be the most important? Which characters seem less important?

**2** What do you learn about the characters from what they say and do or from what others say about them? Which characters do you like? Why?

**3** What is happening in Act 1? Who is plotting against Caesar? Why do they dislike him? Who supports Caesar?

## Vocabulary

Here are some difficult words that appear in the selection that follows. Study the words and their definitions, as well as the sentences that show how the words are used. This will help you get the most from your reading.

**beseech**  beg. *The woman will beseech the hospital to admit her sick child.*

**servile**  cringingly submissive. *The servile waiter annoyed us by constantly refolding our napkins.*

**wont**  accustomed to. *Last Sunday I did not take the nap I am usually wont to have.*

**countenance**  the face as an indication of mood, emotion, or character. *The troubled look on her countenance hinted that she was distressed about something.*

**vexed**  troubled; agitated. *Sue was vexed that George's plane was several hours late.*

**construe**  interpret. *This sentence is so vague that I can construe no meaning from it.*

**fawn**  to court favor by a cringing or flattering manner. *That man will often flatter and fawn on his friends when he wants to borrow money from them.*

**sinews**  muscles. *The sinews of long-distance runners are strong and well developed.*

**entreat** beg. *During a severe storm, the innkeeper would entreat his guests to stay safely by the fire.*

**tempests** violent storms accompanied by high winds. *The sailors described the terrifying tempests that battered their small ship.*

**incenses** angers. *Careless treatment of our natural resources incenses people who care about the environment.*

**portentous** relating to a coming event. *The gray sky is portentous of an approaching rainstorm.*

**offal** garbage; refuse. *Despite sanitation regulations, many residents continue to pollute the reservoir with offal.*

**gait** step or walk. *The horse trotted around the show ring with a smooth and stylish gait.*

# *Julius Caesar*

## ACT 1

WILLIAM SHAKESPEARE

## Characters

Julius Caesar

Octavius Caesar ⎫
Marcus Antonius ⎬ *triumvirs after the death of Julius Caesar*
M. Aemilius Lepidus ⎭

Cicero ⎫
Publius ⎬ *senators*
Popilius Lena ⎭

Marcus Brutus ⎫
Cassius ⎪
Casca ⎪
Trebonius ⎬ *conspirators against Julius Caesar*
Caius Ligarius ⎪
Decius Brutus ⎪
Metellus Cimber ⎪
Cinna ⎭

Flavius and Marullus   *tribunes (elected representatives of the people)*
Artemidorus   *a teacher*
A Soothsayer   *(fortune-teller)*
Cinna   *a poet*
Another Poet

Lucilius  
Titinius  
Messala } *friends to Brutus and Cassius*  
Young Cato  
Volumnius  

Varro  
Clitus  
Claudius  
Strato } *servants or officers to Brutus*  
Lucius  
Dardanius  

Pindarus   *servant to Cassius*  
Commoners of Rome  
Calpurnia   *wife to Caesar*  
Portia   *wife to Brutus*  
The Ghost of Caesar  
Senators, Guards, Servants,  
Attendants, etc.

# ACT 1

## Scene 1

*The play begins with Flavius and Marullus, two Roman officials, scolding a group of workers who are celebrating in the streets. The workers are enjoying a holiday that has been declared in honor of Julius Caesar's victory over his rival, Pompey. Flavius and Marullus were supporters of Pompey, and they tell the people to go home. They then go off to tear down the decorations that were put up in honor of Caesar.*

*Rome. A street. Enter* **Flavius, Marullus** *and certain* **Commoners.**

**Flavius**   Hence! home, you idle creatures, get you home:
Is this a holiday? What, know you not,
Being mechanical,° you ought not walk
Upon a labouring day without the sign
Of your profession? Speak, what trade art thou?                    5

**1st Commoner**   Why, sir, a carpenter.

**Marullus**   Where is thy leather apron, and thy rule?
What dost thou with thy best apparel on?
You, sir, what trade are you?

**2nd Commoner**   Truly, sir, in respect of a fine workman, I am        10
but, as you would say, a cobbler.

**Marullus**   But what trade art thou? Answer me directly.

**2nd Commoner**   A trade, sir, that I hope I may use with a safe
conscience; which is, indeed, sir, a mender of bad soles.°

**Marullus**   What trade, thou knave? thou naughty knave,° what      15
trade?

**2nd Commoner**   Nay, I beseech you, sir, be not out with me:
yet, if you be out, sir, I can mend you.

**Marullus**   What meanest thou by that? Mend me, thou saucy
fellow?                                                              20

---

**3. mechanical:** people who make and repair things.   **14. mender of bad soles:** a pun on the words *soles* and *souls*.   **15. naughty knave:** worthless liar.

**2nd Commoner**   Why, sir, cobble you.

**Flavius**   Thou art a cobbler, art thou?

**2nd Commoner**   Truly, sir, all that I live by is with the awl:° I
meddle with no tradesman's matters, nor women's matters;
but withal I am, indeed, sir, a surgeon to old shoes: when          25
they are in great danger, I recover them. As proper men as
ever trod upon neat's leather have gone upon my handiwork.

**Flavius**   But wherefore° art not in thy shop today?
Why dost thou lead these men about the streets?

**2nd Commoner**   Truly, sir, to wear out their shoes, to get          30
myself into more work. But indeed, sir, we make holiday to
see Caesar, and to rejoice in his triumph.

**Marullus**   Wherefore rejoice? What conquest brings he home?
What tributaries follow him to Rome,
To grace in captive bonds his chariot wheels?          35
You blocks, you stones, you worse than senseless things!
O you hard hearts, you cruel men of Rome,
Knew you not Pompey? Many a time and oft
Have you climb'd up to walls and battlements,
To towers and windows, yea, to chimney-tops,          40
Your infants in your arms, and there have sat
The livelong day, with patient expectation,
To see great Pompey pass the streets of Rome:
And when you saw his chariot but appear,
Have you not made an universal shout,          45
That Tiber° trembled underneath her banks
To hear the replication of your sounds
Made in her concave shores?°
And do you now put on your best attire?
And do you now cull out a holiday?          50
And do you now strew flowers in his way,

---

**23. awl:** a shoemaker's tool.   **28. wherefore:** why.   **46. Tiber:** the Tiber River, in Rome.   **47–48. To
hear . . . shores?:** when your voice echoed along the river's shores?

That comes in triumph over Pompey's blood?
Be gone!
Run to your houses, fall upon your knees,
Pray to the gods to intermit the plague°                               55
That needs must light on this ingratitude.

**Flavius**   Go, go, good countrymen, and for this fault
Assemble all the poor men of your sort;
Draw them to Tiber banks, and weep your tears
Into the channel, till the lowest stream                               60
Do kiss the most exalted shores of all.

*(Exeunt° all the* **Commoners***)*

See where their basest mettle° be not mov'd;
They vanish tongue-tied in their guiltiness.
Go you down that way towards the Capitol;
This way will I. Disrobe the images,                                   65
If you do find them deck'd with ceremonies.°

**Marullus**   May we do so?
You know it is the feast of Lupercal.°

**Flavius**   It is no matter; let no images
Be hung with Caesar's trophies. I'll about                             70
And drive away the vulgar from the streets;
So do you too, where you perceive them thick.
These growing feathers pluck'd from Caesar's wing
Will make him fly an ordinary pitch,
Who else would soar above the view of men                             75
And keep us all in servile fearfulness.

*(Exeunt)*

----

**55. intermit the plague:** not to send a plague as punishment. The Romans believed that the gods caused evils such as disease to punish sin.   **After 61. Exeunt:** Latin meaning "They go out."   **62. basest mettle:** vulgar feelings.   **65–66. Disrobe . . . ceremonies:** remove any decorations from the statues. Ceremonies were the wreaths worn by rulers on special occasions.   **68. Lupercal:** a Roman holiday in honor of Lupercus, the god of shepherds.

# Scene 2

*Caesar enters with companions, followed by a crowd. Among those with him are his wife, Calpurnia, and a friend, Mark Antony. They are all celebrating a religious holiday that includes a foot race in which Antony will take part. A soothsayer, or fortuneteller, warns Caesar that danger threatens him on the ides (the 15th) of March, which is the next day. Caesar ignores the warning.*

*Brutus and Cassius, two Roman senators, have a private conversation. Cassius, jealous of Caesar, complains bitterly about Caesar's growing power. He tries to find out how Brutus feels about it. Casca, another senator, joins them and tells them that Antony has just offered a crown to Caesar, who refused it in front of the applauding crowd. Cassius uses that news to persuade Brutus, who is a friend of Caesar's, that something must be done to stop Caesar.*

*A public place. Enter* **Caesar, Antony, Calpurnia, Portia, Decius, Cicero, Brutus, Cassius, Casca, a Soothsayer,** *and a crowd.*

**Caesar**    Calpurnia!

**Casca**                          Peace, ho! Caesar speaks.

**Caesar**                                              Calpurnia!

**Calpurnia**    Here, my lord.

**Caesar**    Stand you directly in Antonius' way
   When he doth run his course. Antonius!

**Antony**    Caesar, my lord?                                              5

**Caesar**    Forget not, in your speed, Antonius,
   To touch Calpurnia; for our elders say,
   The barren touched in this holy chase,
   Shake off their sterile curse.°

**Antony**                          I shall remember:
   When Caesar says, 'do this,' it is perform'd.          10

**Caesar**    Set on, and leave no ceremony out.

**Soothsayer**    Caesar!

**Caesar**    Ha! Who calls?

**Casca**    Bid every noise be still; peace yet again!

---

**7–9. To touch . . . curse:** Our wise men say that a runner in this religious festival can cure a woman of sterility.

**Caesar**  Who is it in the press that calls on me?            15
    I hear a tongue shriller than all the music
    Cry 'Caesar!' Speak: Caesar is turn'd to hear.
**Soothsayer**  Beware the ides of March.°
**Caesar**                                What man is that?
**Brutus**  A soothsayer bids you beware the ides of March.
**Caesar**  Set him before me; let me see his face.        20
**Cassius**  Fellow, come from the throng; look upon Caesar.
**Caesar**  What say'st thou to me now? Speak once again.
**Soothsayer**  Beware the ides of March.
**Caesar**  He is a dreamer. Let us leave him. Pass.

*(Exeunt all except* **Brutus** *and* **Cassius***)*

**Cassius**  Will you go see the order of the course?      25
**Brutus**  Not I.
**Cassius**          I pray you, do.
**Brutus**  I am not gamesome:° I do lack some part
    Of that quick spirit that is in Antony.
    Let me not hinder, Cassius, your desires;
    I'll leave you.                                    30
**Cassius**  Brutus, I do observe you now of late:
    I have not from your eyes that gentleness
    And show of love as I was wont to have.
    You bear too stubborn and too strange a hand
    Over your friend that loves you.
**Brutus**                          Cassius,      35
    Be not deceiv'd: if I have veil'd my look,
    I turn the trouble of my countenance
    Merely upon myself. Vexed I am
    Of late with passions of some difference,
    Conceptions only proper to myself,           40
    Which give some soil, perhaps, to my behaviours;

---

**18. ides of March:** March 15.   **27. gamesome:** athletic, or fond of sports.

But let not therefore my good friends be griev'd—
Among which number, Cassius, be you one—
Nor construe any further my neglect,
Than that poor Brutus, with himself at war, 45
Forgets the shows of love to other men.

**Cassius** Then, Brutus, I have much mistook your passion;
By means whereof this breast of mine hath buried
Thoughts of great value, worthy cogitations.
Tell me, good Brutus, can you see your face? 50

**Brutus** No, Cassius; for the eye sees not itself
But by reflection, by some other things.

**Cassius** 'Tis just;
And it is very much lamented, Brutus,
That you have no such mirrors as will turn 55
Your hidden worthiness into your eye,
That you might see your shadow. I have heard,
Where many of the best respect in Rome,
Except immortal Caesar, speaking of Brutus,
And groaning underneath this age's yoke,° 60
Have wish'd that noble Brutus had his eyes.

**Brutus** Into what dangers would you lead me, Cassius,
That you would have me seek into myself
For that which is not in me?

**Cassius** Therefore, good Brutus, be prepar'd to hear; 65
And since you know you cannot see yourself
So well as by reflection, I, your glass,°
Will modestly discover to yourself
That of yourself which you yet know not of.
And be not jealous on me, gentle Brutus: 70
Were I a common laugher, or did use
To stale° with ordinary oaths my love

---

**60. And groaning . . . yoke:** suffering under burden of these times.  **67. glass:** mirror.  **72. stale:** spoil;
cheapen.

*Character and Plot*

To every new protester; if you know
That I do fawn on men and hug them hard,
And after scandal them; or if you know 75
That I profess myself in banqueting
To all the rout,° then hold me dangerous.

*(Flourish° and shout)*

**Brutus**   What means this shouting? I do fear the people
Choose Caesar for their king.
**Cassius**                               Ay, do you fear it?
Then must I think you would not have it so. 80
**Brutus**   I would not, Cassius; yet I love him well.
But wherefore do you hold me here so long?
What is it that you would impart to me?
If it be aught toward the general good,
Set honour in one eye, and death i' th' other, 85
And I will look on both indifferently;
For let the gods so speed me as I love
The name of honour more than I fear death.
**Cassius**   I know that virtue to be in you, Brutus,
As well as I do know your outward favour. 90
Well, honour is the subject of my story.
I cannot tell what you and other men
Think of this life; but for my single self,
I had as lief not be° as live to be
In awe of such a thing as I myself. 95
I was born free as Caesar; so were you;
We both have fed as well, and we can both
Endure the winter's cold as well as he:
For once, upon a raw and gusty day,

---

**76–77. That I profess . . . rout:** that I announce my friendship when I have been drinking to any of the common rabble, or low life.   **After 76. Flourish:** trumpet notes to signal the arrival of an important person.   **94. I had as lief not be:** I would just as soon be dead.

The troubled Tiber chafing with her shores,                           100
Caesar said to me, 'Dar'st thou, Cassius, now
Leap in with me into this angry flood,
And swim to yonder point?' Upon the word,
Accoutred° as I was, I plunged in
And bade him follow; so indeed he did.                                105
The torrent roar'd, and we did buffet it
With lusty sinews, throwing it aside
And stemming it with hearts of controversy.
But ere we could arrive the point propos'd,
Caesar cried, 'Help me, Cassius, or I sink.'                          110
I, as Aeneas, our great ancestor,
Did from the flames of Troy upon his shoulder
The old Anchises bear,° so from the waves of Tiber
Did I the tired Caesar. And this man
Is now become a god, and Cassius is                                   115
A wretched creature, and must bend his body
If Caesar carelessly but nod on him.
He had a fever when he was in Spain,
And when the fit was on him, I did mark
How he did shake; 'tis true, this god did shake;                      120
His coward lips did from their colour fly,
And that same eye whose bend doth awe the world
Did lose his lustre; I did hear him groan;
Ay, and that tongue of his, that bade the Romans
Mark him and write his speeches in their books,                       125
Alas, it cried, 'Give me some drink, Titinius,'
As a sick girl. Ye gods, it doth amaze me
A man of such a feeble temper should

---

**104. Accoutred:** dressed.  **111–113. I, as Aeneas . . . bear:** Cassius is comparing himself to Aeneas, the legendary founder of Rome. According to legend, Aeneas carried his father, Anchises, on his shoulders from the burning city of Troy.

So get the start of the majestic world,
And bear the palm alone.°

*(Flourish and shout)*

**Brutus**                              Another general shout?          130
I do believe that these applauses are
For some new honours that are heap'd on Caesar.
**Cassius**   Why, man, he doth bestride the narrow world
Like a Colossus,° and we petty men
Walk under his huge legs, and peep about          135
To find ourselves dishonourable graves.
Men at some time are masters of their fates:
The fault, dear Brutus, is not in our stars,
But in ourselves, that we are underlings.°
Brutus and Caesar: what should be in that 'Caesar'?          140
Why should that name be sounded more than yours?
Write them together, yours is as fair a name;
Sound them, it doth become the mouth as well;
Weigh them, it is as heavy; conjure° with 'em,
'Brutus' will start a spirit as soon as 'Caesar'.          145
Now in the names of all the gods at once,
Upon what meat doth this our Caesar feed,
That he is grown so great? Age, thou art sham'd!
Rome, thou hast lost the breed of noble bloods!
When went there by an age, since the great flood,          150
But it was fam'd with more than with one man?
When could they say, till now, that talk'd of Rome,
That her wide walks encompass'd but one man?

---

**130. bear the palm alone:** become sole ruler of Rome.   **134. Colossus:** a huge, one hundred-foot statue called the Colossus of Rhodes is one of the seven wonders of the world. Cassius compares Caesar to that huge statue.   **138–139. The fault . . . underlings:** It is not fate (our stars), but our own weakness that has made Caesar so powerful. In ancient Rome, many people believed that the stars influenced a person's destiny. Cassius denies that power to the stars and says that men control their own fates.   **144. conjure:** call up spirits.

Now is it Rome indeed, and room enough,
When there is in it but one only man. 155
O, you and I have heard our fathers say,
There was a Brutus once° that would have brook'd
Th' eternal devil to keep his state in Rome
As easily as a king.
**Brutus**   That you do love me, I am nothing jealous; 160
What you would work me to, I have some aim:
How I have thought of this, and of these times,
I shall recount hereafter. For this present,
I would not, so with love I might entreat you,
Be any further mov'd. What you have said 165
I will consider; what you have to say
I will with patience hear, and find a time
Both meet° to hear and answer such high things.
Till then, my noble friend, chew upon this:
Brutus had rather be a villager 170
Than to repute himself° a son of Rome
Under these hard conditions as this time
Is like to lay upon us.
**Cassius**                              I am glad
That my weak words have struck but thus much show
Of fire from Brutus. 175

*(Enter **Caesar** and his train)*

**Brutus**   The games are done and Caesar is returning.
**Cassius**   As they pass by, pluck Casca by the sleeve,
And he will, after his sour fashion, tell you
What hath proceeded worthy note today.
**Brutus**   I will do so. But look you, Cassius, 180
The angry spot doth glow on Caesar's brow,

---

157. **There was a Brutus once:** Cassius is referring to Lucius Junius Brutus, a Roman hero and an ancestor of Marcus Brutus.   **168. meet:** suitable; fitting.   **171. repute himself:** call himself.

And all the rest look like a chidden train:°
Calpurnia's cheek is pale, and Cicero
Looks with such ferret° and such fiery eyes
As we have seen him in the Capitol,                                              185
Being cross'd in conference by some senators.
**Cassius**   Casca will tell us what the matter is.
**Caesar**   Antonius!
**Antony**                    Caesar?
**Caesar**   Let me have men about me that are fat,
Sleek-headed men, and such as sleep a-nights.                           190
Yond Cassius has a lean and hungry look;
He thinks too much: such men are dangerous.
**Antony**   Fear him not, Caesar, he's not dangerous.
He is a noble Roman, and well given.
**Caesar**   Would he were fatter! But I fear him not:                 195
Yet if my name were liable to fear,
I do not know the man I should avoid
So soon as that spare Cassius. He reads much,
He is a great observer, and he looks
Quite through the deeds of men. He loves no plays,             200
As thou dost, Antony; he hears no music.
Seldom he smiles, and smiles in such a sort
As if he mock'd himself, and scorn'd his spirit
That could be mov'd to smile at any thing.
Such men as he be never at heart's ease                                      205
Whiles they behold a greater than themselves,
And therefore are they very dangerous.
I rather tell thee what is to be fear'd
Than what I fear; for always I am Caesar.
Come on my right hand, for this ear is deaf,                             210
And tell me truly what thou think'st of him.

---

**182. chidden train:** group of embarrassed people.   **184. ferret:** bloodshot with anger.

*(Exeunt* **Caesar** *and his train)*

**Casca**   You pull'd me by the cloak. Would you speak with me?

**Brutus**   Ay, Casca. Tell us what hath chanc'd today,
That Caesar looks so sad.

**Casca**   Why, you were with him, were you not?                    215

**Brutus**   I should not then ask Casca what had chanc'd.

**Casca**   Why, there was a crown offer'd him; and, being offer'd
him, he put it by with the back of his hand, thus; and then the
people fell a-shouting.

**Brutus**   What was the second noise for?                    220

**Casca**   Why, for that too.

**Brutus**   They shouted thrice: what was the last cry for?

**Casca**   Why, for that too.

**Brutus**   Was the crown offer'd him thrice?

**Casca**   Ay, marry,° was't, and he put it by thrice, every time           225
gentler than other; and at every putting-by mine honest
neighbours shouted.

**Cassius**   Who offered him the crown?

**Casca**   Why, Antony.

**Brutus**   Tell us the manner of it, gentle Casca.                    230

**Casca**   I can as well be hang'd as tell the manner of it: it was
mere foolery; I did not mark it. I saw Mark Antony offer him
a crown; yet 'twas not a crown neither, 'twas one of these
coronets;° and, as I told you, he put it by once; but for all that,
to my thinking, he would fain° have had it. Then he offered it           235
to him again; then he put it by again; but to my thinking, he
was very loath to lay his fingers off it. And then he offered it
the third time. He put it the third time by; and still as he
refus'd it, the rabblement hooted, and clapp'd their chopt
hands, and threw up their sweaty night-caps, and uttered           240
such a deal of stinking breath because Caesar refus'd the

---

**225. marry:** indeed.   **234. coronets:** wreaths made of leaves.   **235. fain:** willingly.

*Character and Plot*

crown, that it had, almost, choked Caesar; for he swounded,°
and fell down at it. And for mine own part, I durst not laugh,
for fear of opening my lips and receiving the bad air.

**Cassius**   But soft, I pray you; what, did Caesar swound?          245

**Casca**   He fell down in the market-place, and foam'd at
mouth, and was speechless.

**Brutus**   'Tis very like; he hath the falling-sickness.°

**Cassius**   No, Caesar hath it not; but you, and I,
And honest Casca, we have the falling-sickness.          250

**Casca**   I know not what you mean by that, but I am sure Caesar
fell down. If the tag-rag people did not clap him and hiss him,
according as he pleas'd and displeas'd them, as they use to do
the players in the theatre, I am no true man.

**Brutus**   What said he when he came unto himself?          255

**Casca**   Marry, before he fell down, when he perceiv'd the
common herd was glad he refus'd the crown, he pluck'd me
ope his doublet,° and offer'd them his throat to cut. And I had
been a man of any occupation, if I would not have taken him
at a word, I would I might go to hell among the rogues. And so          260
he fell. When he came to himself again, he said, if he had done
or said anything amiss, he desir'd their worships to think it
was his infirmity. Three or four wenches, where I stood,
cried, 'Alas, good soul,' and forgave him with all their hearts;
but there's no heed to be taken of them; if Caesar had stabb'd          265
their mothers, they would have done no less.

**Brutus**   And after that, he came, thus sad, away?

**Casca**   Ay.

**Cassius**   Did Cicero say anything?

**Casca**   Ay, he spoke Greek.          270

**Cassius**   To what effect?

**Casca**   Nay, and I tell you that, I'll ne'er look you i' th' face

---

**242. swounded:** fainted.   **248. the falling-sickness:** epilepsy.   **258. ope his doublet:** loosened his jacket.

again. But those that understood him smil'd at one another, and shook their heads; but for mine own part, it was Greek to me. I could tell you more news too: Marullus and Flavius, for pulling scarfs off Caesar's images, are put to silence.° Fare you well. There was more foolery yet, if I could remember it. 275

**Cassius**  Will you sup with me tonight, Casca?

**Casca**  No, I am promis'd forth.

**Cassius**  Will you dine with me tomorrow? 280

**Casca**  Ay, if I be alive, and your mind hold, and your dinner worth the eating.

**Cassius**  Good. I will expect you.

**Casca**  Do so. Farewell, both.

*(Exit* **Casca***)*

**Brutus**  What a blunt fellow is this grown to be! 285
He was quick mettle° when he went to school.

**Cassius**  So is he now in execution
Of any bold or noble enterprise,
However he puts on this tardy form.
This rudeness is a sauce to his good wit, 290
Which gives men stomach to digest his words
With better appetite.

**Brutus**  And so it is. For this time I will leave you.
Tomorrow, if you please to speak with me,
I will come home to you; or if you will, 295
Come home to me, and I will wait for you.

**Cassius**  I will do so: till then, think of the world.

*(Exit* **Brutus***)*

Well, Brutus, thou art noble; yet I see
Thy honourable mettle may be wrought
From that it is dispos'd: therefore 'tis meet 300

---

276. **put to silence:** removed from office; perhaps put to death.  286. **quick mettle:** smart.

That noble minds keep ever with their likes;
For who so firm that cannot be seduc'd?
Caesar doth bear me hard; but he loves Brutus.
If I were Brutus now, and he were Cassius,
He should not humour me. I will this night,          305
In several hands, in at his windows throw,
As if they came from several citizens,
Writings, all tending to the great opinion
That Rome holds of his name; wherein obscurely
Caesar's ambition shall be glanced at.          310
And after this, let Caesar seat him sure,
For we will shake him, or worse days endure.

*(Exit)*

## Scene 3

*That night a terrible storm shakes Rome. It is, however, not an
ordinary storm. Ghosts and other strange apparitions are seen in
the streets of the city. Casca and Cicero talk of the strange elements
and wonder what they mean. Casca and Cassius then agree to a
plan to kill Caesar. Cinna joins them. In an effort to persuade
Brutus to join in the plot against Caesar, Cassius tells Cinna to
go to Brutus's house to secretly leave letters urging Brutus to take
action against Caesar.*

*A street. Thunder and lightning. Enter **Casca** and **Cicero**.*

**Cicero**   Good even, Casca: brought you Caesar home?
    Why are you breathless? and why stare you so?
**Casca**   Are you not mov'd, when all the sway of earth
    Shakes like a thing unfirm? O Cicero,
    I have seen tempests, when the scolding winds     5
    Have riv'd° the knotty oaks; and I have seen

---

6. riv'd: split.

Th' ambitious ocean swell and rage and foam,
To be exalted with the threat'ning clouds:
But never till tonight, never till now,
Did I go through a tempest dropping fire.                    10
Either there is a civil strife in heaven,
Or else the world, too saucy with the gods,
Incenses them to send destruction.
**Cicero**   Why, saw you any thing more wonderful?
**Casca**   A common slave, you know him well by sight,        15
Held up his left hand, which did flame and burn
Like twenty torches join'd; and yet his hand,
Not sensible of fire, remain'd unscorch'd.
Besides (I ha' not since put up my sword)
Against the Capitol I met a lion,                            20
Who glaz'd upon me, and went surly by,
Without annoying me. And there were drawn
Upon a heap a hundred ghastly women,
Transformed with their fear, who swore they saw
Men, all in fire, walk up and down the streets.             25
And yesterday the bird of night did sit,
Even at noonday, upon the market place,
Hooting and shrieking. When these prodigies°
Do so conjointly meet, let not men say,
'These are their reasons, they are natural';                30
For I believe, they are portentous things
Unto the climate that they point upon.
**Cicero**   Indeed, it is a strange-disposed° time:
But men may construe things, after their fashion,
Clean from the purpose of the things themselves.°           35
Comes Caesar to the Capitol tomorrow?
**Casca**   He doth; for he did bid Antonius

---

**28. prodigies:** omens, or strange events.   **33. strange-disposed:** odd.   **34–35. But men . . . themselves:**
People may imagine meanings that are not really there.

Send word to you he would be there tomorrow.

**Cicero**   Good night then, Casca: this disturbed sky
Is not to walk in.

**Casca**                               Farewell, Cicero.                               40

*(Exit **Cicero**)*

*(Enter **Cassius**)*

**Cassius**   Who's there?

**Casca**                       A Roman.

**Cassius**                                 Casca, by your voice.

**Casca**   Your ear is good. Cassius, what night is this!

**Cassius**   A very pleasing night to honest men.

**Casca**   Who ever knew the heavens menace so?

**Cassius**   Those that have known the earth so full of faults.   45
For my part, I have walk'd about the streets,
Submitting me unto the perilous night,
And, thus unbraced,° Casca, as you see,
Have bar'd my bosom to the thunder-stone;
And when the cross blue lightning seem'd to open   50
The breast of heaven, I did present myself
Even in the aim and very flash of it.

**Casca**   But wherefore did you so much tempt the heavens?
It is the part of men to fear and tremble
When the most mighty gods by tokens send   55
Such dreadful heralds to astonish us.

**Cassius**   You are dull, Casca, and those sparks of life
That should be in a Roman you do want,
Or else you use not. You look pale, and gaze,
And put on fear, and cast yourself in wonder,   60
To see the strange impatience of the heavens;
But if you would consider the true cause

---

**48. thus unbraced:** with my coat opened.

Why all these fires, why all these gliding ghosts,
Why birds and beasts from quality and kind,
Why old men, fools, and children calculate,                    65
Why all these things change from their ordinance,
Their natures, and pre-formed faculties,
To monstrous quality, why, you shall find
That heaven hath infus'd° them with these spirits
To make them instruments of fear and warning          70
Unto some monstrous state.
Now could I, Casca, name to thee a man
Most like this dreadful night,
That thunders, lightens, opens graves, and roars
As doth the lion in the Capitol;                               75
A man no mightier than thyself, or me,
In personal action, yet prodigious grown,
And fearful, as these strange eruptions° are.

**Casca**    'Tis Caesar that you mean, is it not, Cassius?

**Cassius**   Let it be who it is: for Romans now          80
Have thews° and limbs like to their ancestors;
But, woe the while! our fathers' minds are dead,
And we are govern'd with our mothers' spirits;
Our yoke and sufferance show us womanish.

**Casca**   Indeed, they say the senators tomorrow       85
Mean to establish Caesar as a king;
And he shall wear his crown by sea and land,
In every place, save here in Italy.

**Cassius**   I know where I will wear this dagger then;
Cassius from bondage will deliver Cassius:°               90
Therein, ye gods, you make the weak most strong;
Therein, ye gods, you tyrants do defeat.
Nor stony tower, nor walls of beaten brass,

---

**69. infus'd:** filled.    **78. strange eruptions:** odd happenings.    **81. thews:** muscles.    **89–90. I know . . .**
**Cassius:** I will use this knife to free myself by committing suicide.

Nor airless dungeon, nor strong links of iron,
Can be retentive to° the strength of spirit;                              95
But life, being weary of these worldly bars
Never lacks power to dismiss itself.
If I know this, know all the world besides,
That part of tyranny that I do bear
I can shake off at pleasure.

**Casca**                   So can I:                                     100
So every bondman° in his own hand bears
The power to cancel his captivity.

**Cassius**   And why should Caesar be a tyrant then?
Poor man! I know he would not be a wolf,
But that he sees the Romans are but sheep;                              105
He were no lion, were not Romans hinds.°
Those that with haste will make a mighty fire
Begin it with weak straws. What trash is Rome,
What rubbish, and what offal, when it serves
For the base matter to illuminate                                        110
So vile a thing as Caesar! But, O grief,
Where hadst thou led me? I, perhaps, speak this
Before a willing bondman; then I know
My answer must be made. But I am arm'd,
And dangers are to me indifferent.                                       115

**Casca**   You speak to Casca, and to such a man
That is no fleering tell-tale.° Hold,° my hand:
Be factious for redress of all these griefs,°
And I will set this foot of mine as far
As who goes furthest.

**Cassius**                   There's a bargain made.                    120
Now know you, Casca, I have mov'd already
Some certain of the noblest-minded Romans

---

95. **be retentive to:** hold back.   101. **bondman:** slave.   106. **hinds:** female deer.   117. **fleering tell-tale:** smirking tattle-tale.   **Hold:** here is.   118. **Be factious . . . griefs:** form a group to avenge these wrongs.

To undergo with me an enterprise
Of honourable-dangerous consequence;
And I do know, by this they stay for me                                     125
In Pompey's porch: for now, this fearful night,
There is no stir or walking in the streets;
And the complexion of the element
In favour's like the work we have in hand,
Most bloody, fiery, and most terrible.                                      130

*(Enter* **Cinna***)*

**Casca**   Stand close awhile, for here comes one in haste.

**Cassius**   'Tis Cinna. I do know him by his gait.

He is a friend. Cinna, where haste you so?

**Cinna**   To find out you. Who's that? Metellus Cimber?

**Cassius**   No, it is Casca, one incorporate                              135

To our attempts. Am I not stay'd for, Cinna?

**Cinna**   I am glad on 't. What a fearful night is this!

There's two or three of us have seen strange sights.

**Cassius**   Am I not stay'd for? Tell me.

**Cinna**                                            Yes, you are.

O Cassius, if you could                                                     140

But win the noble Brutus to our party —

**Cassius**   Be you content. Good Cinna, take this paper,

And look you lay it in the praetor's chair,°

Where Brutus may but find it; and throw this

In at his window; set this up with wax                                      145

Upon old Brutus's statue: all this done,

Repair to Pompey's porch,° where you shall find us.

Is Decius Brutus and Trebonius there?

**Cinna**   All but Metellus Cimber, and he's gone

To seek you at your house. Well, I will hie,                                150

---

143. **praetor's chair:** a judge's chair. Brutus was a praetor (judge) of Rome.   147. **Repair to Pompey's porch:** go to the entrance of Pompey's theatre, where the Senate meets.

*Character and Plot*

And so bestow these papers as you bade me.

**Cassius**   That done, repair to Pompey's theatre.

*(Exit* **Cinna***)*

Come, Casca, you and I will yet ere day
See Brutus at his house: three parts of him
Is ours already, and the man entire                                         155
Upon the next encounter yields him ours.

**Casca**   O, he sits high in all the people's hearts:
And that which would appear offence in us
His countenance, like richest alchemy,°
Will change to virtue and to worthiness.                                    160

**Cassius**   Him and his worth and our great need of him
You have right well conceited.° Let us go,
For it is after midnight; and ere day
We will awake him and be sure of him.

*(Exeunt)*

---

**159. alchemy:** in Shakespeare's time, alchemy was a science devoted to finding ways of making various worthless metals into gold. Casca says that Brutus has such high respect that any project he supports becomes worthy and virtuous.   **162. conceited:** judged.

# Reviewing the Selection

Answer each of the following questions without looking back at the play.

*Recalling Facts*

1. While Caesar attends ceremonial games and races, he
   - ☐ a. is crowned king of Rome.
   - → ☐ b. refuses to accept a crown that is offered to him.
   - ☐ c. offers a crown to Antony.
   - ☐ d. announces that he is leaving Rome.

*Understanding Main Ideas*

2. Which of the following statements best sums up the point Cassius makes in his argument with Brutus?
   - ☐ a. Caesar is no better than Cassius or Brutus, so they must prevent him from becoming a dictator.
   - ☐ b. Cassius should become king of Rome instead of Caesar.
   - ☐ c. Fate has determined that Caesar will rule Rome, and they can do nothing about it.
   - ☐ d. Caesar must be stopped before the ides of March.

*Placing Events in Order*

3. The soothsayer warns Caesar to "Beware the ides of March"
   - ☐ a. before the tribunes Flavius and Marullus tell about Pompey's defeat.
   - ☐ b. during a dangerous storm.
   - ☐ c. after Caesar has turned down the crown.
   - ⌐ ☐ d. as Caesar is going to the ceremonial games.

4. In Act 1 Shakespeare gives hints or warnings of dangers that lie ahead. Which of the following is an example of such a warning?
   - ☐ a. the commoners decorating the statues
   - ☐ b. Caesar's victory over Pompey
   - ☒ ☐ c. the terrible thunderstorm that strikes Rome
   - ☐ d. Mark Antony's offering Caesar the crown

5. "He put it the third time by; and still as he refus'd it, the <u>rabblement</u> hooted, and clapp'd their chopt hands . . ." In this context *rabblement* means
   - ☐ a. runners.
   - ☐ b. enemies.
   - ☐ c. crowd.
   - ☐ d. soldiers.

## Interpreting the Selection

Answer each of the following questions. You may look back at the play if necessary.

6. When Caesar says that "Yond Cassius has a lean and hungry look," and that he prefers to be surrounded by men who are fat and who sleep well, he means that
   - ☐ a. Cassius is poor and therefore he is dangerous.
   - ☐ b. Cassius always seems tired and confused.
   - ☐ c. he feels threatened by Cassius.
   - ☐ d. only fat men sleep well at night.

7. Caesar's behavior in refusing the crown three times shows that he
   - ☐ a. is afraid to accept it.
   - ☐ b. does not want to rule Rome.
   - ☐ c. wants the people to think he is humble.
   - ☐ d. wants Cassius to be king.

8. In Act 1 Shakespeare uses Casca to
   - ☐ a. let you know what has occurred at the ceremony.
   - ☐ b. warn Caesar about the thunderstorm.
   - ☐ c. show you how powerful Caesar's enemies are.
   - ☐ d. inform Caesar of the plans of Cassius and Brutus.

9. What does Brutus mean in Scene 2, line 45, when he says he is at war with himself?
   - ☐ a. He has had a fight with his wife and is angry at both himself and her.
   - ☐ b. He has joined the army but does not want to fight Pompey.
   - ☐ c. He is angry with Cassius and is afraid of what Cassius might do to him.
   - ☐ d. He is torn between his love for Caesar and his fear that Caesar will become a dictator.

10. In Act 1 you can conclude that
   - ☐ a. Antony is plotting against Caesar.
   - ☐ b. Antony is a loyal friend to Caesar.
   - ☐ c. Antony does not like Calpurnia.
   - ☐ d. Cassius is a loyal friend to Caesar.

# *Character and Plot*

The actions of a play, like the actions in a short story or a novel, are carried out by the characters. As you will discover in *Julius Caesar* and the other plays in this book, the characters can be major or minor, depending on their importance to the action.

Characters carry out the plot, or sequence of events, of a play. A plot can be simple and straightforward, or it can have many twists and turns. The actions of the characters and the results of those actions are what moves the plot along.

In a play characters and events are revealed differently than they are in a novel or a short story. The playwright cannot explain directly to the reader or to the audience who each character is or what is happening. A play is made up of the words the characters speak to each other. So the characters and the plot must be revealed through the <u>dialogue</u>—the actual conversation between the characters. In *Julius Caesar*, as in other plays, the dialogue does two important things: It shows you the personalities of the characters and it moves the plot along smoothly. Part of Shakespeare's genius is his ability to create effective dialogue.

# Major and Minor Characters

Some plays have only a few characters. In such plays each character has an important part in the drama. A playwright develops the major, or most important, characters as fully as possible.

Other plays, including *Julius Caesar*, have a large cast of characters. In such plays you will find both major and minor, or less important, characters. Although you usually do not learn much about the minor characters, they do contribute to the play. Minor characters often reveal background information. They can also help you to understand the actions of the major characters.

At the beginning of most plays, you will find a list of characters. The list includes the characters' names and often adds some information about them. The list may put the names in the order in which the characters appear in the play, or it may put the names of the most important characters first.

   1. *Read the list of characters at the beginning of* Julius Caesar. *How many characters appear in the play? Make a list of the characters you have met in Act 1. Circle the names of those that you think are major characters. Explain how you can tell which characters are important.*

# Characterization

Playwrights reveal the personalities of their characters in a number of ways. Characterization refers to the methods by which a writer develops a character's personality. Characterization is sometimes called character development. In *Julius Caesar* Shakespeare uses four common methods of characterization: (1) He gives physical descriptions, (2) he shows the character's actions, (3) he reveals the character's thoughts and words, and (4) he shows how one character feels about another.

   In Act 1 of *Julius Caesar*, Shakespeare begins to develop several major characters, including Caesar, Cassius, and Brutus. In later acts he continues to develop those characters, giving you a more complete picture of them.

**Physical Description.** In a play physical description is usually limited.

Playwrights do not take a lot of time to explain what their characters look like. Instead, since they expect their plays to be performed, they rely on the actors and the costumes to give that information to the audience.

In *Julius Caesar* Shakespeare gives little physical description, although you do get some information about how the characters look. Early in Act 1, Scene 1, Marullus asks the first commoner: "Where is thy leather apron, and thy rule? / What dost thou with thy best apparel on?" Through that dialogue, you get an idea of how the first commoner is dressed.

Sometimes you learn how a person looks from what another character says. In Act 1, Scene 2 (lines 180 to 186), Brutus describes Caesar and the people with him:

> But look you, Cassius,
> The angry spot doth glow on Caesar's brow,
> And all the rest look like a chidden train:

*2. In that same speech, how does Brutus describe the appearances of Calpurnia and Cicero? What do you learn is the reason for Caesar's anger?*

*3. Read Caesar's dialogue with Antony, Act 1, Scene 2, starting at line 189. What does Caesar say about Cassius's physical appearance? How does Shakespeare connect Cassius's physical attributes to Cassius's character?*

**A Character's Actions.** A person's behavior in any difficult situation reveals a lot about his or her character. In *Julius Caesar* the characters are all under stress. Caesar's enemies are plotting against him. They are not confident of one another, but they are determined to stop Caesar from gaining more power. Caesar knows he is surrounded by danger, but he does not want to look like a coward. Brutus is uncertain about what to do. He is torn between respect for Caesar and fear of Caesar's growing power.

Unlike Brutus, Cassius is sure of his goal. He is determined to kill Caesar. Cassius wants to persuade Brutus to join the conspirators who are plotting against Caesar. In Act 1, Scene 2 (lines 99 to 130), he describes how Caesar behaved on two different occasions in the past. He hopes his stories will have an effect on Brutus.

*4. Reread those lines. Why is Cassius telling Brutus those stories about Caesar?*

*5. Describe the actions of one character in Act 1 and explain what you think those actions reveal about that character.*

**A Character's Thoughts and Words.** In a play the characters are revealed mainly by the words they speak. In Act 1, Scene 2, Caesar asks his wife, Calpurnia, to step into Antony's path during the race. Caesar then reminds Antony to touch Calpurnia as he runs by her. In that scene Caesar quotes "our elders." Like them, he seems to believe that Calpurnia's barrenness—her inability to have a child—might be cured by Antony's touch as he runs a holy race.

Soon after that dialogue about the race, the soothsayer warns Caesar to "Beware the ides of March." Caesar rejects the warning, saying, "He is a dreamer. Let us leave him."

*6. What do Caesar's words in those two incidents tell you about his character?*

In Act 1 Shakespeare focuses a great deal of attention on two major characters, Cassius and Brutus. Each man reveals much about himself through his own words. Cassius is a close observer of people. He is clever with words and a manipulator of people. He is bitterly opposed to Caesar's rise to power.

*7. Find at least three passages in which Cassius reveals his character through his words. Explain what you think each passage shows about him.*

Brutus's personality and outlook are very different from Cassius's. Brutus does not hate Caesar, as Cassius does. Brutus wants to collect information and think carefully before he acts.

*8. Find two passages in which Brutus's own words reveal something about his character. Explain what you think his words reveal.*

**How One Character Feels About Another.** Shakespeare also uses characterization to show how one character feels about another character. In Act 1 you see Caesar through the eyes of several people.

*9. How do the following characters see Caesar: (a) Flavius and Marullus, (b) Brutus, (c) Cassius?*

# Plot and Conflict

Characters are closely connected to plot because the characters perform the action of a play. Plot helps you to understand the characters by showing you how the characters respond to situations and events.

The plot of a play always involves some kind of <u>conflict</u>, a struggle or tension between two opposing forces. In *Julius Caesar* the conflict is between the people who oppose Caesar and those who support him. This conflict begins in Act 1 and continues throughout the rest of the play.

A plot usually has five sections. The <u>exposition</u> is the first part of the plot in which the playwright introduces the characters and conflicts, and provides whatever background information is necessary to the story. In the exposition, which is contained in Act 1, Scene 1, of *Julius Caesar*, Shakespeare uses several minor characters to give you background information.

*10. What do the characters in Act 1, Scene 1, tell you about the events taking place in Rome? To what conflicts do they introduce you?*

In Acts 2 and 3 the plot builds through the <u>rising action</u>, the second part of the plot in which the tension builds and complications develop. In Act 3 the plot reaches the <u>climax</u>—the point of greatest tension and highest interest for the audience. The climax is the third part of the plot and the turning point in the play. Following the climax is the <u>falling action</u>, the fourth part of the plot in which the tension eases and the action begins to slow down. In Acts 4 and 5 the falling action moves the play toward the last part of the plot, the <u>resolution</u>, which is the conclusion of the play. The resolution contains the outcome of the conflict.

**Conflict.** Shakespeare begins to develop the conflict early in the play. By Act 1, Scene 2, you know that Caesar has enemies who are plotting his downfall. Early in that scene, the soothsayer calls out to Caesar from the crowd. Caesar has the man brought before him but dismisses his warning. Caesar will not admit before his followers that he is in danger.

In Scene 2 you also see Cassius trying to persuade Brutus to join the conspirators. Brutus faces a personal conflict as he tries to decide what to do. Cassius flatters Brutus and tries to convince him that Caesar is weak. Cassius is determined to bring the well-respected Brutus into the plot against Caesar.

*11. At the end of Scene 2, what does Cassius plan to do to get Brutus to join the conspiracy? How does he carry out that plan in Scene 3?*

**Subplots.** In many plays and stories a series of minor actions is woven into the main action. This secondary series of actions is called a subplot. A subplot is always related to the main action. It may emphasize what is happening in the main plot, or it may reveal more about the main characters. Sometimes you will find more than one subplot within a story.

In *Julius Caesar* there are several subplots. One subplot begins in Act 1, Scene 1 (lines 64 to 66), when Flavius tells Marullus:

> Go you down that way towards the Capitol;
> This way will I. Disrobe the images,
> If you do find them deck'd with ceremonies.

The two men go offstage to remove the decorations that the people have put on the statues of Caesar. In Act 1, Scene 2, you learn that the two tribunes were "put to silence."

In that brief subplot Shakespeare shows how the two tribunes, elected officials of Rome, dared to oppose Caesar. As a result, they were arrested and put to death. The subplot is short and might seem unimportant, but notice Shakespeare's timing in revealing its outcome: Casca mentions the tribunes' fate just after telling Brutus and Cassius about Caesar's refusal of the crown.

*12. Notice what Cassius and Brutus are discussing early in Scene 2 before Casca enters and tells his story. How might the news about Marullus and Flavius affect what Cassius is trying to do? How is the subplot of Marullus and Flavius related to the main plot?*

Another subplot begins early in Scene 2 when the soothsayer warns Caesar to beware the ides of March. Unlike the subplot involving Marullus and Flavius, this one is not resolved in Act 1. As you read later acts, watch for references to the ides of March. You will see how Shakespeare develops this subplot, concluding it in Act 3.

## Questions for Thought and Discussion

The questions and activities that follow will help you explore *Julius Caesar*, Act 1, in more depth and at the same time develop your critical thinking skills.

1. **Understanding the Role of the Director.** When a play is staged, the play's director has a very important job. The director coordinates the work of all the actors and decides with the actors how each character can best be portrayed. In small groups select part of any scene in Act 1 to perform. Choose a director to work with the actors. Then prepare your scene so that it carries the message that Shakespeare intended. For example, you might choose the place in Scene 2 where Julius Caesar appears for the first time. The director and actors need to develop this scene to show that Caesar is the most powerful man in the Roman world.

2. **Comparing.** In Act 1 Cassius and Brutus talk at length, mostly about Caesar. What does each man think of Caesar? How are their views similar? How are they different?

3. **Analyzing Character.** Scene 3 takes place in the middle of an extraordinary storm that frightens Casca. During the storm Casca sees a man with a burning hand, a lion roaming the streets, and several other fantastic sights. When Cassius enters, he and Casca have a conversation that shows an interesting contrast between the two men. How do the two men's reactions to the storm differ? What does the difference tell you about the two men? Which man do you think is more dangerous? Why?

## Writing About Literature

Several suggestions for writing projects follow. You may be asked to complete one or more of these projects. If you have any questions about how to begin a writing assignment, review Using the Writing Process, beginning on page 385.

1. **Interpreting Shakespeare's Language.** Some of the best-known lines in all of Shakespeare's plays appear in *Julius Caesar.* Part of Cassius's speech in Act 1, Scene 2 (lines 133 to 159), is often quoted. Read the entire speech. Then look at the first nine lines. In your own words explain what Cassius is saying in those lines. Then compare the language in your summary to Shakespeare's language. What are some of the differences you notice?

2. **Explaining an Argument.** Imagine that you have to give a speech in which you explain Cassius's reasons for opposing Caesar. In two or three paragraphs, explain why Cassius is plotting against Caesar.

3. **Writing Dialogue.** On the basis of what you have learned so far about the major characters, write a dialogue between Caesar and Brutus. In the dialogue Brutus should ask Caesar about the incident in which he turned down the crown. You may use present-day language or try to use Shakespearean language.

## Chapter 2

**Selection**       *Julius Caesar, Acts 2 & 3*
WILLIAM SHAKESPEARE

**Lesson**       *Dialogue, Monologue, and Soliloquy*

## About the Selection

In Act 1 Shakespeare introduced you to the major characters in *Julius Caesar.* You learned about them through their words and actions. You saw two groups in conflict and heard about the plot to topple Caesar from power.

Cassius is the leader of the conspirators. He wants to persuade the noble and highly respected Brutus to join the plot. You have learned how different the two men are. Cassius is a flatterer. He is outspoken in his hatred of Caesar. He is angry and determined to achieve his purpose.

By contrast, Brutus examines his personal motives, or reasons, for acting in a certain way. He is concerned with choosing the honorable course. He weighs both sides of the issue—whether to join the plot or not. He wants to do what is best for Rome. He is unsure about what action to take. At the close of Act 1, Cassius and Cinna try to make sure that Brutus will join them.

During the rising action in Acts 2 and 3, the tension builds. As Act 2 opens, Brutus is debating what to do. Cassius and the other conspirators are again urging him to join them. As you read the opening scene, think about what you already know about the various characters. Notice how each behaves and speaks. Once you are familiar with the personalities of the characters, you can understand more clearly why the plot develops as it does.

In two separate incidents in Act 2, you see both Brutus and Caesar with their wives. Although you meet Portia, Brutus's wife, only briefly, you get a clear picture of her. Both women are worried, for different reasons, about what is going on in their husbands' lives. Notice how each woman behaves and what her relationship with her husband is like.

In Act 3 the plot moves toward the climax, or point of highest tension, when Caesar's opponents confront him. The scene takes place outside the Capitol and is among the most famous scenes in all of Shakespeare's work. The action occurs in front of the Roman people.

The people of Rome are important to the play. Before joining the conspiracy, Brutus thinks about how best to serve the interests of the people. In Act 3 the opinions and feelings of the Roman people are crucial to the plot. Both Brutus and Mark Antony make speeches that appeal to the people. Antony's speech is one of Shakespeare's best-known passages. As you read, think about what purpose each speech serves. Think, too, about how the character giving the speech influences the people.

As you have read, Julius Caesar was a historical figure. At the time Shakespeare wrote his play, people were fascinated by the great leaders of the past. Before writing *Julius Caesar,* Shakespeare had written several historical plays about important English kings. Scholars have studied the sources that Shakespeare may have used in writing his historical plays. In Elizabethan times a number of books about Caesar existed, but it is not known whether Shakespeare read any of them.

One source Shakespeare did use was Plutarch's *Parallel Lives of Illustrious Greeks and Romans.* Plutarch was a Greek writer who was born a few years after Caesar was killed. Plutarch died in about A.D. 120. He wrote biographies of many great figures of ancient Greece and Rome. In separate chapters on Julius Caesar, Mark Antony, and Brutus, Plutarch described the events surrounding the plot to kill Caesar.

For the most part, Shakespeare followed Plutarch's stories very closely. Shakespeare, however, was a playwright, not a historian. Though he borrowed ideas and scenes from Plutarch, Shakespeare's language and images are his own. His play differs in other ways from Plutarch's description of the incident. For example, he changed the order of some events to make the story more effective in the theater.

Shakespeare sometimes invented a scene based on Plutarch's stories. Shakespeare created his own dialogue and speeches. He expanded the personalities of various characters to make the play more dramatic.

The characters in *Julius Caesar* are based on people who once lived. The outline of events is factual. But Shakespeare gave personalities, thoughts, and feelings to the characters. He gave them words to speak and created the details of scenes and events. His play gives life to a historical event and tells a dramatic story.

## Lesson Preview

The lesson that follows *Julius Caesar,* Acts 2 and 3, focuses on the types of speeches in the play. As you saw in Act 1, sometimes several characters discuss an event or idea. At other times, one character speaks to others on the stage. In Act 1, for example, Cassius gave several long speeches to which Brutus or others listened. Another type of speech is one in which a character is alone onstage expressing his or her thoughts out loud.

In most plays what the characters say is more important than anything else. Although some modern playwrights give detailed instructions about how actors should move or behave, Shakespeare gave very few instructions. Therefore the words that his characters speak must support the play. The questions that follow will help you identify the various types of speeches in Acts 2 and 3. As you read, think about how you would answer these questions.

**1** In Acts 2 and 3, which characters spend the most time onstage?

**2** Which characters have the most spoken lines? To whom are they speaking?

**3** Which actions take place onstage or offstage? How do you learn about the offstage actions?

**4** What do the speeches reveal about the plot and about the speakers themselves?

# Vocabulary

Here are some difficult words that appear in the selection that follows. Study the words and their definitions, as well as the sentences that show how the words are used. This will help you get the most from your reading.

**interpose**  come between; intrude. *The teacher had to interpose herself between the quarreling students.*

**disclose**  reveal. *What did the investigation disclose about the company's profits?*

**prevail**  succeed. *I hope that the second-place runner will prevail over the current world champion.*

**suit**  petition. *We presented our suit to the town council, and they will study it carefully before making a decision.*

**doomsday**  the end of the world; judgment day. *Although many predictions have been made about doomsday's arrival, none of these predictions have proven to be accurate.*

**abridged**  shortened. *An abridged novel is an incomplete version of the original book.*

**vouchsafe**  grant. *The country may vouchsafe us permission to stay and work there for a year.*

**leagues**  units of measurement similar to miles. *We walked along the road for several leagues before we ever saw a house.*

**oration**  speech. *After the voting results came in, the successful candidate gave a brief, joyful oration.*

**reverence**  great love or respect. *Tourists who visit the Baseball Hall of Fame often feel great reverence for many of the legendary baseball players.*

**parchment**  document. *This ancient parchment is one of the earliest records of a complex mathematical system.*

**compel**  force. *Because she had already eaten her candy bar, Sue tried to compel George to give her the rest of his.*

# *Julius Caesar*

## ACTS 2 & 3

WILLIAM SHAKESPEARE

## ACT 2

### Scene 1

*Brutus, unable to sleep, walks in his orchard, thinking about how to stop Caesar from becoming the tyrant of Rome. He finally realizes that Caesar must be killed. His servant Lucius brings him a letter that he found in the house. Though supposedly written by a Roman citizen, it is actually one of the letters Cassius composed and directed Cinna to throw in Brutus's window. The letter convinces Brutus that his decision is just. Cassius and the other conspirators arrive, and the men make plans to assassinate Caesar at the Capitol the next day, the ides of March. Brutus's wife, Portia, later asks Brutus what is troubling him, but he avoids answering her.*

### Rome. Brutus's orchard. Enter **Brutus**.

**Brutus**   What, Lucius, ho!
   I cannot, by the progress of the stars,

Give guess how near to day. Lucius, I say!
I would it were my fault to sleep so soundly.
When, Lucius, when? Awake, I say! What, Lucius!                    5

*(Enter **Lucius**)*

**Lucius**   Call'd you, my lord?
**Brutus**   Get me a taper° in my study, Lucius:
   When it is lighted, come and call me here.
**Lucius**   I will, my lord.

*(Exit)*

**Brutus**   It must be by his death; and for my part,          10
   I know no personal cause to spurn at° him,
   But for the general. He would be crown'd:
   How that might change his nature, there's the question.
   It is the bright day that brings forth the adder,°
   And that craves wary walking. Crown him?—that?          15
   And then, I grant, we put a sting in him,
   That at his will he may do danger with.
   Th' abuse of greatness is when it disjoins°
   Remorse from power; and, to speak truth of Caesar,
   I have not known when his affections sway'd                 20
   More than his reason. But 'tis a common proof,
   That lowliness is young ambition's ladder,
   Whereto the climber upward turns his face;
   But when he once attains the upmost round,
   He then unto the ladder turns his back,                       25
   Looks in the clouds, scorning the base degrees
   By which he did ascend. So Caesar may;
   Then lest he may, prevent. And since the quarrel
   Will bear no colour for the thing he is,

---

**7. taper:** candle.   **11. spurn at:** oppose.   **14. adder:** a poisonous snake. Brutus observes that favorable
conditions often bring out the evil in people.   **18. disjoins:** separates.

Fashion it thus: that what he is, augmented,° 30
Would run to these and these extremities;
And therefore think him as a serpent's egg,
Which hatch'd would, as his kind, grow mischievous,
And kill him in the shell.

*(Enter **Lucius**)*

**Lucius**   The taper burneth in your closet,° sir. 35
Searching the window for a flint, I found
This paper, thus seal'd up; and I am sure
It did not lie there when I went to bed.
**Brutus**   Get you to bed again; it is not day.
Is not tomorrow, boy, the ides of March? 40
**Lucius**   I know not, sir.
**Brutus**   Look in the calendar, and bring me words.
**Lucius**   I will, sir.

*(Exit)*

**Brutus**   The exhalations° whizzing in the air
Give so much light that I may read by them. 45

*(Reads)*

'Brutus, thou sleep'st; awake, and see thyself.
Shall Rome, etc. Speak, strike, redress!'°

Brutus, thou sleep'st; awake! . . .
Such instigations° have been often dropp'd
Where I have took them up. 50
'Shall Rome, etc.' Thus must I piece it out:
Shall Rome stand under one man's awe? What, Rome?

---

**30. augmented:** enlarged.   **35. closet:** room.   **44. exhalations:** meteors.   **46–47. Brutus, thou sleep'st
. . . redress:** This is one of many unsigned notes that Cassius ordered placed in Brutus's house to make
him think they were from Roman citizens. The notes told him to wake up to what was happening
and to correct (redress) the evils.   **49. instigations:** recommendations.

My ancestors did from the streets of Rome
The Tarquin° drive, when he was call'd a king.
'Speak, strike, redress!' Am I entreated                                55
To speak, and strike? O Rome, I make thee promise,
If the redress will follow, thou receivest
Thy full petition at the hand of Brutus.

*(Enter Lucius)*

**Lucius**  Sir, March is wasted fourteen days.
**Brutus**  'Tis good. Go to the gate; somebody knocks.                  60

*(Exit Lucius)*

Since Cassius first did whet° me against Caesar,
I have not slept.
Between the acting of a dreadful thing
And the first motion, all the interim is
Like a phantasma,° or a hideous dream:                                  65
The genius and the mortal instruments
Are then in council; and the state of man,
Like to a little kingdom, suffers then
The nature of an insurrection.°

*(Enter Lucius)*

**Lucius**  Sir, 'tis your brother Cassius,                             70
Who doth desire to see you.
**Brutus**                          Is he alone?
**Lucius**  No sir, there are more with him.
**Brutus**                          Do you know them?
**Lucius**  No, sir, their hats are pluck'd about their ears,
And half their faces buried in their cloaks,

---

**54. The Tarquin:** people who once ruled Rome. Brutus's famous ancestor, Lucius Junius Brutus, led the Romans when they overthrew the Tarquins. **61. whet:** arouse. **65. phantasma:** ghost. **69. insurrection:** rebellion.

That by no means I may discover them                                    75
By any mark of favour.
**Brutus**                                    Let 'em enter.

*(Exit* **Lucius***)*

They are the faction.° O conspiracy,
Sham'st thou to show thy dangerous brow by night,
When evils are most free? O, then by day
Where wilt thou find a cavern dark enough                               80
To mask thy monstrous visage?° Seek none, conspiracy;
Hide it in smiles and affability:°
For if thou path, thy native semblance on,°
Not Erebus° itself were dim enough
To hide thee from prevention.                                           85

*(Enter the Conspirators,* **Cassius, Casca, Decius, Cinna, Metellus
Cimber** *and* **Trebonius***)*

**Cassius**   I think we are too bold upon your rest:
Good morrow, Brutus. Do we trouble you?
**Brutus**   I have been up this hour, awake all night.
Know I these men that come along with you?
**Cassius**   Yes, every man of them; and no man here                   90
But honours you; and every one doth wish
You had but that opinion of yourself
Which every noble Roman bears of you.
This is Trebonius.
**Brutus**                                    He is welcome hither.
**Cassius**   This, Decius Brutus.
**Brutus**                                    He is welcome too.        95
**Cassius**   This, Casca; this, Cinna; and this, Metellus Cimber.

---

77. **faction:** group.   81. **visage:** face; appearance.   82. **affability:** friendliness.   83. **For if thou path . . .
semblance on:** if you go about just as you are.   84. **Erebus:** in Roman mythology, a dark place between
earth and Hades (the underworld).

**Brutus**  They are all welcome.
　　What watchful cares do interpose themselves
　　Betwixt your eyes and night?°
**Cassius**  Shall I entreat a word?　　　　　　　　　100
**Decius**  Here lies the east: doth not the day break here?
**Casca**  No.
**Cinna**  O, pardon, sir, it doth; and yon grey lines
　　That fret° the clouds are messengers of day.
**Casca**  You shall confess that you are both deceiv'd.　　105
　　Here, as I point my sword, the sun arises,
　　Which is a great way growing on the south,
　　Weighing the youthful season of the year.
　　Some two months hence, up higher toward the north
　　He first presents his fire; and the high east　　　110
　　Stands, as the Capitol, directly here.
**Brutus**  Give me your hands all over, one by one.
**Cassius**  And let us swear our resolution.
**Brutus**  No, not an oath. If not the face of men,
　　The sufferance of our souls, the time's abuse—　　115
　　If these be motives weak, break off betimes,
　　And every man hence to his idle bed;°
　　So let high-sighted tyranny range on,
　　Till each man drop by lottery. But if these,
　　As I am sure they do, bear fire enough　　　　120
　　To kindle cowards and to steel with valour
　　The melting spirits of women, then, countrymen,
　　What need we any spur but our own cause
　　To prick us to redress? what other bond
　　Than secret Romans, that have spoke the word,　　125
　　And will not palter?° and what other oath

---

**98–99. What watchful cares . . . night:** What worries keep you from sleeping?　**104. fret:** decorate. **114–117. No, not an oath . . . to his idle bed:** If we need a pledge to bind us together, we should stop right now and go to bed.　**126. palter:** use tricks.

Than honesty to honesty engag'd,
That this shall be, or we will fall for it?
Swear priests and cowards, and men cautelous,°
Old feeble carrions,° and such suffering souls                    130
That welcome wrongs; unto bad causes swear
Such creatures as men doubt; but do not stain
The even virtue of our enterprise,
Nor th' insuppressive mettle° of our spirits,
To think that or our cause or our performance              135
Did need an oath; when every drop of blood
That every Roman bears, and nobly bears,
Is guilty of a several bastardy,
If he do break the smallest particle
Of any promise that hath pass'd from him                        140

**Cassius** But what of Cicero? Shall we sound him?
I think he will stand very strong with us.

**Casca** Let us not leave him out.

**Cinna**                                   No, by no means.

**Metellus** O, let us have him, for his silver hairs
Will purchase us a good opinion,                                  145
And buy men's voices to commend our deeds.
It shall be said his judgment rul'd our hands;
Our youths and wildness shall no whit appear,
But all be buried in his gravity.

**Brutus** O, name him not; let us not break with him;   150
For he will never follow any thing
That other men begin.

**Cassius**                                Then leave him out.

**Casca** Indeed he is not fit.

**Decius** Shall no man else be touch'd but only Caesar?

**Cassius** Decius, well urg'd. I think it is not meet,      155

---

**129. men cautelous:** lying people.  **130. carrions:** people near death.  **134. insuppressive mettle:** unbeatable strength.

Mark Antony, so well belov'd of Caesar,
Should outlive Caesar: we shall find of him
A shrewd contriver;° and you know, his means,
If he improve them, may well stretch so far
As to annoy us all; which to prevent,                                     160
Let Antony and Caesar fall together.

**Brutus**   Our course will seem too bloody, Caius Cassius,
To cut the head off and then hack the limbs,
Like wrath in death and envy afterwards;
For Antony is but a limb of Caesar.                                        165
Let's be sacrificers, but not butchers, Caius.
We all stand up against the spirit of Caesar,
And in the spirit of men there is no blood.
O, that we then could come by Caesar's spirit,
And not dismember Caesar! But, alas,                                       170
Caesar must bleed for it. And, gentle friends,
Let's kill him boldly, but not wrathfully;
Let's carve him as a dish fit for the gods,
Not hew him as a carcass fit for hounds.
And let our hearts, as subtle masters do,                                  175
Stir up their servants to an act of rage,
And after seem to chide° 'em. This shall make
Our purpose necessary, and not envious;
Which so appearing to the common eyes,
We shall be call'd purgers,° not murderers.                               180
And for Mark Antony, think not of him;
For he can do no more than Caesar's arm
When Caesar's head is off.

**Cassius**                          Yet I fear him;
For the ingrafted love he bears to Caesar—

**Brutus**   Alas, good Cassius, do not think of him:                     185
    If he love Caesar, all that he can do

---

**158. contriver:** trickster.   **177. chide:** blame; scold.   **180. purgers:** purifiers.

Is to himself: take thought, and die for Caesar.
And that were much he should; for he is given
To sports, to wildness, and much company.
**Trebonius**　There is no fear in him; let him not die;　　　190
For he will live, and laugh at this hereafter.

*(Clock strikes)*

**Brutus**　Peace! count the clock.
**Cassius**　　　　　　　　　The clock hath stricken three.
**Trebonius**　'Tis time to part.
**Cassius**　　　　　　　　　But it is doubtful yet
Whether Caesar will come forth today or no;
For he is superstitious grown of late,　　　195
Quite from the main opinion he held once
Of fantasy, of dreams, and ceremonies.
It may be these apparent prodigies,
The unaccustom'd terror of this night,
And the persuasion of his augurers,°　　　200
May hold him from the Capitol today.
**Decius**　Never fear that: if he be so resolv'd,
I can o'ersway him; for he loves to hear
That unicorns may be betray'd with trees,
And bears with glasses, elephants with holes,　　　205
Lions with toils, and men with flatterers;°
But when I tell him he hates flatterers,
He says he does, being then most flattered.
Let me work;
For I can give his humour° the true bent,　　　210
And I will bring him to the Capitol.
**Cassius**　Nay, we will all of us be there to fetch him.

**200. augurers:** fortunetellers.　**202–206. Never fear . . . with flatterers:** Don't worry, I can change his mind. Caesar loves to hear how unicorns can be turned into trees, how bears can be fooled with mirrors, how elephants can be caught in ditches, lions in nets, and men fooled by flatterers.　**210. humour:** mood.

**Brutus**  By the eighth hour: is that the uttermost?

**Cinna**  Be that the uttermost, and fail not then.

**Metellus**  Caius Ligarius doth bear Caesar hard,     215
    Who rated° him for speaking well of Pompey:
    I wonder none of you have thought of him.

**Brutus**  Now good Metellus, go along by him:
    He loves me well, and I have given him reasons;
    Send him but hither, and I'll fashion him.     220

**Cassius**  The morning comes upon 's: we'll leave you, Brutus.
    And friends, disperse yourselves; but all remember
    What you have said, and show yourselves true Romans.

**Brutus**  Good gentlemen, look fresh and merrily.
    Let not our looks put on our purposes,     225
    But bear it as our Roman actors do,
    With untir'd spirits and formal constancy.
    And so good morrow to you every one.

*(Exeunt all but* **Brutus***)*

    Boy! Lucius! Fast asleep? It is no matter;
    Enjoy the honey-heavy dew of slumber:     230
    Thou hast no figures nor no fantasies
    Which busy care draws in the brains of men;
    Therefore thou sleep'st so sound.

*(Enter* **Portia***)*

**Portia**                   Brutus, my lord!

**Brutus**  Portia, what mean you? Wherefore rise you now?
    It is not for your health thus to commit     235
    Your weak condition to the raw cold morning.

**Portia**  Nor for yours neither. You've ungently, Brutus,
    Stole from my bed; and yesternight at supper
    You suddenly arose, and walk'd about,

---

**216. rated:** drove away by scolding.

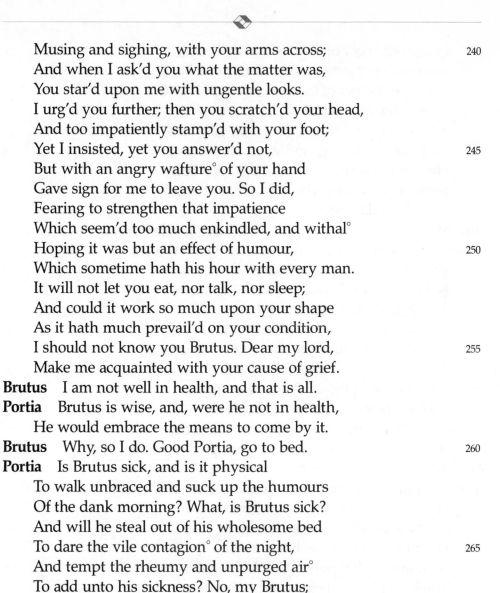

Musing and sighing, with your arms across; 240
And when I ask'd you what the matter was,
You star'd upon me with ungentle looks.
I urg'd you further; then you scratch'd your head,
And too impatiently stamp'd with your foot;
Yet I insisted, yet you answer'd not, 245
But with an angry wafture° of your hand
Gave sign for me to leave you. So I did,
Fearing to strengthen that impatience
Which seem'd too much enkindled, and withal° 250
Hoping it was but an effect of humour,
Which sometime hath his hour with every man.
It will not let you eat, nor talk, nor sleep;
And could it work so much upon your shape
As it hath much prevail'd on your condition,
I should not know you Brutus. Dear my lord, 255
Make me acquainted with your cause of grief.
**Brutus**   I am not well in health, and that is all.
**Portia**   Brutus is wise, and, were he not in health,
He would embrace the means to come by it.
**Brutus**   Why, so I do. Good Portia, go to bed. 260
**Portia**   Is Brutus sick, and is it physical
To walk unbraced and suck up the humours
Of the dank morning? What, is Brutus sick?
And will he steal out of his wholesome bed
To dare the vile contagion° of the night, 265
And tempt the rheumy and unpurged air°
To add unto his sickness? No, my Brutus;
You have some sick offence within your mind,
Which by the right and virtue of my place,

---

**246. wafture:** wave.   **249. withal:** at the same time.   **265. vile contagion:** The Romans considered the night air unhealthful.   **266. rheumy and unpurged air:** sickly and unclean air. Romans feared fog as a cause of disease.

I ought to know of; and, upon my knees, 270
I charm you, by my once commended beauty,
By all your vows of love, and that great vow
Which did incorporate and make us one,
That you unfold to me, your self, your half,
Why you are heavy,° and what men tonight 275
Have had resort to you; for here have been
Some six or seven, who did hide their faces
Even from darkness.

**Brutus**                              Kneel not, gentle Portia.

**Portia**    I should not need, if you were gentle Brutus.
Within the bond of marriage, tell me, Brutus, 280
Is it excepted I should know no secrets
That appertain° to you? Am I your self
But, as it were, in sort or limitation,
To keep with you at meals, comfort your bed,
And talk to you sometimes? Dwell I but in the suburbs 285
Of your good pleasure? If it be no more,
Portia is Brutus's harlot, not his wife.

**Brutus**    You are my true and honourable wife,
As dear to me as are the ruddy drops°
That visit my sad heart. 290

**Portia**    If this were true, then should I know this secret.
I grant I am a woman; but withal
A woman that Lord Brutus took to wife;
I grant I am a woman; but withal
A woman well reputed, Cato's daughter. 295
Think you I am no stronger than my sex,
Being so father'd, and so husbanded?
Tell me your counsels,° I will not disclose 'em.
I have made a strong proof of my constancy,

---

275. **heavy:** troubled.    282. **appertain:** relate.    289. **ruddy drops:** drops of blood.    298. **counsels:** secrets.

Giving myself a voluntary wound                    300
Here, in the thigh: can I bear that with patience,
And not my husband's secrets?

**Brutus**                          O ye gods,
Render me worthy of this noble wife!
Hark, hark! one knocks. Portia, go in awhile;
And by and by thy bosom shall partake              305
The secrets of my heart.
All my engagements I will construe to thee,
All the charactery of my sad brows.
Leave me with haste.

*(Exit* **Portia***)*

*(Enter* **Lucius** *and* **Ligarius***)*

                          Lucius, who's that knocks?

**Lucius**   Here is a sick man that would speak with you.   310

**Brutus**   Caius Ligarius, that Metellus spake of.
     Boy, stand aside. Caius Ligarius, how?

**Ligarius**   Vouchsafe° good morrow from a feeble tongue.

**Brutus**   O, what a time have you chose out, brave Caius,
     To wear a kerchief! Would you were not sick!      315

**Ligarius**   I am not sick if Brutus have in hand
     Any exploit° worthy the name of honour.

**Brutus**   Such an exploit have I in hand, Ligarius,
     Had you a healthful ear to hear of it.

**Ligarius**   By all the gods that Romans bow before,    320
     I here discard my sickness. Soul of Rome!
     Brave son, deriv'd from honourable loins!
     Thou, like an exorcist, hast conjur'd up

---

**313. Vouchsafe:** accept.   **317. exploit:** deed.

My mortified° spirit. Now bid me run,
And I will strive with things impossible,                    325
Yea, get the better of them. What's to do?
**Brutus**  A piece of work that will make sick men whole.
**Ligarius**  But are not some whole that we must make sick?
**Brutus**  That must we also. What it is, my Caius,
I shall unfold to thee, as we are going                      330
To whom it must be done.
**Ligarius**                    Set on your foot,
And with a heart new-fir'd I follow you,
To do I know not what; but it sufficeth
That Brutus leads me on.
**Brutus**                              Follow me then.

*(Exeunt)*

## Scene 2

*Because of a terrifying dream, Calpurnia begs Caesar not to go to
the Capitol as he has planned. Caesar at first agrees, but then
he allows Decius, one of the conspirators, to flatter him into
changing his mind. Accompanied by several of the conspirators,
Caesar departs for the Capitol.*

*Caesar's house. Thunder and lightning. Enter* **Caesar** *in his nightgown.*

**Caesar**  Nor heaven nor earth have been at peace tonight:
Thrice hath Calpurnia in her sleep cried out,
'Help, ho! they murder Caesar!' Who's within?
*(Enter a* **Servant***)*

**Servant**  My lord?

---

**324. mortified:** dead.

**Caesar**   Go bid the priests do present sacrifice,          5
And bring me their opinions of success.
**Servant**   I will, my lord.

*(Exit)*

*(Enter **Calpurnia**)*

**Calpurnia**   What mean you, Caesar? Think you to walk forth?
You shall not stir out of your house today.
**Caesar**   Caesar shall forth. The things that threaten'd me          10
Ne'er look'd but on my back; when they shall see
The face of Caesar, they are vanished.
**Calpurnia**   Caesar, I never stood on ceremonies,°
Yet now they fright me. There is one within,
Besides the things that we have heard and seen,          15
Recounts most horrid sights seen by the watch.
A lioness hath whelped° in the streets,
And graves have yawn'd and yielded up their dead;
Fierce fiery warriors fight upon the clouds
In ranks and squadrons and right form of war,          20
Which drizzled blood upon the Capitol;
The noise of battle hurtled in the air,
Horses did neigh, and dying men did groan,
And ghosts did shriek and squeal about the streets.
O Caesar, these things are beyond all use,          25
And I do fear them.
**Caesar**                                   What can be avoided
Whose end is purpos'd by the mighty gods?
Yet Caesar shall go forth; for these predictions
Are to the world in general as to Caesar.
**Calpurnia**   When beggars die, there are no comets seen;          30
The heavens themselves blaze forth the death of princes.

---

**13. I never stood on ceremonies:** I never paid attention to supernatural signs.   **17. whelped:** gave birth to her offspring.

**Caesar**  Cowards die many times before their deaths;
         The valiant never taste of death but once.
         Of all the wonders that I yet have heard,
         It seems to me most strange that men should fear,          35
         Seeing that death, a necessary end,
         Will come when it will come.

                    *(Enter a* **Servant)**

                              What say the augurers?
**Servant**  They would not have you to stir forth today.
          Plucking the entrails of an offering forth,
          They could not find a heart within the beast.          40
**Caesar**  The gods do this in shame of cowardice:
         Caesar should be a beast without a heart
         If he should stay at home today for fear.
         No, Caesar shall not. Danger knows full well
         That Caesar is more dangerous than he.                 45
         We are two lions litter'd in one day,°
         And I the elder and more terrible,
         And Caesar shall go forth.
**Calpurnia**                      Alas, my lord,
          Your wisdom is consum'd in confidence.
          Do not go forth today: call it my fear                 50
          That keeps you in the house, and not your own.
          We'll send Mark Antony to the Senate House,
          And he shall say you are not well today.
          Let me upon my knee prevail in this.
**Caesar**  Mark Antony shall say I am not well,                 55
         And for thy humour I will stay at home.

                    *(Enter* **Decius)**

          Here's Decius Brutus; he shall tell them so.

_____
**46. litter'd in one day:** born together of the same mother.

**Decius**  Caesar, all hail! Good morrow, worthy Caesar.
　　　I come to fetch you to the Senate House.

**Caesar**  And you are come in very happy time　　　　　　60
　　　To bear my greeting to the senators,
　　　And tell them that I will not come today:
　　　Cannot is false; and that I dare not, falser;
　　　I will not come today. Tell them so, Decius.

**Calpurnia**  Say he is sick.

**Caesar**　　　　　　　　　　Shall Caesar send a lie?　　　65
　　　Have I in conquest stretch'd mine arm so far,
　　　To be afeard to tell greybeards the truth?
　　　Decius, go tell them Caesar will not come.

**Decius**  Most mighty Caesar, let me know some cause,
　　　Lest I be laugh'd at when I tell them so.　　　　　70

**Caesar**  The cause is in my will: I will not come;
　　　That is enough to satisfy the Senate.
　　　But for your private satisfaction,
　　　Because I love you, I will let you know:
　　　Calpurnia here, my wife, stays me at home.　　　75
　　　She dreamt tonight she saw my statue,
　　　Which like a fountain with an hundred spouts
　　　Did run pure blood; and many lusty Romans
　　　Came smiling, and did bathe their hands in it.
　　　And these does she apply for warnings and portents　80
　　　And evils imminent;° and on her knee
　　　Hath begg'd that I will stay at home today.

**Decius**  This dream is all amiss interpreted;
　　　It was a vision fair and fortunate:
　　　Your statue spouting blood in many pipes,　　　85
　　　In which so many smiling Romans bath'd,
　　　Signifies that from you great Rome shall suck
　　　Reviving blood, and that great men shall press

**81. imminent:** near and threatening.

For tinctures, stains, relics, and cognizance.°
This by Calpurnia's dream is signified.                               90
**Caesar**  And this way have you well expounded it.
**Decius**  I have, when you have heard what I can say:
And know it now. The Senate have concluded
To give this day a crown to mighty Caesar.
If you shall send them word you will not come,                        95
Their minds may change. Besides, it were a mock
Apt to be render'd, for some one to say,
'Break up the Senate till another time,
When Caesar's wife shall meet with better dreams.'
If Caesar hide himself, shall they not whisper,                       100
'Lo, Caesar is afraid'?
Pardon me, Caesar; for my dear dear love
To your proceeding bids me tell you this,
And reason to my love is liable.
**Caesar**  How foolish do your fears seem now, Calpurnia!            105
I am ashamed I did yield to them.
Give me my robe, for I will go.

*(Enter* **Publius, Brutus, Ligarius, Metellus, Casca, Trebonius** *and* **Cinna***)*

And look where Publius is come to fetch me.
**Publius**  Good morrow, Caesar.
**Caesar**                            Welcome, Publius.
What, Brutus, are you stirr'd so early too?                           110
Good morrow, Casca. Caius Ligarius,
Caesar were ne'er so much your enemy

---

**89. For tinctures . . . cognizance:** Decius's interpretation of Calpurnia's dream has a double meaning. First, he suggests that Romans will honor Caesar, seeking "tinctures" (coats of arms) and "cognizances" (badges worn by a great man's servant) from him. Second, he suggests to the audience the image of Caesar as a martyr, with men dipping handkerchiefs in his blood to preserve as "relics" (sacred remains).

As that same ague° which hath made you lean.
What is't a clock?

**Brutus**                              Caesar, 'tis strucken eight.

**Caesar**   I thank you for your pains and courtesy.          115

*(Enter **Antony**)*

See! Antony, that revels long a-nights,
Is notwithstanding up. Good morrow, Antony.

**Antony**   So to most noble Caesar.

**Caesar**                              Bid them prepare within.
I am to blame to be thus waited for.
Now, Cinna; now, Metellus; what, Trebonius:          120
I have an hour's talk in store for you;
Be near me, that I may remember you.

**Trebonius**   Caesar, I will: *(Aside)* and so near will I be,
That your best friends shall wish I had been further.

**Caesar**   Good friends, go in, and taste some wine with me;          125
And we, like friends, will straightway go together.

**Brutus**   *(Aside)* That every like is not the same, O Caesar!°
The heart of Brutus yearns to think upon.

*(Exeunt)*


# Scene 3

*Artemidorus waits outside the Capitol, hoping to warn Caesar of
the plot against his life.*

*A street near the Capitol. Enter **Artemidorus**, reading a paper.*

**Artemidorus**   Caesar, beware of Brutus; take heed of Cassius;
come not near Casca; have an eye to Cinna; trust not
Trebonius; mark well Metellus Cimber; Decius Brutus loves

---

**113. ague:** sickness; fever.   **127. That every like . . . Caesar:** being like friends is not the same as being
friends.

thee not; thou hast wrong'd Caius Ligarius. There is but one
mind in all these men, and it is bent against Caesar. If thou     5
beest not immortal, look about you: security gives way to
conspiracy. The mighty gods defend thee! Thy lover,
Artemidorus.
Here will I stand till Caesar pass along,
And as a suitor° will I give him this.
My heart laments that virtue cannot live                          10
Out of the teeth of emulation.
If thou read this, O Caesar, thou may'st live;
If not, the Fates with traitors do contrive.

*(Exit)*


## Scene 4

*Portia sends Lucius to the Capitol to find out what is happening.
She sees the soothsayer on his way to the Capitol to warn Caesar
once again of the ides of March.*

*Before the house of Brutus. Enter* **Portia** *and* **Lucius.**

**Portia**   I prithee, boy, run to the Senate House.
    Stay not to answer me, but get thee gone.
    Why dost thou stay?
**Lucius**                          To know my errand, madam.
**Portia**   I would have had thee there and here again
    Ere I can tell thee what thou should'st do there.     5
    O constancy, be strong upon my side;
    Set a huge mountain 'tween my heart and tongue!
    I have a man's mind, but a woman's might.
    How hard it is for women to keep counsel!
    Art thou here yet?

---

9. **suitor:** petitioner.

**Lucius**                              Madam, what should I do?                              10
　　　Run to the Capitol, and nothing else?
　　　And so return to you, and nothing else?
**Portia**   Yes, bring me word, boy, if thy lord look well,
　　　For he went sickly forth; and take good note
　　　What Caesar doth, what suitors press to him.                              15
　　　Hark, boy, what noise is that?
**Lucius**   I hear none, madam.
**Portia**                              Prithee, listen well.
　　　I heard a bustling rumour, like a fray,°
　　　And the wind brings it from the Capitol.
**Lucius**   Sooth, madam, I hear nothing.                              20

### (Enter the **Soothsayer**)

**Portia**   Come hither, fellow. Which way hast thou been?
**Soothsayer**   At mine own house, good lady.
**Portia**   What is 't a clock?
**Soothsayer**                              About the ninth hour, lady.
**Portia**   Is Caesar yet gone to the Capitol?                              25
**Soothsayer**   Madam, not yet. I go to take my stand,
　　　To see him pass on to the Capitol.
**Portia**   Thou hast some suit to Caesar, hast thou not?
**Soothsayer**   That I have, lady, if it will please Caesar
　　　To be so good to Caesar as to hear me:                              30
　　　I shall beseech him to befriend himself.
**Portia**   Why, know'st thou any harm's intended towards him?
**Soothsayer**   None that I know will be, much that I fear may
　　　chance.
　　　Good morrow to you. Here the street is narrow.
　　　The throng that follows Caesar at the heels,                              35
　　　Of Senators, of praetors, common suitors,
　　　Will crowd a feeble man almost to death:

---

**18. fray:** public disturbance.

I'll get me to a place more void,° and there
Speak to great Caesar as he comes along.
**Portia**   I must go in. Ay me, how weak a thing                    40
The heart of woman is! O Brutus,
The heavens speed thee in thine enterprise!
*(Aside)* Sure, the boy heard me. Brutus hath a suit
That Caesar will not grant. *(Aside)* O, I grow faint.
Run, Lucius, and commend me to my lord;                            45
Say I am merry; come to me again,
And bring me word what he doth say to thee.

*(Exeunt)*

---

38. **more void:** a less crowded space.

# ACT 3

## Scene 1

*Accompanied by a group of senators, Caesar arrives at the Capitol after ignoring the warnings of Artemidorus and the soothsayer. Brutus and several other senators beg Caesar to revoke his punishment of Publius Cimber, whom Caesar has ordered deported from Rome. Caesar refuses, insisting that he never changes his mind once he has made a decision. The conspirators then attack Caesar, each stabbing him. After he is dead, they bathe their hands in his blood. Antony arrives, and Brutus agrees to let him speak at Caesar's funeral after he himself has explained why it was necessary to kill Caesar. Left alone with Caesar's bloody corpse, Antony vows revenge against the murderers. He then learns that Octavius, Caesar's adopted son, is on his way to Rome with an army.*

*Rome. Before the Capitol. Enter* **Caesar, Brutus, Cassius, Casca, Decius, Metellus, Trebonius, Cinna, Antony, Lepidus, Artemidorus, Publius, Popilius,** *and the* **Soothsayer.**

**Caesar**   The ides of March are come.
**Soothsayer**   Ay, Caesar, but not gone.
**Artemidorus**   Hail, Caesar! Read this schedule.
**Decius**   Trebonius doth desire you to o'er-read,
 At your best leisure, this his humble suit.                    5
**Artemidorus**   O Caesar, read mine first; for mine's a suit
 That touches Caesar nearer. Read it, great Caesar.
**Caesar**   What touches us ourself shall be last serv'd.
**Artemidorus**   Delay not, Caesar. Read it instantly.
**Caesar**   What, is the fellow mad?
**Publius**                           Sirrah, give place.        10
**Cassius**   What, urge you your petitions in the street?
 Come to the Capitol.

**(Caesar** *goes up to the Senate House, the rest following)*

**Popilius**  I wish your enterprise today may thrive.
**Cassius**  What enterprise, Popilius?
**Popilius**                              Fare you well.

*(Leaves him and joins **Caesar**)*

**Brutus**  What said Popilius Lena?                              15
**Cassius**  He wish'd today our enterprise might thrive.
    I fear our purpose is discovered.
**Brutus**  Look how he makes to Caesar: mark him.
**Cassius**  Casca, be sudden, for we fear prevention.
    Brutus, what shall be done? If this be known,                              20
    Cassius or Caesar never shall turn back,
    For I will slay myself.
**Brutus**                              Cassius, be constant:
    Popilius Lena speaks not of our purposes;
    For look, he smiles, and Caesar doth not change.
**Cassius**  Trebonius knows his time; for look you, Brutus,                              25
    He draws Mark Antony out of the way.

*(Exeunt **Antony** and **Trebonius**)*

**Decius**  Where is Metellus Cimber? Let him go,
    And presently prefer his suit to Caesar.
**Brutus**  He is address'd. Press near and second him.
**Cinna**  Casca, you are the first that rears your hand.                              30
**Caesar**  Are we all ready? What is now amiss°
    That Caesar and his senate must redress?
**Metellus**  Most high, most mighty, and most puissant° Caesar,
    Metellus Cimber throws before thy seat
    An humble heart,—
**Caesar**                              I must prevent thee, Cimber.                              35
    These couchings and these lowly courtesies
    Might fire the blood of ordinary men,

---

**31. amiss:** wrong.   **33. puissant:** powerful.

And turn pre-ordinance and first decree
Into the law of children.° Be not fond,°
To think that Caesar bears such rebel blood                40
That will be thaw'd from the true quality
With that which melteth fools—I mean sweet words,
Low-crooked curtsies, and base spaniel fawning.
Thy brother by decree is banished:
If thou dost bend and pray and fawn for him,              45
I spurn thee like a cur° out of my way.
Know, Caesar doth not wrong, nor without cause
Will he be satisfied.

**Metellus**   Is there no voice more worthy than my own,
To sound more sweetly in great Caesar's ear              50
For the repealing of my banish'd brother?

**Brutus**   I kiss thy hand, but not in flattery, Caesar,
Desiring thee that Publius Cimber may
Have an immediate freedom of repeal.

**Caesar**   What, Brutus?

**Cassius**                           Pardon, Caesar; Caesar, pardon:   55
As low as to thy foot doth Cassius fall,
To beg enfranchisement° for Publius Cimber.

**Caesar**   I could be well mov'd, if I were as you;
If I could pray to move, prayers would move me;
But I am constant as the northern star,                  60
Of whose true-fix'd and resting quality
There is no fellow in the firmament.
The skies are painted with unnumber'd sparks,
They are all fire, and every one doth shine;
But there's but one in all doth hold his place.          65
So in the world: 'tis furnish'd well with men,

---

**38–39. And turn . . . law of children:** You would have me treat established laws as though they were childish nothings.   **39. fond:** foolish.   **46. cur:** dog.   **57. enfranchisement:** release from confinement.

And men are flesh and blood, and apprehensive;°
Yet in the number I do know but one
That unassailable° holds on his rank,
Unshak'd of motion; and that I am he, 70
Let me a little show it, even in this,
That I was constant Cimber should be banish'd,
And constant do remain to keep him so.

**Cinna** O Caesar—

**Caesar** Hence! Wilt thou lift up Olympus?

**Decius** Great Caesar—

**Caesar** Doth not Brutus bootless° kneel? 75

**Casca** Speak hands for me!

*(They stab* **Caesar***)*

**Caesar** Et tu, Brute?° Then fall Caesar!

*(He dies)*

**Cinna** Liberty! Freedom! Tyranny is dead!
Run hence, proclaim, cry it about the streets.

**Cassius** Some to the common pulpits, and cry out, 80
'Liberty, freedom, and enfranchisement'.

**Brutus** People and senators, be not affrighted.
Fly not; stand still; ambition's debt is paid.

**Casca** Go to the pulpit, Brutus.

**Decius** And Cassius too.

**Brutus** Where's Publius? 85

**Cinna** Here, quite confounded° with this mutiny.

**Metellus** Stand fast together, lest some friend of Caesar's
Should chance—

**Brutus** Talk not of standing. Publius, good cheer;

---

**67. apprehensive:** intelligent.   **69. unassailable:** stubbornly.   **75. bootless:** without success. Caesar is pointing out that even Brutus's begging cannot move him.   **77. Et tu, Brute?:** Shocked that his friend is part of the plot, Caesar says, in Latin, "Even you, Brutus?"   **86. confounded:** shocked.

There is no harm intended to your person,                90
Nor to no Roman else. So tell them, Publius.

**Cassius**   And leave us, Publius, lest that the people
Rushing on us, should do your age some mischief.

**Brutus**   Do so; and let no man abide this deed
But we the doers.                                        95

*(Enter* **Trebonius***)*

**Cassius**   Where is Antony?
**Trebonius**                     Fled to his house amaz'd.
Men, wives, and children stare, cry out, and run,
As it were doomsday.
**Brutus**                     Fates, we will know your pleasures.
That we shall die, we know; 'tis but the time
And drawing days out, that men stand upon.              100
**Casca**   Why, he that cuts off twenty years of life
Cuts off so many years of fearing death.
**Brutus**   Grant that, and then is death a benefit:
So are we Caesar's friends, that have abridg'd
His time of fearing death. Stoop, Romans, stoop,        105
And let us bathe our hands in Caesar's blood
Up to the elbows, and besmear our swords:
Then walk we forth, even to the market-place,
And waving our red weapons o'er our heads,
Let's all cry, 'Peace, freedom, and liberty!'           110
**Cassius**   Stoop then, and wash. How many ages hence
Shall this our lofty scene be acted over,
In states unborn, and accents yet unknown!
**Brutus**   How many times shall Caesar bleed in sport,
That now on Pompey's basis lies along,                  115
No worthier than the dust!
**Cassius**                     So oft as that shall be,
So often shall the knot of us be call'd

The men that gave their country liberty.

**Decius**     What, shall we forth?

**Cassius**                                    Ay, every man away.

Brutus shall lead, and we will grace his heels                                    120
With the most boldest and best hearts of Rome.

*(Enter a **Servant**)*

**Brutus**   Soft, who comes here? A friend of Antony's.

**Servant**   Thus, Brutus, did my master bid me kneel;
Thus did Mark Antony bid me fall down;
And, being prostrate,° thus he bade me say:                                    125
Brutus is noble, wise, valiant, and honest;
Caesar was mighty, bold, royal, and loving:
Say I love Brutus, and I honour him;
Say I fear'd Caesar, honour'd him, and lov'd him.
If Brutus will vouchsafe that Antony                                    130
May safely come to him, and be resolv'd
How Caesar hath deserv'd to lie in death,
Mark Antony shall not love Caesar dead
So well as Brutus living; but will follow
The fortunes and affairs of noble Brutus                                    135
Through the hazards of this untrod state,°
With all true faith. So says my master Antony.

**Brutus**   Thy master is a wise and valiant Roman;
I never thought him worse.
Tell him, so please him come unto this place,                                    140
He shall be satisfied; and, by my honour,
Depart untouch'd.

**Servant**                                    I'll fetch him presently.

*(Exit **Servant**)*

**Brutus**   I know that we shall have him well to friend.

---

**125. being prostrate:** lying face down.   **136. untrod state:** new situation.

**Cassius**   I wish we may: but yet have I a mind
     That fears him much; and my misgiving still        145
     Falls shrewdly to the purpose.
                     *(Enter* **Antony***)*

**Brutus**   But here comes Antony. Welcome, Mark Antony.
**Antony**   O mighty Caesar! dost thou lie so low?
     Are all thy conquests, glories, triumphs, spoils,
     Shrunk to this little measure? Fare thee well.        150
     I know not, gentlemen, what you intend,
     Who else must be let blood, who else is rank:°
     If I myself, there is no hour so fit
     As Caesar's death's hour; nor no instrument
     Of half that worth as those your swords, made rich     155
     With the most noble blood of all this world.
     I do beseech ye, if you bear me hard,
     Now, whilst your purpled hands do reek° and smoke,
     Fulfil your pleasure. Live a thousand years,
     I shall not find myself so apt to die:        160
     No place will please me so, no mean of death,
     As here by Caesar, and by you cut off,
     The choice and master spirits of this age.
**Brutus**   O Antony, beg not your death of us.
     Though now we must appear bloody and cruel,       165
     As by our hands and this our present act
     You see we do, yet see you but our hands
     And this the bleeding business they have done.
     Our hearts you see not; they are pitiful;
     And pity to the general wrong of Rome—       170
     As fire drives out fire, so pity pity—
     Hath done this deed on Caesar. For your part,
     To you our swords have leaden points, Mark Antony:

---

**152. rank:** ready to bleed.  **158. reek:** stink.

Our arms in strength of malice, and our hearts
Of brothers' temper, do receive you in                                        175
With all kind love, good thoughts, and reverence.
**Cassius**   Your voice shall be as strong as any man's
In the disposing° of new dignities.
**Brutus**   Only be patient till we have appeas'd°
The multitude, beside themselves with fear,                                    180
And then we will deliver you the cause
Why I, that did love Caesar when I struck him,
Have thus proceeded.
**Antony**                                  I doubt not of your wisdom.
Let each man render me his bloody hand.
First, Marcus Brutus, will I shake with you;                                   185
Next Caius Cassius, do I take your hand;
Now, Decius Brutus, yours; now yours, Metellus;
Yours, Cinna; and, my valiant Casca, yours;
Though last, not least in love, yours, good Trebonius.
Gentlemen all—alas, what shall I say?                                          190
My credit now stands on such slippery ground,
That one of two bad ways you must conceit me,
Either a coward, or a flatterer.
That I did love thee, Caesar, O, 'tis true!
If then thy spirit look upon us now,                                           195
Shall it not grieve thee dearer than thy death,
To see thy Antony making his peace,
Shaking the bloody fingers of thy foes,
Most noble, in the presence of thy corse?°
Had I as many eyes as thou hast wounds,                                        200
Weeping as fast as they stream forth thy blood,
It would become me better than to close
In terms of friendship with thine enemies.

---

**178. disposing:** assigning; granting.   **179. appeas'd:** calmed.   **199. corse:** corpse.

Pardon me, Julius! Here wast thou bay'd, brave hart;°
Here didst thou fall; and here thy hunters stand, 205
Sign'd in thy spoil, and crimson'd in thy lethe.°
O world, thou wast the forest to this hart;
And this indeed, O world, the heart of thee.
How like a deer, strucken by many princes,
Dost thou here lie! 210

**Cassius**  Mark Antony—
**Antony**                              Pardon me, Caius Cassius:
The enemies of Caesar shall say this;
Then, in a friend, it is cold modesty.

**Cassius**  I blame you not for praising Caesar so;
But what compact° mean you to have with us? 215
Will you be prick'd in number of our friends,
Or shall we on, and not depend on you?

**Antony**  Therefore I took your hands, but was indeed
Sway'd from the point by looking down on Caesar.
Friends am I with you all, and love you all, 220
Upon this hope, that you shall give me reasons
Why, and wherein, Caesar was dangerous.

**Brutus**  Or else were this a savage spectacle.
Our reasons are so full of good regard,
That were you, Antony, the son of Caesar, 225
You should be satisfied.

**Antony**                              That's all I seek;
And am moreover suitor that I may
Produce his body to the market-place,
And in the pulpit, as becomes a friend,
Speak in the order of his funeral. 230

**Brutus**  You shall, Mark Antony.

---

**204. Here wast . . . brave hart:** Here you were surrounded and trapped by barking hounds, brave
deer. A hart is a male red deer. Shakespeare is comparing the plot against and murder of Caesar to
the hunting down of a deer.  **206. Sign'd . . . thy lethe:** splattered with your ruins and red with your
blood.  **215. compact:** agreement.

**Cassius**                              Brutus, a word with you.
    You know not what you do. Do not consent
    That Antony speak in his funeral.
    Know you how much the people may be mov'd
    By that which he will utter?
**Brutus**                              By your pardon:                    235
    I will myself into the pulpit first,
    And show the reason of our Caesar's death.
    What Antony shall speak, I will protest
    He speaks by leave and by permission:
    And that we are contented Caesar shall              240
    Have all true rites° and lawful ceremonies.
    It shall advantage more than do us wrong.
**Cassius**   I know not what may fall; I like it not.
**Brutus**   Mark Antony, here, take you Caesar's body.
    You shall not in your funeral speech blame us,      245
    But speak all good you can devise of Caesar,
    And say you do 't by our permission;
    Else shall you not have any hand at all
    About his funeral. And you shall speak
    In the same pulpit whereto I am going,              250
    After my speech is ended.
**Antony**                              Be it so;
    I do desire no more.
**Brutus**   Prepare the body, then, and follow us.

*(Exeunt all except* **Antony***)*

**Antony**   O pardon me, thou bleeding piece of earth,
    That I am meek and gentle with these butchers.     255
    Thou art the ruins of the noblest man
    That ever lived in the tide of times.
    Woe to the hand that shed this costly blood!

**241. rites:** rituals.

Over thy wounds now do I prophesy
(Which like dumb mouths do ope their ruby lips,                     260
To beg the voice and utterance of my tongue),
A curse shall light upon the limbs of men;
Domestic fury and fierce civil strife
Shall cumber° all the parts of Italy;
Blood and destruction shall be so in use,                          265
And dreadful objects so familiar,
That mothers shall but smile when they behold
Their infants quartered with the hands of war,
All pity chok'd with custom of fell deeds;
And Caesar's spirit, ranging for revenge,                          270
With Ate° by his side come hot from hell,
Shall in these confines with a monarch's voice
Cry havoc and let slip the dogs of war,
That this foul deed shall smell above the earth
With carrion men, groaning for burial.                             275

*(Enter a **Servant**)*

You serve Octavius Caesar, do you not?
**Servant**   I do, Mark Antony.
**Antony**   Caesar did write for him to come to Rome.
**Servant**   He did receive his letters, and is coming,
And bid me say to you by word of mouth—                            280
O Caesar!
**Antony**   Thy heart is big; get thee apart and weep.
Passion, I see, is catching; for mine eyes,
Seeing those beads of sorrow stand in thine,
Began to water. Is thy master coming?                              285
**Servant**   He lies tonight within seven leagues of Rome.
**Antony**   Post back with speed, and tell him what hath chanc'd.
Here is a mourning Rome, a dangerous Rome,

---

**264. cumber:** burden.   **271. Ate** (AY-tee): the goddess of discord and conflict.

*Dialogue, Monologue, and Soliloquy*

No Rome of safety for Octavius yet;
Hie hence and tell him so. Yet stay awhile;                290
Thou shalt not back till I have borne this corse
Into the market place; there shall I try,
In my oration, how the people take
The cruel issue of these bloody men;
According to the which thou shalt discourse               295
To young Octavius of the state of things.
Lend me your hand.

*(Exeunt, with* **Caesar's** *body)*


## Scene 2

*Brutus speaks to the people outside the Capitol, explaining why Caesar had to be killed. They cheer and give him their support. Satisfied that the people are on his side, Brutus introduces Antony and leaves. Antony then makes a powerful speech in which he sways the crowd to the opposite opinion, inciting their anger against the assassins.*

*The Forum. Enter* **Brutus** *and* **Cassius,** *with a throng of* **Plebeians**.

**Plebeians**    We will be satisfied: let us be satisfied.
**Brutus**    Then follow me, and give me audience, friends.
  Cassius, go you into the other street,
  And part the numbers.
  Those that will hear me speak, let 'em stay here;        5
  Those that will follow Cassius, go with him;
  And public reasons shall be rendered
  Of Caesar's death.
**1st Pleb**                            I will hear Brutus speak.
**2nd Pleb**    I will hear Cassius, and compare their reasons,
  When severally we hear them rendered.°                   10

---

10. **When severally . . . rendered:** When we hear them given separately.

*(Exit **Cassius,** with some of the **Plebeians**)*

**3rd Pleb**   The noble Brutus is ascended: silence!

**Brutus**   Be patient till the last.

Romans, countrymen, and lovers, hear me for my cause, and
be silent, that you may hear. Believe me for mine honour, and
have respect to mine honour, that you may believe. Censure     15
me° in your wisdom, and wake your senses, that you may the
better judge. If there be any in this assembly, any dear friend
of Caesar's, to him I say that Brutus's love to Caesar was no less
than his. If then that friend demand why Brutus rose against
Caesar, this is my answer: Not that I loved Caesar less, but     20
that I loved Rome more. Had you rather Caesar were living,
and die all slaves, than that Caesar were dead, to live all free
men? As Caesar loved me, I weep for him; as he was
fortunate, I rejoice at it; as he was valiant, I honour him; but,
as he was ambitious, I slew him. There is tears, for his love;     25
joy, for his fortune; honour, for his valour; and death, for his
ambition. Who is here so base, that would be a bondman? If
any, speak; for him have I offended. Who is here so rude, that
would not be a Roman? If any, speak; for him have I
offended. Who is here so vile, that will not love his country? If     30
any, speak; for him have I offended. I pause for a reply.

**All**   None, Brutus, none.

**Brutus**   Then none have I offended. I have done no more to
Caesar than you shall do to Brutus. The question of his death
is enroll'd in the Capitol; his glory not extenuated,° wherein he     35
was worthy; nor his offences enforc'd, for which he suffered
death.

*(Enter **Mark Antony** with **Caesar's** body)*

Here comes his body, mourned by Mark Antony, who though

---

**15–16. Censure me:** judge me.   **35. extenuated:** diminished.

*Dialogue, Monologue, and Soliloquy*

he had no hand in his death, shall receive the benefit of his
dying, a place in the commonwealth, as which of you shall
not? With this I depart, that, as I slew my best lover for the
good of Rome, I have the same dagger for myself, when it
shall please my country to need my death.

**All**   Live, Brutus! live! live!

**1st Pleb**   Bring him with triumph home unto his house.

**2nd Pleb**   Give him a statue with his ancestors.

**3rd Pleb**   Let him be Caesar.

**4th Pleb**                       Caesar's better parts
  Shall be crown'd in Brutus.

**1st Pleb**   We'll bring him to his house with shouts and
  clamours.

**Brutus**   My countrymen—

**2nd Pleb**                       Peace! Silence! Brutus speaks.

**1st Pleb**   Peace, ho!

**Brutus**   Good countrymen, let me depart alone,
  And, for my sake, stay here with Antony.
  Do grace to Caesar's corpse, and grace his speech
  Tending to Caesar's glories, which Mark Antony,
  By our permission, is allow'd to make.
  I do entreat you, not a man depart,
  Save I alone, till Antony have spoke.

**1st Pleb**   Stay, ho! and let us hear Mark Antony.

**3rd Pleb**   Let him go up into the public chair.
  We'll hear him. Noble Antony, go up.

**Antony**   For Brutus's sake, I am beholding to you.

**4th Pleb**   What does he say of Brutus?

**3rd Pleb**                       He says, for Brutus's sake
  He finds himself beholding to us all.

**4th Pleb**   'Twere best he speak no harm of Brutus here!

**1st Pleb**   This Caesar was a tyrant.

**3rd Pleb**                       Nay, that's certain.

We are blest that Rome is rid of him.

**2nd Pleb**  Peace! let us hear what Antony can say.

**Antony**  You gentle Romans—

**All**                                    Peace, ho! let us hear him.            70

**Antony**  Friends, Romans, countrymen, lend me your ears;
I come to bury Caesar, not to praise him.
The evil that men do lives after them,
The good is oft interred with their bones;
So let it be with Caesar. The noble Brutus            75
Hath told you Caesar was ambitious.
If it were so, it was a grievous fault,
And grievously hath Caesar answer'd it.
Here, under the leave of Brutus and the rest,
—For Brutus is an honourable man;                    80
So are they all, all honourable men—
Come I to speak in Caesar's funeral.
He was my friend, faithful and just to me;
But Brutus says he was ambitious,
And Brutus is an honourable man.                     85
He hath brought many captives home to Rome,
Whose ransom did the general coffers° fill:
Did this in Caesar seem ambitious?
When that the poor have cried, Caesar hath wept;
Ambition should be made of sterner stuff:            90
Yet Brutus says he was ambitious,
And Brutus is an honourable man.
You all did see that on the Lupercal
I thrice presented him a kingly crown,
Which he did thrice refuse. Was this ambition?       95
Yet Brutus says he was ambitious,
And sure he is an honourable man.
I speak not to disprove what Brutus spoke,

87. **general coffers:** treasury.

But here I am to speak what I do know.
You all did love him once, not without cause; 100
What cause withholds you then to mourn for him?
O judgment, thou art fled to brutish beasts,
And men have lost their reason. Bear with me.
My heart is in the coffin there with Caesar,
And I must pause till it come back to me. 105

**1st Pleb**   Methinks there is much reason in his sayings.

**2nd Pleb**   If thou consider rightly of the matter,
Caesar has had great wrong.

**3rd Pleb**                             Has he, masters?
I fear there will a worse come in his place.

**4th Pleb**   Mark'd ye his words? He would not take the crown; 110
Therefore 'tis certain he was not ambitious.

**1st Pleb**   If it be found so, some will dear abide it.

**2nd Pleb**   Poor soul! His eyes are red as fire with weeping.

**3rd Pleb**   There's not a nobler man in Rome than Antony.

**4th Pleb**   Now mark him; he begins again to speak. 115

**Antony**   But yesterday the word of Caesar might
Have stood against the world; now lies he there,
And none so poor to do him reverence.
O masters! if I were dispos'd to stir
Your hearts and minds to mutiny and rage, 120
I should do Brutus wrong, and Cassius wrong,
Who, you all know, are honourable men.
I will not do them wrong; I rather choose
To wrong the dead, to wrong myself and you,
Than I will wrong such honourable men. 125
But here's a parchment with the seal of Caesar;
I found it in his closet; 'tis his will.
Let but the commons hear this testament,
Which, pardon me, I do not mean to read,
And they would go and kiss dead Caesar's wounds 130

And dip their napkins in his sacred blood,
Yea, beg a hair of him for memory,
And, dying, mention it within their wills,
Bequeathing it as a rich legacy
Unto their issue.                                                    135

**4th Pleb**  We'll hear the will. Read it, Mark Antony.
**All**   The will, the will! We will hear Caesar's will!
**Antony**   Have patience, gentle friends; I must not read it.
It is not meet you know how Caesar lov'd you.
You are not wood, you are not stones, but men;                        140
And being men, hearing the will of Caesar,
It will inflame you, it will make you mad.
'Tis good you know not that you are his heirs;
For if you should, O, what would come of it?

**4th Pleb**   Read the will! We'll hear it, Antony!                  145
You shall read us the will, Caesar's will!
**Antony**   Will you be patient? Will you stay awile?
I have o'ershot myself to tell you of it.
I fear I wrong the honourable men
Whose daggers have stabb'd Caesar; I do fear it.                      150

**4th Pleb**   They were traitors. Honourable men!
**All**   The will!—The testament!
**2nd Pleb**   They were villains, murderers! The will! Read the
will!
**Antony**   You will compel me then to read the will?                155
Then make a ring about the corpse of Caesar,
And let me show you him that made the will.
Shall I descend? and will you give me leave?
**All**   Come down.
**2nd Pleb**   Descend.                                               160

(**Antony** *comes down*)

**3rd Pleb**   You shall have leave.

**4th Pleb**   A ring; stand round.

**1st Pleb**   Stand from the hearse!° stand from the body!

**2nd Pleb**   Room for Antony, most noble Antony!

**Antony**   Nay, press not so upon me; stand far off.      165

**All**   Stand back! Room! Bear back!

**Antony**   If you have tears, prepare to shed them now.
You all do know this mantle.° I remember
The first time ever Caesar put it on;
'Twas on a summer's evening in his tent,      170
That day he overcame the Nervii.°
Look, in this place ran Cassius's dagger through:
See what a rent the envious Casca made:
Through this the well-beloved Brutus stabb'd;
And as he pluck'd his cursed steel away,      175
Mark how the blood of Caesar follow'd it,
As rushing out of doors, to be resolv'd
If Brutus so unkindly knock'd or no;
For Brutus, as you know, was Caesar's angel.
Judge, O you gods, how dearly Caesar lov'd him.      180
This was the most unkindest cut of all;
For when the noble Caesar saw him stab,
Ingratitude, more strong than traitors' arms,
Quite vanquish'd him: then burst his mighty heart;
And in his mantle muffling up his face,      185
Even at the base of Pompey's statue
(Which all the while ran blood) great Caesar fell.
O, what a fall was there, my countrymen!
Then I, and you, and all of us fell down,
Whilst bloody treason flourish'd over us.      190
O, now you weep, and I perceive you feel
The dint of pity. These are gracious drops.

---

**163. hearse:** casket.   **168. mantle:** cloak or coat.   **171. the Nervii:** a fierce tribe of Belgians defeated by Caesar in a brutal battle. That victory made Caesar very popular with his soldiers.

Kind souls, what weep you when you but behold
Our Caesar's vesture° wounded? Look you here!
Here is himself, marr'd, as you see, with traitors.                           195

**1st Pleb**   O piteous spectacle!

**2nd Pleb**   O noble Caesar!

**3rd Pleb**   O woeful day!

**4th Pleb**   O traitors! villains!

**1st Pleb**   O most bloody sight!                                            200

**2nd Pleb**   We will be revenged.

**All**   Revenge! About! Seek! Burn! Fire! Kill! Slay!
Let not a traitor live.

**Antony**   Stay, countrymen.

**1st Pleb**   Peace there! Hear the noble Antony.                             205

**2nd Pleb**   We'll hear him, we'll follow him, we'll die with him.

**Antony**   Good friends, sweet friends, let me not stir you up
To such a sudden flood of mutiny.
They that have done this deed are honourable.
What private griefs they have, alas, I know not,                              210
That made them do it. They are wise and honourable,
And will, no doubt, with reasons answer you.
I come not, friends, to steal away your hearts.
I am no orator, as Brutus is,
But, as you know me all, a plain blunt man,                                  215
That love my friend; and that they know full well
That gave me public leave to speak of him.
For I have neither wit, nor words, nor worth,
Action, nor utterance, nor the power of speech
To stir men's blood; I only speak right on.                                  220
I tell you that which you yourselves do know,
Show you sweet Caesar's wounds, poor poor dumb mouths,
And bid them speak for me. But were I Brutus,
And Brutus Antony, there were an Antony

**194. vesture:** clothing.

Would ruffle up your spirits, and put a tongue 225
In every wound of Caesar that should move
The stones of Rome to rise and mutiny.

**All**  We'll mutiny.

**1st Pleb**  We'll burn the house of Brutus.

**3rd Pleb**  Away then! Come, seek the conspirators. 230

**Antony**  Yet hear me, countrymen. Yet hear me speak.

**All**  Peace, ho! Hear Antony, most noble Antony.

**Antony**  Why, friends, you go to do you know not what.
Wherein hath Caesar thus deserv'd your loves?
Alas! you know not: I must tell you then. 235
You have forgot the will I told you of.

**All**  Most true. The will! Let's stay and hear the will.

**Antony**  Here is the will, and under Caesar's seal.
To every Roman citizen he gives,
To every several man, seventy-five drachmas.° 240

**2nd Pleb**  Most noble Caesar! We'll revenge his death.

**3rd Pleb**  O royal Caesar!

**Antony**  Hear me with patience.

**All**  Peace, ho!

**Antony**  Moreover, he hath left you all his walks, 245
His private arbours, and new-planted orchards,
On this side Tiber; he hath left them you,
And to your heirs for ever: common pleasures,
To walk abroad and recreate yourselves.
Here was a Caesar! when comes such another? 250

**1st Pleb**  Never, never! Come, away, away!
We'll burn his body in the holy place,
And with the brands fire the traitors' houses.
Take up the body.

**2nd Pleb**  Go fetch fire. 255

---

240. **drachmas:** units of Roman money.

**3rd Pleb**  Pluck down benches.

**4th Pleb**  Pluck down forms, windows, any thing.

*(Exeunt **Plebeians** with the body)*

**Antony**  Now let it work. Mischief, thou art afoot,
　　　Take thou what course thou wilt! How now, fellow?

*(Enter a **Servant**)*

**Servant**  Sir, Octavius is already come to Rome.　　　　　　　260

**Antony**  Where is he?

**Servant**  He and Lepidus are at Caesar's house.

**Antony**  And thither° will I straight to visit him.
　　　He comes upon a wish. Fortune is merry,
　　　And in this mood will give us any thing.　　　　　　　265

**Servant**　 I heard him say Brutus and Cassius
　　　Are rid° like madmen through the gates of Rome.

**Antony**  Belike they had some notice of the people,
　　　How I had mov'd them.° Bring me to Octavius.

*(Exeunt)*

## Scene 3

*The enraged mob comes upon a poet named Cinna. Confusing him
with one of Caesar's murderers who has the same name, they
attack and kill him.*

*A street. Enter **Cinna** the poet, and after him the **Plebeians**.*

**Cinna**　I dreamt tonight that I did feast with Caesar,
　　　And things unlucky charge my fantasy.°
　　　I have no will to wander forth of doors,
　　　Yet something leads me forth.

---

**263. thither:** there.　**267. Are rid:** have ridden out.　**268–269. Belike . . . mov'd them:** They have probably had some warning of how the Roman people have been moved to anger.　**2. And things unlucky
charge my fantasy:** My imagination is filled with thoughts of bad luck.

**1st Pleb**   What is your name?                                          5
**2nd Pleb**   Whither are you going?
**3rd Pleb**   Where do you dwell?
**4th Pleb**   Are you a married man or a bachelor?
**2nd Pleb**   Answer every man directly.
**1st Pleb**   Ay, and briefly.                                            10
**4th Pleb**   Ay, and wisely.
**3rd Pleb**   Ay, and truly, you were best.
**Cinna**   What is my name? Whither am I going? Where do I
    dwell? Am I a married man or a bachelor? Then, to answer
    every man directly and briefly, wisely and truly: wisely I    15
    say, I am a bachelor.
**2nd Pleb**   That's as much as to say they are fools that marry.
    You'll bear me a bang for that, I fear. Proceed, directly.
**Cinna**   Directly, I am going to Caesar's funeral.
**1st Pleb**   As a friend or an enemy?                                    20
**Cinna**   As a friend.
**2nd Pleb**   The matter is answered directly.
**4th Pleb**   For your dwelling, briefly.
**Cinna**   Briefly, I dwell by the Capitol.
**3rd Pleb**   Your name, sir, truly.                                      25
**Cinna**   Truly, my name is Cinna.
**1st Pleb**   Tear him to pieces! He's a conspirator.
**Cinna**   I am Cinna the poet, I am Cinna the poet.
**4th Pleb**   Tear him for his bad verses, tear him for his bad
    verses.                                                        30
**Cinna**   I am not Cinna the conspirator.
**1st Pleb**   It is no matter, his name's Cinna; pluck but his name
    out of his heart, and turn him going.
**3rd Pleb**   Tear him, tear him! come, brands, ho! firebrands!
    To Brutus's, to Cassius's; burn all! Some to Decius's house, and    35
    some to Casca's; some to Ligarius's. Away! go!

*(Exeunt all the* **Plebeians**, *dragging off* **Cinna**)

# Reviewing the Selection

Answer each of the following questions without looking back at the play.

*Recalling Facts*

1. Portia is
   - ☐ a. Caesar's wife.
   - ☐ b. Antony's servant.
   - ☐ c. Caesar's nephew.
   - ☐ d. Brutus's wife.

*Understanding Main Ideas*

2. Brutus makes his speech at Caesar's funeral before Mark Antony speaks. What is the main idea of Brutus's words to the Roman people?
   - ☐ a. He explains why he loved Caesar better than anyone else.
   - ☐ b. He wants the people to accept Cassius as ruler in Caesar's place.
   - ☐ c. He tries to show that Caesar was too ambitious and would have become a tyrant.
   - ☐ d. He warns the people of Mark Antony's ambitions.

*Placing Events in Order*

3. At Caesar's funeral Mark Antony reads Caesar's will
   - ☐ a. before Brutus makes his speech.
   - ☐ b. after he learns that Octavius is near Rome.
   - ☐ c. at the beginning of his speech.
   - ☐ d. at the end of his speech.

*Dialogue, Monologue, and Soliloquy*

4. Courage is important to Caesar. He wants to appear brave to himself and to others. Which of the following actions supports this view?
   ☐ a. Caesar goes to the Senate on the ides of March.
   ☐ b. Caesar listens to the petitions of the Romans.
   ☐ c. Caesar asks what the augurers have to say.
   ☐ d. Caesar allows Calpurnia to keep him from going to the Senate.

*Recognizing Words*
*in Context*

5. "The evil that men do lives after them, The good is oft <u>interred</u> with their bones." In this context *interred* means
   ☐ a. buried.
   ☐ b. broken.
   ☐ c. praised.
   ☐ d. worshipped.

## Interpreting the Selection

Answer each of the following questions. You may look back at the play if necessary.

*Making*
*Inferences*

6. When Brutus speaks after Caesar has been killed, the crowd agrees with what he says. When Mark Antony speaks, the crowd turns against Brutus and agrees with Antony. Which of the following statements is *not* true?
   ☐ a. The people trust Mark Antony.
   ☐ b. The crowd is easily influenced.
   ☐ c. The people are upset by Caesar's death.
   ☐ d. The people have no respect for Mark Antony.

7. For Brutus, what is the most important reason
   for killing Caesar?
   ☐ a. to prevent tyranny
   ☐ b. to gain power for himself
   ☐ c. to gain a pardon for Publius Cimber
   ☐ d. to form a more honest government

8. What is Shakespeare's purpose for including
   the dream in which Calpurnia cries out in
   her sleep?
   ☐ a. to let Caesar know that Brutus will
        betray him
   ☐ b. to show that Calpurnia is crazy
   ☐ c. to increase the tension in the play
   ☐ d. to show the audience that Calpurnia is
        smarter than Caesar

9. Portia pleads with Brutus to confide in her.
   From what she says, you can see that she is
   ☐ a. aware that Brutus wants to kill Caesar.
   ☐ b. a loving and sensitive wife.
   ☐ c. afraid that Brutus no longer loves her.
   ☐ d. unable to keep a secret.

10. What conclusion can you draw from the
    contents of Caesar's will?
    ☐ a. Caesar did not have many possessions.
    ☐ b. Caesar loved the people of Rome.
    ☐ c. Caesar wanted his money buried
         with him.
    ☐ d. Caesar cared more for his wife than for
         anyone else.

# Dialogue, Monologue, and Soliloquy

Plays such as *Julius Caesar* are dependent on conversations, or dialogue, between different characters. You will also find two other types of speeches in William Shakespeare's plays: monologues and soliloquies. A monologue is an extended speech delivered by one character. It is heard but uninterrupted by the other character or characters. A soliloquy is a speech in which a character speaks his or her thoughts aloud while alone.

In Acts 2 and 3 of *Julius Caesar*, you can find examples of dialogue, monologue, and soliloquy. In this lesson you will study what purpose each type of speech serves.

## Dialogue

As you have learned, dialogue is the actual conversation between the characters. Playwrights use dialogue for several purposes. One obvious purpose is to move along the action of the play. Early in Act 2, Scene 1, for example, the conspirators visit Brutus in his home.

*1. Read the dialogue between Brutus and the six other conspirators in*

*Act 2, Scene 1 (lines 86 to 228). What do the men discuss? What decisions do they make? How does that dialogue move along the action of the play?*

A second function of dialogue is to let the audience know what is happening onstage or what has happened offstage. In many plays only part of the action of the story occurs onstage. The audience knows that other events are taking place offstage while they are watching a particular scene. But they do not know what the results are. Therefore the playwright must let the audience know what has taken place offstage. The playwright often chooses to have action take place offstage and to have the characters report the action.

In Act 1, you will recall, Shakespeare did not actually show the scene in which Mark Antony offered Caesar the crown. Instead, he had Casca, who had witnessed the incident, describe the incident to Brutus and Cassius, who had not been there.

In Act 2, Scene 2 (lines 8 to 56), Shakespeare introduces a dialogue between Calpurnia, Caesar, and a servant. In the dialogue you learn about some strange occurrences offstage.

*2. What does Calpurnia report is happening in Rome? What does the servant report? What does Calpurnia want Caesar to do? Does he agree?*

Through dialogue, the playwright also builds suspense. Suspense is the interest, excitement, and anticipation you feel about what will happen in the play. In the dialogue between Calpurnia and Caesar, you learn about the frightening happenings in the streets of Rome and the strange omens of the augurers—priests who claimed that they could foretell the future by explaining certain signs. That news, together with earlier warnings, creates uncertainty about what will happen. Calpurnia pleads with her husband to stay home. He agrees, but then Decius appears.

*3. What does Decius want Caesar to do? Why? How does the dialogue between Caesar, Calpurnia, and Decius contribute to the suspense?*

As you learned in Chapter 1, dialogue also reveals a character's personality. In Act 2 Shakespeare develops the characters you met in Act 1, especially Brutus, Cassius, and Caesar. At the beginning of Act 2,

Brutus does much of the talking when the conspirators meet. The others accept his lead because they know he is more respected than they are. By arranging the scene in this way, Shakespeare shows Brutus as a strong leader.

   *4. Study Act 2, Scene 1 (lines 141 to 153), at the point when Cassius suggests that the conspirators ask Cicero to join their plot. Briefly summarize what is said. What does the dialogue tell you about Brutus, Cassius, and Casca?*

   *5. Skim Acts 2 and 3. Choose a dialogue in which the personality of the characters is revealed more fully. Summarize the dialogue and explain what you learn about the character or characters.*

## Irony and Asides

Occasionally, Shakespeare uses asides in the middle of a dialogue. An aside is a brief speech in which a character expresses his or her thoughts in words not meant to be heard by other characters onstage. An aside lets the audience know what a character really thinks, as opposed to what he or she is saying to the other characters. In Act 2, Scene 2 (lines 120 to 122), Caesar asks Trebonius to stand near him so they can talk. In lines 123 and 124, you hear Trebonius's reply, with an aside.

> **Trebonius:**   Caesar, I will: *[Aside]* and so near will I be,
>                       That your best friends shall wish I had been further.

   In delivering an aside such as this one, the actor playing Trebonius would speak in an undertone. He would probably turn away from Caesar as he spoke. The aside reminds the audience that Caesar is surrounded by enemies.
   Asides often contribute to the irony of a dialogue. Irony refers to the contrast between appearance and reality or between what is expected and what actually happens. Trebonius's aside is an example of a particular kind of irony called dramatic irony. Dramatic irony is the contrast that occurs when the audience has information or an understanding of events that a character or characters in a play do not have. Dramatic irony adds

suspense to a play because the audience wonders when the characters will learn the truth.

*6. What is the dramatic irony surrounding Caesar's dialogue with Trebonius in Act 2, Scene 2?*

*7. Find another aside in Act 2 or Act 3 and explain its importance to the scene.*

# Monologue

Unlike a dialogue, a monologue is not a shared exchange between characters. Instead, one character delivers his or her thoughts or opinions while others listen. Shakespeare uses monologues in the same ways he uses dialogue. That is, he includes monologues to move along the plot and to develop characters.

Early in Act 2, Scene 1, Brutus delivers two monologues. In the first, he gives his reasons for why the conspirators should not take an oath. In the second, he explains why he opposes Cassius's plan to kill Mark Antony as well as Caesar.

*8. Reread both monologues in Act 2, Scene 1 (lines 114 to 140 and 162 to 183). What does each monologue tell you about Brutus's character?*

**Public Speeches.** Shakespeare also uses monologues in the same way they are used in everyday life—as public speeches. In Act 3, Scene 2, you read two public speeches. Both Brutus and Antony address the people of Rome after Caesar's murder. The two speeches are among the most famous monologues in all of Shakespeare's plays. Brutus speaks to the crowd because the people are disturbed by the frightening events that have just taken place. Brutus is straightforward and honest with the people. He tells the crowd that he loved and admired Caesar as much as they did. Like them, he honored Caesar's bravery.

*9. Read Brutus's speech in Act 3, Scene 2 (lines 12 to 43). How is this speech written differently from much of the rest of the play? Why do you think it is written in this way?*

*10. What reasons does Brutus give for killing Caesar? How does the crowd respond to his speech? Give examples to show their response.*

**The Art of Persuasion.** At the end of his speech (lines 53 to 59), Brutus introduces Mark Antony to the crowd. The people are not particularly friendly toward Antony or respectful of the dead Caesar. In this hostile atmosphere Antony begins to speak. His speech is a masterpiece of persuasion, or <u>rhetoric</u>—the art of using words effectively to sway an audience's opinions.

*11. Antony's speech is actually made up of four separate monologues. Skim the speech beginning in Act 2, Scene 2 (line 71), to find each of the four monologues. Write the first line of each.*

In his speech Antony uses several techniques to win the audience to his side. He begins by appearing detached and statesmanlike. He is clear and reasonable. In a few words he states his purpose. He reviews the facts. He weighs both sides in the controversy. He praises his enemies. At the end of the first part, he reluctantly gives way to his emotions.

*12. In what way is Antony's pause after line 105 well timed?*

*13. Notice how often Antony repeats: "But Brutus says he [Caesar] was ambitious, / And Brutus is an honourable man." What kinds of details does Antony mention before he repeats those lines? In what tone of voice do you think Mark Antony talks about Brutus?*

In his second monologue Antony introduces the topic of Caesar's will, which he says he will not read. He also allows himself to get more emotional. In the remainder of the speech, he builds his emotions until he has inspired the people.

*14. In your own words, describe several other techniques that Antony uses in his speech to win the Roman people to his side. What does this speech tell you about Antony?*

## Soliloquy

Another type of speech you find in *Julius Caesar* is a soliloquy. It is given by a character who is alone onstage. Shakespeare uses a soliloquy to show you the character's inner thoughts and feelings. Today's play-wrights do not often use soliloquies or asides. However, soliloquies and asides were both frequently included in Elizabethan plays.

Like a dialogue or a monologue, a soliloquy moves along the plot and reveals a character's personality. It also gives the audience information that other characters do not know.

In Act 3, at the end of Scene 1, Antony is alone onstage after Caesar's murder. Caesar lies dead at his feet. Antony has just assured Brutus and the others that he understands their reasons for killing Caesar. As a result, Brutus has agreed to let Mark Antony speak to the crowd.

*15. Reread Mark Antony's soliloquy (Act 3, Scene 1, lines 254 to 275). Think about the information you learn here that Brutus and the other con-spirators do not have. Was Antony sincere when he shook hands with Caesar's murderers? What promise does Antony make to Caesar's corpse? How is the audience better prepared for Antony's speech to the crowd than Brutus is?*

As you read the rest of the play, notice whether you are reading a dialogue, a monologue, or a soliloquy. Think about what purpose Shakespeare is achieving with each kind of speech.

## Questions for Thought and Discussion

The questions and activities that follow will help you explore *Julius Caesar*, Acts 2 and 3, in more depth and at the same time develop your critical thinking skills.

1. **Analyzing.** Mark Antony was an admirer and a loyal friend of Caesar's. Yet he shakes hands with the men who murdered Caesar. Why is Antony friendly to Caesar's murderers? What kind of person do Antony's actions show him to be? Use evidence from the play to support your answer.

2. **Expressing an Opinion.** Which character do you think was more honest and sincere in his feelings—Mark Antony or Brutus? Give evidence from the play to support your opinion.

3. **Comparing.** Both Antony and Cassius are shrewd and clever men. What evidence shows that they have those characteristics? How is Brutus different from them? Use examples to support the comparison.

4. **Evaluating.** Divide the class into small groups. Each group should prepare two lists, one headed "Positive" and the other headed "Negative." Under each heading, list the positive and negative characteristics that Shakespeare reveals about Caesar in the first three acts of the play. Now make two more lists, using the same headings. In those lists write the positive and negative feelings that Brutus has toward Caesar. As a group, try to agree on why Brutus made the decision he did. Then compare your lists and your decision with those of the other groups.

## Writing About Literature

Several suggestions for writing projects are given below. You may be asked to complete one or more of these projects. If you have any questions about how to begin a writing assignment, review Using the Writing Process, beginning on page 385.

1. **Interpreting Shakespearean Language.** Study the main part of Brutus's speech to the crowd in Act 3, Scene 2 (lines 12 to 31). Imagine that Brutus is giving the speech today. In a paragraph write the same message in modern language.

2. **Preparing Staging Plans.** Imagine that you are directing *Julius Caesar*. You must write detailed plans about how you will stage each scene and what instructions you want to give the actors. Prepare the plans for staging the speeches of Brutus and Antony in Act 3, Scene 2. Be sure to include where the crowd stands, how the different characters sound, what movements occur onstage, and so on. You may want to illustrate your plans.

3. **Explaining.** Reread Act 2, Scene 2, where Calpurnia begs Caesar not to go to the Capitol and Decius counters her arguments. Write a paragraph explaining why Caesar was unlikely to stay at home because of his wife's fears. Explain what kind of man he was and how he viewed himself.

## Chapter 3

Selection      *Julius Caesar, Acts 4 & 5*
               WILLIAM SHAKESPEARE

Lesson         *Tragedy and Theme*

## About the Selection

At the end of Act 3, the tension in *Julius Caesar* is high. Julius Caesar, the popular Roman general, has been murdered by friends who feared his growing power. Rome is in turmoil. The people have been swayed first toward Caesar's murderers and then toward his supporters.

In his funeral speech Mark Antony has rallied the Roman mob in favor of Caesar and against the assassins. The mob leaves to burn the homes of Brutus, Cassius, and the other conspirators. In the final scene they find and attack a poet named Cinna, whom they mistake for one of the conspirators of the same name.

In Acts 1 and 2 the conspirators plan Caesar's downfall. In Act 3 they assassinate him. In Acts 4 and 5 you will learn the consequences of the conspirators' actions.

As the play moves toward its conclusion, the friendship between Brutus and Cassius, the two main conspirators, is severely tested. On the other side, Mark Antony forms an alliance with Octavius, Caesar's nephew and heir. The two sides prepare to do battle.

In the final act of *Julius Caesar,* the opposing forces fight. When you read the battle scenes in Act 5, try to imagine how the two armies are situated. The actual battle is not enacted onstage. Instead, the events are reported by several characters. If you were watching the play, you might hear the sounds of battle offstage as you learned about the fighting from what the various characters say. When reading the play, you need to use

Shakespeare's words and your own imagination to picture the scene.

In the battle scene, as in other scenes, you also need to imagine how the actors say their lines. For example, how would an actor report the news of someone's death? How would the character most affected by the death respond? Let your imagination help to move along the action.

Most plays in Shakespeare's time were performed by acting companies. An acting company was a group of men who worked full time putting on plays. In Elizabethan times women were not allowed to act on the stage. As a result, all women's parts were played by males, usually boys whose voices were not deep.

Wealthy nobles sponsored the major acting companies. A company was named for its sponsor. Shakespeare's company was called the Lord Chamberlain's Men. It was among the most popular groups in England. Its success was probably due to the plays that Shakespeare wrote for the company. In 1603 King James I became the company's sponsor, so the group changed its name to the King's Men.

Shakespeare's company had its own theater, called the Globe. The Globe was built around a courtyard. On three sides of the courtyard, the building held roofed galleries in which members of the audience who could afford the price sat. The stage projected into the courtyard, which was called the pit. Other members of the audience stood in the pit, either at the front of the stage or along the sides.

The theater was open to the weather, so when it rained, no performance was held. Because lighting in the theater was limited, plays were performed in the afternoon. The stage had no curtain and little scenery. The playwright had to use dialogue to let the audience know where a scene was taking place.

Actors wore costumes, but the costumes were based on current fashions. If the acting company had money, the actors wore expensive silks and brocades. In *Julius Caesar*, therefore, Caesar and Brutus would wear the fine clothes of wealthy Elizabethans, not the togas of ancient Rome. In modern times Shakespeare has sometimes been staged with actors in contemporary clothing.

During the play the audience often talked or moved about in the pit. People also bought food to eat. Sometimes they threw food at the actors if they did not like a performance. Women seldom attended plays at public theaters such as the Globe. When they did go, they wore masks to hide their identities.

## Lesson Preview

*Julius Caesar* is a type of play called a tragedy. The lesson that follows Acts 4 and 5 examines the play as a tragedy. A <u>tragedy</u> is a play that involves serious and important actions which turn out disastrously for the main character or characters.

Like any serious piece of literature, Shakespeare's *Julius Caesar* has a <u>theme</u>, the underlying message or central idea of a piece of writing. In this play, as in many works of literature, the author treats more than one theme.

The questions that follow will help you identify the elements of tragedy in *Julius Caesar* and discover the themes in the play. As you read, think about how you would answer these questions.

**1** Who is the main character of *Julius Caesar*? What other characters are important to the play?

**2** What is the chief problem facing the main character? How does he try to solve the problem? What are the results of his actions?

**3** What happens to the main character? How do you feel about the turn of events?

**4** What relationships exist among the various characters? Do these relationships change in the course of the play? If so, how do they change?

**5** What serious ideas does Shakespeare treat in this play?

## Vocabulary

Here are some difficult words that appear in the selection that follows. Study the words and their definitions, as well as the sentences that show how the words are used. This will help you get the most from your reading.

**divers** various. *Although we were all close friends in college, we went our divers ways after graduation.*

**wrangle** argue. *The unhappy couple will often wrangle about very insignificant problems.*

**contaminate** poison; dirty. *The health authorities warned that the factory might contaminate our town's water supply.*

**infirmities** weaknesses; sicknesses. *The elderly farmer did not let his infirmities prevent him from working.*

**indirection** devious means; deceitfulness. *She managed by indirection to take several hundred dollars from the cash register.*

**covetous** greedy; envious. *The covetous girls envied their sister's beautiful new dress.*

**chides** scolds. *A good trainer always chides a disobedient dog, but she should never hit the dog.*

**repose** rest. *George sought repose in the garden hammock.*

**apparition** ghost. *The ghost story was so vivid that I almost believed I saw the apparition itself listening to the tale.*

# *Julius Caesar*

## ACTS 4 & 5

WILLIAM SHAKESPEARE

## ACT 4

### Scene 1

*Antony, Octavius, and Lepidus, who now control Rome, make a list of those people who will be executed for having taken part in the conspiracy to murder Caesar. Lepidus leaves, and Antony tells Octavius that he thinks little of Lepidus. The two men then plan their campaign against the armies of Cassius and Brutus.*

**Antony's house. Enter Antony, Octavius *and* Lepidus.**

**Antony**  These many then shall die; their names are prick'd.°
**Octavius**  Your brother too must die; consent you, Lepidus?
**Lepidus**  I do consent—
**Octavius**                             Prick him down, Antony.
**Lepidus**  Upon condition Publius shall not live,
  Who is your sister's son, Mark Antony.                               5

---

**1. prick'd:** marked.

**Antony**    He shall not live. Look, with a spot I damn him.
      But Lepidus, go you to Caesar's house;
      Fetch the will hither, and we shall determine
      How to cut off some charge in legacies.
**Lepidus**    What, shall I find you here?                                    10
**Octavius**    Or here or at the Capitol.

*(Exit* **Lepidus***)*

**Antony**    This is a slight unmeritable man,
      Meet to be sent on errands. Is it fit,
      The three-fold world divided,° he should stand
      One of the three to share it?
**Octavius**                          So you thought him,                      15
      And took his voice who should be prick'd to die
      In our black sentence and proscription.°
**Antony**    Octavius, I have seen more days than you:
      And though we lay these honours on this man,
      To ease ourselves of divers sland'rous loads,°                          20
      He shall but bear them as the ass bears gold,
      To groan and sweat under the business,
      Either led or driven, as we point the way;
      And having brought our treasure where we will,
      Then take we down his load, and turn him off,                           25
      Like to the empty ass, to shake his ears,
      And graze in commons.°
**Octavius**                          You may do your will;
      But he's a tried and valiant soldier.
**Antony**    So is my horse, Octavius, and for that
      I do appoint him store of provender:°                                   30

---

**14. The three-fold world divided:** Antony, Octavius, and Lepidus formed a triumvirate—a three-part government—that ruled Rome.    **17. In our black sentence and proscription:** on our death list.    **20. To ease . . . sland'rous loads:** to be free of some of the blame that is laid on us.    **27. graze in commons:** eat grass on public grounds.    **30. appoint him store of provender:** feed him.

It is a creature that I teach to fight,
To wind, to stop, to run directly on,
His corporal motion govern'd by my spirit.
And, in some taste, is Lepidus but so:
He must be taught, and train'd, and bid go forth:          35
A barren-spirited fellow; one that feeds
On objects, arts, and imitations,
Which, out of use and stal'd by other men,
Begin his fashion. Do not talk of him
But as a property. And now, Octavius,                      40
Listen great things: Brutus and Cassius
Are levying powers:° we must straight make head.
Therefore let our alliance be combin'd,
Our best friends made, our means stretch'd;
And let us presently go sit in council,                    45
How covert matters may be best disclos'd,
And open perils surest answered.

**Octavius**   Let us do so: for we are at the stake,
And bay'd about with many enemies;
And some that smile have in their hearts, I fear,          50
Millions of mischiefs.

*(Exeunt)*

## Scene 2

*At Sardis, Brutus and his army are preparing for battle. Two of Cassius's soldiers arrive to announce the approach of their general. Cassius soon follows them into the camp.*

*Camp near Sardis. Before Brutus's tent. Drum. Enter* **Brutus**, **Lucilius** *and the soldiers.* **Titinius** *and* **Pindarus** *meet them.*

**Brutus**   Stand ho!

---

**42. Are levying powers:** are raising armies.

**Lucilius**   Give the word, ho! and stand.

**Brutus**   What now, Lucilius, is Cassius near?

**Lucilius**   He is at hand, and Pindarus is come

    To do you salutation from his master.             5

**Brutus**   He greets me well. Your master, Pindarus,

    In his own change, or by ill officers,

    Hath given me some worthy cause to wish

    Things done undone: but if he be at hand,

    I shall be satisfied.

**Pindarus**               I do not doubt      10

    But that my noble master will appear

    Such as he is, full of regard and honour.

**Brutus**   He is not doubted. A word, Lucilius;

    How he receiv'd you, let me be resolv'd.°

**Lucilius**   With courtesy and with respect enough,      15

    But not with such familiar instance,

    Nor with such free and friendly conference,°

    As he hath us'd of old.

**Brutus**               Thou hast describ'd

    A hot friend cooling. Ever note, Lucilius,

    When love begins to sicken and decay      20

    It useth an enforced ceremony.

    There are no tricks in plain and simple faith;

    But hollow men, like horses hot at hand,

    Make gallant show and promise of their mettle;

    But when they should endure the bloody spur,      25

    They fall their crests, and like deceitful jades

    Sink in the trial.° Comes his army on?

**Lucilius**   They mean this night in Sardis to be quarter'd;

    The greater part, the horse in general,°

---

**14. How he . . . be resolv'd:** Tell me how he [Cassius] received you.   **17. conference:** conversation.
**26–27. They fall . . . trial:** They lower their heads and, like liars, fail the test. In this speech, Brutus compares the false show of emotions of a fading friendship to the showiness of horses who act strong and willing but won't perform when they're needed.   **29. the horse in general:** most of the cavalry.

Are come with Cassius.

*(Enter **Cassius** and his Powers)*

**Brutus**                                    Hark! he is arriv'd.                    30
    March gently on to meet him.
**Cassius**   Stand ho!
**Brutus**   Stand ho! Speak the word along.
**1st Soldier**   Stand!
**2nd Soldier**   Stand!                                              35
**3rd Soldier**   Stand!
**Cassius**   Most noble brother, you have done me wrong.
**Brutus**   Judge me, you gods; wrong I mine enemies?
    And if not so, how should I wrong a brother?
**Cassius**   Brutus, this sober form of yours hides wrongs;   40
    And when you do them—
**Brutus**                                    Cassius, be content.
    Speak your griefs softly; I do know you well.
    Before the eyes of both our armies here,
    Which should perceive nothing but love from us,
    Let us not wrangle. Bid them move away;          45
    Then in my tent, Cassius, enlarge your griefs,
    And I will give you audience.
**Cassius**                                   Pindarus,
    Bid our commanders lead their charges off
    A little from this ground.
**Brutus**   Lucius, do you the like; and let no man           50
    Come to our tent till we have done our conference.
    Lucilius and Titinius guard our door.

*(Exeunt)*

# Scene 3

*Cassius and Brutus argue violently and almost come to blows over Cassius's refusal to help Brutus pay for his army. When the two men calm down, Brutus explains his hot temper by revealing that Portia has killed herself. Their allies arrive, and a war council is held at which Brutus's battle plan is accepted. When Brutus tries to sleep, he sees the ghost of Julius Caesar, who predicts that they will meet again at Philippi, the scene of the upcoming battle.*

## *The same*

**Cassius**   That you have wrong'd me doth appear in this:
You have condemn'd and noted Lucius Pella
For taking bribes here of the Sardians;
Wherein my letters, praying on his side,
Because I knew the man, was slighted off.°                              5
**Brutus**   You wrong'd yourself to write in such a case.
**Cassius**   In such a time as this it is not meet
That every nice° offence should bear his comment.
**Brutus**   Let me tell you, Cassius, you yourself
Are much condemn'd to have an itching palm,                             10
To sell and mart your offices for gold°
To undeservers.
**Cassius**                              I an itching palm!
You know that you are Brutus that speaks this,
Or, by the gods, this speech were else your last.
**Brutus**   The name of Cassius honours this corruption,                 15
And chastisement° doth therefore hide his head.
**Cassius**   Chastisement!
**Brutus**   Remember March, the ides of March remember.
Did not great Julius bleed for justice' sake?
What villain touch'd his body, that did stab,                           20

---

**4–5. Wherein my letters . . . slighted off:** You ignored my letters, in which I defended him because I knew him.   **8. nice:** small.   **10–11. Are much condemn'd . . . offices for gold:** are believed to have taken bribes and to have dealt in the selling of public offices.   **16. chastisement:** punishment.

And not for justice? What, shall one of us,
That struck the foremost man of all this world
But for supporting robbers, shall we now
Contaminate our fingers with base bribes,
And sell the mighty space of our large honours          25
For so much trash as may be grasped thus?
I had rather be a dog, and bay the moon,
Than such a Roman.

**Cassius**                                 Brutus, bait not me;
I'll not endure it. You forget yourself,
To hedge me in. I am a soldier, I,                        30
Older in practice, abler than yourself
To make conditions.

**Brutus**                                  Go to! you are not, Cassius.
**Cassius**   I am.
**Brutus**   I say you are not.
**Cassius**   Urge me no more, I shall forget myself;     35
Have mind upon your health; tempt me no farther.
**Brutus**   Away, slight man!
**Cassius**   Is't possible?
**Brutus**                                  Hear me, for I will speak.
Must I give way and room to your rash choler?°
Shall I be frighted when a madman stares?                 40
**Cassius**   O ye gods, ye gods! Must I endure all this?
**Brutus**   All this? ay, more: fret till your proud heart break;
Go show your slaves how choleric you are,
And make your bondmen tremble. Must I budge?
Must I observe you? Must I stand and crouch               45
Under your testy humour? By the gods,
You shall digest the venom of your spleen,
Though it do split you; for, from this day forth,
I'll use you for my mirth, yea, for my laughter,

**39. rash choler:** uncontrolled temper.

When you are waspish.°

**Cassius**                        Is it come to this?           50

**Brutus**    You say you are a better soldier:
    Let it appear so; make your vaunting° true,
    And it shall please me well. For mine own part,
    I shall be glad to learn of noble men.

**Cassius**    You wrong me every way; you wrong me, Brutus.    55
    I said, an elder soldier, not a better:
    Did I say better?

**Brutus**                    If you did, I care not.

**Cassius**    When Caesar liv'd, he durst not thus have mov'd me.°

**Brutus**    Peace, peace! you durst not so have tempted him.

**Cassius**    I durst not?                                60

**Brutus**    No

**Cassius**    What? durst not tempt him?

**Brutus**                     For your life you durst not.

**Cassius**    Do not presume too much upon my love.
    I may do that I shall be sorry for.

**Brutus**    You have done that you should be sorry for.    65
    There is no terror, Cassius, in your threats;
    For I am arm'd so strong in honesty
    That they pass by me as the idle wind,
    Which I respect not. I did send to you
    For certain sums of gold, which you denied me;    70
    For I can raise no money by vile means:
    By heaven, I had rather coin my heart,
    And drop my blood for drachmas, than to wring
    From the hard hands of peasants their vile trash
    By any indirection. I did send    75
    To you for gold to pay my legions,
    Which you denied me: was that done like Cassius?

---

**49. waspish:** cranky.   **52. vaunting:** bragging.   **58. he durst not . . . thus have mov'd me:** he dared not speak to me this way.

Should I have answer'd Caius Cassius so?
When Marcus Brutus grows so covetous,
To lock such rascal counters from his friends,                    80
Be ready, gods, with all your thunderbolts,
Dash him to pieces!

**Cassius**                              I denied you not.

**Brutus**   You did.

**Cassius**                              I did not. He was but a fool
That brought my answer back. Brutus hath riv'd my heart.
A friend should bear his friend's infirmities;                    85
But Brutus makes mine greater than they are.

**Brutus**   I do not, till you practise them on me.

**Cassius**   You love me not.

**Brutus**                              I do not like your faults.

**Cassius**   A friendly eye could never see such faults.

**Brutus**   A flatterer's would not, though they do appear        90
As huge as high Olympus.

**Cassius**   Come, Antony, and young Octavius, come,
Revenge yourselves alone on Cassius,
For Cassius is aweary of the world:
Hated by one he loves; brav'd by his brother;                    95
Check'd like a bondman; all his faults observ'd,
Set in a note-book, learn'd, and conn'd by rote,°
To cast into my teeth. O, I could weep
My spirit from mine eyes! There is my dagger,
And here my naked breast; within, a heart                        100
Dearer than Pluto's mine,° richer than gold:
If that thou be'st a Roman, take it forth.
I, that denied thee gold, will give my heart:
Strike, as thou didst at Caesar; for I know,
When thou didst hate him worst, thou lov'dst him better          105

---

**97. conn'd by rote:** memorized.    **101. Dearer than Pluto's mine:** more precious than the mine of Plutus, the god of riches.

Than ever thou lov'dst Cassius.

**Brutus**                                    Sheathe your dagger.
Be angry when you will, it shall have scope;
Do what you will, dishonour shall be humour.°
O Cassius, you are yoked with a lamb
That carries anger as the flint bears fire,                          110
Who, much enforced, shows a hasty spark,
And straight is cold again.

**Cassius**                                    Hath Cassius liv'd
To be but mirth and laughter to his Brutus,
When grief and blood ill-temper'd vexeth him?

**Brutus**   When I spoke that, I was ill-temper'd too.          115

**Cassius**   Do you confess so much? Give me your hand.

**Brutus**   And my heart too.

**Cassius**                            O Brutus!

**Brutus**                            What's the matter?

**Cassius**   Have not you love enough to bear with me,
When that rash humour which my mother gave me
Makes me forgetful?

**Brutus**                            Yes, Cassius; and from henceforth          120
When you are over-earnest with your Brutus,
He'll think your mother chides, and leave you so.

*(Enter a **Poet** followed by **Lucilius**, **Titinius** and **Lucius**)*

**Poet**   Let me go in to see the generals.
There is some grudge between 'em; 'tis not meet
They be alone.                                                              125

**Lucilius**   You shall not come to them.

**Poet**   Nothing but death shall stay me.

**Cassius**   How now? What's the matter?

**Poet**   For shame, you generals! What do you mean?
Love, and be friends, as two such men should be;          130

---

**108. dishonour shall be humour:** I will attribute your insults to bad temper.

For I have seen more years, I'm sure, than ye.

**Cassius**  Ha, ha! how vilely doth this cynic rhyme!

**Brutus**  Get you hence, sirrah! Saucy fellow, hence!

**Cassius**  Bear with him, Brutus; 'tis his fashion.

**Brutus**  I'll know his humour, when he knows his time.                    135

What should the wars do with these jigging fools?

Companion, hence!

**Cassius**                              Away, away, be gone!

*(Exit **Poet**)*

**Brutus**  Lucilius and Titinius, bid the commanders

Prepare to lodge their companies tonight.

**Cassius**  And come yourselves, and bring Messala with you                 140

Immediately to us.

*(Exeunt **Lucilius** and **Titinius**)*

**Brutus**                      Lucius, a bowl of wine!

*(Exit **Lucius**)*

**Cassius**  I did not think you could have been so angry.

**Brutus**  O Cassius, I am sick of many griefs.

**Cassius**  Of your philosophy you make no use,

If you give place to accidental evils.°                                     145

**Brutus**  No man bears sorrow better. Portia is dead.

**Cassius**  Ha? Portia?

**Brutus**  She is dead.

**Cassius**  How 'scap'd I killing, when I cross'd you so?

O insupportable and touching loss!                                          150

Upon what sickness?

**Brutus**                              Impatient of my absence,

And grief that young Octavius with Mark Antony

---

**144–145. Of your philosophy . . . evils:** Brutus believed in stoicism, a philosophy that taught acceptance of one's fate.

*Tragedy and Theme*

Have made themselves so strong; for with her death
That tidings came. With this she fell distract,°
And, her attendants absent, swallow'd fire.                    155
**Cassius**   And died so?
**Brutus**                          Even so.
**Cassius**                                     O ye immortal gods!

*(Enter* **Lucius** *with wine and taper)*

**Brutus**   Speak no more of her. Give me a bowl of wine.
In this I bury all unkindness, Cassius.
**Cassius**   My heart is thirsty for that noble pledge.
Fill, Lucius, till the wine o'erswell the cup.                 160
I cannot drink too much of Brutus's love.

*(Exit* **Lucius***)*

*(Enter* **Titinius** *and* **Messala***)*

**Brutus**   Come in, Titinius. Welcome, good Messala.
Now sit we close about this taper here,
And call in question our necessities.
**Cassius**   Portia, art thou gone?
**Brutus**                              No more, I pray you.        165
Messala, I have here received letters,
That young Octavius and Mark Antony
Come down upon us with a mighty power,
Bending their expedition toward Philippi.
**Messala**   Myself have letters of the self-same tenor.°        170
**Brutus**   With what addition?
**Messala**   That by proscription and bills of outlawry
Octavius, Antony, and Lepidus
Have put to death an hundred senators.
**Brutus**   Therein our letters do not well agree.              175

---

**154. fell distract:** lost her mind.   **170. self-same tenor:** saying the same thing.

Mine speak of seventy senators that died
By their proscriptions, Cicero being one.

**Cassius**   Cicero one?

**Messala**                          Cicero is dead,
And by that order of proscription.

**Brutus**   Well, to our work alive. What do you think          180
Of marching to Philippi presently?

**Cassius**   I do not think it good.

**Brutus**                          Your reason?

**Cassius**                                This it is:
'Tis better that the enemy seek us;
So shall he waste his means, weary his soldiers,
Doing himself offence, whilst we, lying still,          185
Are full of rest, defence, and nimbleness.

**Brutus**   Good reasons must of force give place to better.
The people 'twixt Philippi and this ground
Do stand but in a forc'd affection;
For they have grudg'd us contribution.          190
The enemy, marching along by them,
By them shall make a fuller number up,°
Come on refresh'd, new-added, and encourag'd;
From which advantage shall we cut him off
If at Philippi we do face him there,          195
These people at our back.

**Cassius**                          Hear me, good brother.

**Brutus**   Under your pardon. You must note beside
That we have tried the utmost of our friends,
Our legions are brim-full, our cause is ripe:
The enemy increaseth every day;          200
We, at the height, are ready to decline.
There is a tide in the affairs of men,
Which, taken at the flood, leads on to fortune;

---

192. **make a fuller number up:** recruit more soldiers.

Omitted, all the voyage of their life
Is bound in shallows and in miseries.                                    205
On such a full sea are we now afloat,
And we must take the current when it serves,
Or lose our ventures.

**Cassius**                          Then, with your will, go on;
We'll along ourselves, and meet them at Philippi.

**Brutus**   The deep of night is crept upon our talk,                    210
And nature must obey necessity,
Which we will niggard° with a little rest.
There is no more to say?

**Cassius**                          No more. Good night.
Early tomorrow will we rise, and hence.

**Brutus**   Lucius!

*(Enter **Lucius**)*

My gown.

*(Exit **Lucius**)*

Farewell, good Messala.                    215
Goodnight, Titinius. Noble, noble Cassius,
Goodnight, and good repose.

**Cassius**                          O my dear brother,
This was an ill beginning of the night.
Never come such division 'tween our souls!
Let it not, Brutus.

*(Enter **Lucius** with the gown)*

**Brutus**                          Everything is well.                    220
**Cassius**   Goodnight, my lord.

---

**212. niggard:** treat in a stingy way.

| **Brutus** | Goodnight, good brother. |
| **Titinius** ⎫ | |
| **Messala** ⎭ | Goodnight, Lord Brutus. |
| **Brutus** | Farewell, every one. |

*(Exeunt all but **Brutus**)*

Give me the gown. Where is thy instrument?°
**Lucius**   Here in the tent.
**Brutus**                                 What, thou speak'st drowsily?
   Poor knave, I blame thee not; thou art o'er-watch'd.°       225
   Call Claudius and some other of my men;
   I'll have them sleep on cushions in my tent.
**Lucius**   Varro and Claudius!

*(Enter **Varro** and **Claudius**)*

**Varro**   Calls my lord?
**Brutus**   I pray you, sirs, lie in my tent and sleep.       230
   It may be I shall raise you by and by
   On business to my brother Cassius.
**Varro**   So please you, we will stand and watch your pleasure.
**Brutus**   I will not have it so; lie down, good sirs;
   It may be I shall otherwise bethink me.       235

*(**Varro** and **Claudius** lie down)*

Look, Lucius, here's the book I sought for so;
   I put it in the pocket of my gown.
**Lucius**   I was sure your lordship did not give it me.
**Brutus**   Bear with me, good boy, I am much forgetful.
   Canst thou hold up thy heavy eyes awhile,       240
   And touch thy instrument a strain or two?
**Lucius**   Ay, my lord, an't please you.°

---

**223. instrument:** musical instrument, possibly a lute or lyre.   **225. o'er-watch'd:** up too late.   **242. an't please you:** if it pleases you.

**Brutus**                                    It does, my boy.
    I trouble thee too much, but thou art willing.
**Lucius**   It is my duty, sir.
**Brutus**   I should not urge thy duty past thy might;                245
    I know young bloods look for a time of rest.
**Lucius**   I have slept, my lord, already.
**Brutus**   It was well done, and thou shalt sleep again;
    I will not hold thee long. If I do live,
    I will be good to thee.                                        250

*(Music and a song)*

    This is a sleepy tune. O murd'rous slumber!
    Layest thou thy leaden mace° upon my boy,
    That plays thee music? Gentle knave, good night;
    I will not do thee so much wrong to wake thee.
    If thou dost nod, thou break'st thy instrument;              255
    I'll take it from thee; and, good boy, good night.
    Let me see, let me see; is not the leaf turn'd down
    Where I left reading? Here it is, I think.

*(Enter the* **Ghost of Caesar***)*

    How ill this taper burns! Ha! who comes here?
    I think it is the weakness of mine eyes                       260
    That shapes this monstrous apparition.
    It comes upon me. Art thou any thing?
    Art thou some god, some angel, or some devil,
    That mak'st my blood cold, and my hair to stare?
    Speak to me what thou art.                                     265
**Ghost**   Thy evil spirit, Brutus.
**Brutus**                                    Why com'st thou?
**Ghost**   To tell thee thou shalt see me at Philippi.
**Brutus**   Well; then I shall see thee again?

---

**252. mace:** weapon.

**Ghost**  Ay, at Philippi.

**Brutus**  Why, I will see thee at Philippi then.                      270

*(Exit* **Ghost***)*

Now I have taken heart° thou vanishest.
Ill spirit, I would hold more talk with thee.
Boy! Lucius! Varro! Claudius! Sirs, awake!
Claudius!

**Lucius**  The strings, my lord, are false.                          275

**Brutus**  He thinks he still is at his instrument.
Lucius, awake!

**Lucius**  My lord?

**Brutus**  Didst thou dream, Lucius, that thou so criedst out?

**Lucius**  My lord, I do not know that I did cry.                     280

**Brutus**  Yes, that thou didst. Didst see anything?

**Lucius**  Nothing, my lord.

**Brutus**  Sleep again, Lucius. Sirrah Claudius!
Fellow thou, awake!

**Varro**                    My lord!

**Claudius**                      My lord!

**Brutus**  Why did you so cry out, sirs, in your sleep!              285

**Both**  Did we, my lord?

**Brutus**                    Ay. Saw you any thing?

**Varro**  No, my lord, I saw nothing.

**Claudius**                    Nor I, my lord.

**Brutus**  Go and commend me to my brother Cassius.
Bid him set on his powers betimes before,°
And we will follow.

**Both**                    It shall be done, my lord.                290

*(Exeunt)*

---

**271. I have taken heart:** I have my courage back.   **289. Bid him set . . . before:** Tell him to move his army first.

---

*Tragedy and Theme*

# ACT 5

## Scene 1

*On the plains of Philippi, the opposing armies face one another,*
*waiting for the order to attack. Brutus and Cassius ride out to meet*
*Antony and Octavius. After they exchange insults and threats, the*
*battle begins.*

*The Plains of Philippi.° Enter* **Octavius, Antony** *and their Army.*

**Octavius**   Now, Antony, our hopes are answered.
You said the enemy would not come down,
But keep the hills and upper regions.
It proves not so; their battles are at hand;
They mean to warn us at Philippi here,                         5
Answering before we do demand of them.
**Antony**   Tut, I am in their bosoms, and I know
Wherefore they do it. They could be content
To visit other places, and come down
With fearful bravery, thinking by this face                   10
To fasten in our thoughts that they have courage;
But 'tis not so.

*(Enter a* **Messenger***)*

**Messenger**   Prepare you, generals.
The enemy comes on in gallant show;
Their bloody sign of battle is hung out,
And something to be done immediately.                         15
**Antony**   Octavius, lead your battle softly on
Upon the left hand of the even field.
**Octavius**   Upon the right hand I. Keep thou the left.

---

**Plains of Philippi:** in Macedonia, north of Greece, near the coast of the Aegean Sea.

**Antony**   Why do you cross me in this exigent?°
**Octavius**   I do not cross you; but I will do so.                    20

> (*Drum. Enter* **Brutus, Cassius,** *and their Army;* **Lucilius, Titinius,**
> **Messala,** *and others*)

**Brutus**   They stand, and would have parley.°
**Cassius**   Stand fast, Titinius; we must out and talk.
**Octavius**   Mark Antony, shall we give sign of battle?
**Antony**   No, Caesar, we will answer on their charge.
　　　Make forth; the generals would have some words.            25
**Octavius**   Stir not until the signal.
**Brutus**   Words before blows: is it so, countrymen?
**Octavius**   Not that we love words better, as you do.
**Brutus**   Good words are better than bad strokes, Octavius.
**Antony**   In your bad strokes, Brutus, you give good words;       30
　　　Witness the hole you made in Caesar's heart,
　　　Crying, 'Long live! hail, Caesar!'
**Cassius**　　　　　　　　　Antony,
　　　The postures of your blows are yet unknown;
　　　But for your words, they rob the Hybla° bees,
　　　And leave them honeyless.
**Antony**　　　　　　　　　Not stingless too.            35
**Brutus**   O yes, and soundless too;
　　　For you have stol'n their buzzing, Antony,
　　　And very wisely threat before you sting.
**Antony**   Villains! you did not so when your vile daggers
　　　Hack'd one another in the sides of Caesar:                   40
　　　You show'd your teeth like apes, and fawn'd like hounds,
　　　And bow'd like bondmen, kissing Caesar's feet;
　　　Whilst damned Casca, like a cur, behind
　　　Struck Caesar on the neck. O you flatterers!

---

**19. exigent:** tense moment.   **21. would have parley:** want to talk.   **34. Hybla:** a town in ancient Sicily known for its excellent honey. Cassius says Antony's words are sweeter than the honey of the Hybla bees.

*Tragedy and Theme*

**Cassius**  Flatterers? Now, Brutus, thank yourself    45
This tongue had not offended so today,
If Cassius might have rul'd.°
**Octavius**  Come, come, the cause. If arguing make us sweat,
The proof of it will turn to redder drops.
Look,    50
I draw a sword against conspirators.
When think you that the sword goes up again?
Never, till Caesar's three and thirty wounds
Be well aveng'd; or till another Caesar°
Have added slaughter to the sword of traitors.    55
**Brutus**  Caesar, thou canst not die by traitor's hands,
Unless thou bring'st them with thee.
**Octavius**                               So I hope.
I was not born to die on Brutus's sword.
**Brutus**  O, if thou wert the noblest of thy strain,
Young man, thou could'st not die more honourable.    60
**Cassius**  A peevish school-boy, worthless of such honour,
Join'd with a masker and a reveller.°
**Antony**  Old Cassius still!
**Octavius**                             Come, Antony; away!
Defiance, traitors, hurl we in your teeth.
If you dare fight today, come to the field;    65
If not, when you have stomachs.

*(Exeunt* **Octavius**, **Antony**, *and their Army)*

**Cassius**  Why now, blow wind, swell billow, and swim bark!°
The storm is up, and all is on the hazard.
**Brutus**  Ho, Lucilius, hark, a word with you.

---

**46–47. This tongue . . . rul'd:** If you had listened to me and killed Antony, his tongue (words) would not be offending us now.    **54. another Caesar:** after the death of Julius Caesar, Octavius took the name Caesar.    **61–62. A peevish school-boy . . . a reveller:** *peevish* means irritable. Cassius and Brutus see Octavius as too young to be a real threat. Antony, who was known to enjoy partying (revels) is also not taken seriously.    **67. bark:** ship.

**Lucilius**   My lord?                                                                              70

**Cassius**   Messala.

**Messala**   What says my general?

**Cassius**                                    Messala,
  This is my birth-day; as this very day
  Was Cassius born. Give me thy hand, Messala;
  Be thou my witness that against my will,                                           75
  As Pompey was, am I compell'd to set
  Upon one battle all our liberties.
  You know that I held Epicurus strong,
  And his opinion; now I change my mind,
  And partly credit things that do presage.°                                         80
  Coming from Sardis, on our former ensign
  Two mighty eagles fell, and there they perch'd,
  Gorging and feeding from our soldiers' hands,
  Who to Philippi here consorted us.
  This morning are they fled away and gone,                                          85
  And in their steads do ravens, crows, and kites°
  Fly o'er our heads, and downward look on us,
  As we were sickly prey; their shadows seem
  A canopy most fatal, under which
  Our army lies, ready to give up the ghost.                                         90

**Messala**   Believe not so.

**Cassius**                                I but believe it partly,
  For I am fresh of spirit, and resolv'd
  To meet all perils very constantly.

**Brutus**   Even so, Lucilius.

**Cassius**                                Now, most noble Brutus,
  The gods today stand friendly, that we may,                                        95
  Lovers in peace, lead on our days to age!
  But since the affairs of men rests still incertain,

---

**78–80. You know . . . do presage:** Epicurus taught that supernatural signs were meaningless. Cassius says he once agreed with that, but he has now come to believe in omens.   **86. kites:** flesh-eating birds.

Let's reason with the worst that may befall.
If we do lose this battle, then is this
The very last time we shall speak together:                    100
What are you then determined to do?

**Brutus**   Even by the rule of that philosophy
By which I did blame Cato for the death
Which he did give himself, I know not how,
But I do find it cowardly and vile,                            105
For fear of what might fall, so to prevent
The time of life, arming myself with patience
To stay the providence of some high powers
That govern us below.°

**Cassius**                              Then, if we lose this battle,
You are contented to be led in triumph                         110
Through the streets of Rome?

**Brutus**   No, Cassius, no: think not, thou noble Roman,
That ever Brutus will go bound to Rome;
He bears too great a mind. But this same day
Must end that work the ides of March begun;                    115
And whether we shall meet again I know not.
Therefore our everlasting farewell take.
For ever, and for ever, farewell, Cassius.
If we do meet again, why, we shall smile;
If not, why then this parting was well made.                   120

**Cassius**   For ever, and for ever, farewell, Brutus.
If we do meet again, we'll smile indeed;
If not, 'tis true this parting was well made.

**Brutus**   Why then, lead on. O, that a man might know
The end of this day's business ere it come!
But it sufficeth that the day will end,
And then the end is known. Come, ho! away!

---

**108–109. To stay . . . below:** to let the gods decide what should happen to us.

## Scene 2

*Thinking he has spotted a weakness in Octavius's forces, Brutus sends Messala to order an attack.*

*The same. The field of battle. Enter* **Brutus** *and* **Messala**.

**Brutus**   Ride, ride, Messala, ride, and give these bills
Unto the legions on the other side.
Let them set on at once, for I perceive
But cold demeanour° in Octavius's wing,
And sudden push gives them the overthrow.                    5
Ride, ride, Messala; let them all come down.

*(Exeunt)*

## Scene 3

*As Cassius and Titinius watch, their soldiers are forced by Antony's army to retreat. Cassius sends Titinius to learn if a group of soldiers not far off are friends or enemies. Pindarus, Cassius's servant, stands on a hilltop and reports what is happening. Mistakenly, he tells Cassius that Titinius has been captured. Believing that he has sent his friend to his death, Cassius orders Pindarus to kill him. Later, Titinius returns with good news, only to find that Cassius is dead. Titinius then kills himself. Brutus arrives and mourns the deaths of his colleagues.*

*Another part of the field. Enter* **Cassius** *and* **Titinius**.

**Cassius**   O, look, Titinius, look, the villains fly.°
Myself have to mine own turn'd enemy:
This ensign here of mine was turning back;
I slew the coward, and did take it from him.
**Titinius**   O Cassius, Brutus gave the word too early,        5
Who, having some advantage on Octavius,

---

4. **cold demeanour:** a lack of fighting spirit.   1. **the villains fly:** Cassius is horrified to see his own men running from the battle.

---

Took it too eagerly; his soldiers fell to spoil,
Whilst we by Antony are all enclos'd.

*(Enter* **Pindarus***)*

**Pindarus**   Fly further off, my lord fly further off!
Mark Antony is in your tents, my lord.                                    10
Fly, therefore, noble Cassius, fly far off!
**Cassius**   This hill is far enough. Look, look, Titinius!
Are those my tents where I perceive the fire?
**Titinius**   They are, my lord.
**Cassius**                                     Titinius, if thou lov'st me,
Mount thou my horse, and hide thy spurs in him,           15
Till he have brought thee up to yonder troops
And here again, that I may rest assur'd
Whether yond troops are friend or enemy.
**Titinius**   I will be here again, even with a thought.

*(Exit)*

**Cassius**   Go, Pindarus, get higher on that hill;               20
My sight was ever thick. Regard Titinius,
And tell me what thou not'st about the field.

*(Exit* **Pindarus***)*

This day I breathed first. Time is come round,
And where I did begin, there shall I end.
My life is run his compass. Sirrah, what news?            25
**Pindarus**   *(at a distance)* O my lord!
**Cassius**   What news?
**Pindarus**   Titinius is enclosed round about
With horsemen, that make to him on the spur,
Yet he spurs on. Now they are almost on him.              30
Now, Titinius; now some light. O, he lights too!
He's ta'en!

*(Shout)*

And, hark! they shout for joy.

**Cassius**   Come down; behold no more.
O, coward that I am, to live so long,
To see my best friend ta'en before my face! 35

*(Enter Pindarus)*

Come hither, sirrah.
In Parthia° did I take thee prisoner;
And then I swore thee, saving of thy life,
That whatsoever I did bid thee do,
Thou shouldst attempt it. Come now, keep thine oath. 40
Now be a freeman; and with this good sword,
That ran through Caesar's bowels, search this bosom.°
Stand not to answer. Here, take thou the hilts,
And when my face is cover'd, as 'tis now,
Guide thou the sword.—Caesar, thou art reveng'd, 45
Even with the sword that kill'd thee.

*(Dies)*

**Pindarus**   So, I am free; yet would not so have been,
Durst I have done my will. O Cassius!
Far from this country Pindarus shall run,
Where never Roman shall take note of him. 50

*(Exit)*

*(Enter Titinius and Messala)*

**Messala**   It is but change, Titinius; for Octavius
Is overthrown by noble Brutus's power,
As Cassius's legions are by Antony.

---

**37. Parthia:** a region conquered by Roman armies. After a battle, victorious armies either killed their prisoners or made them slaves.   **42. search this bosom:** Cassius asks Pindarus to stab him in the chest.

*Tragedy and Theme*

**Titinius**  These tidings will well comfort Cassius.

**Messala**  Where did you leave him?

**Titinius**                                   All disconsolate,° 55
With Pindarus, his bondman, on this hill.

**Messala**  Is not that he that lies upon the ground?

**Titinius**  He lies not like that living. O my heart!

**Messala**  Is not that he?

**Titinius**                                   No, this was he, Messala,
But Cassius is no more. O setting sun, 60
As in thy red rays thou dost sink to night,
So in his red blood Cassius's day is set.
The sun of Rome is set. Our day is gone;
Clouds, dews, and dangers come; our deeds are done.
Mistrust of my success hath done this deed. 65

**Messala**  Mistrust of good success hath done this deed.
O hateful Error, Melancholy's child,
Why dost thou show to the apt thoughts of men
The things that are not? O Error, soon conceiv'd,
Thou never com'st unto a happy birth, 70
But kill'st the mother that engender'd thee.

**Titinius**  What, Pindarus! Where art thou, Pindarus?

**Messala**  Seek him, Titinius, whilst I go to meet
The noble Brutus, thrusting this report
Into his ears. I may say thrusting it; 75
For piercing steel and darts envenomed°
Shall be as welcome to the ears of Brutus
As tidings of this sight.

**Titinius**                                   Hie you, Messala,
And I will seek for Pindarus the while.

*(Exit **Messala**)*

Why didst thou send me forth, brave Cassius? 80

---

55. **disconsolate:** sad.   76. **envenomed:** poisoned.

Did I not meet thy friends, and did not they
Put on my brows this wreath of victory,
And bid me give it thee? Didst thou not hear their shouts?
Alas, thou hast misconstrued every thing.
But hold thee, take this garland on thy brow;                              85
Thy Brutus bid me give it thee, and I
Will do his bidding. Brutus, come apace,
And see how I regarded Caius Cassius.
By your leave, gods. This is a Roman's part:
Come, Cassius's sword, and find Titinius's heart.                          90

*(Dies)*

*(Enter* **Brutus, Messala, Young Cato, Strato, Volumnius** *and* **Lucilius***)*

**Brutus**   Where, where, Messala, doth his body lie?
**Messala**   Lo, yonder, and Titinius mourning it.
**Brutus**   Titinius's face is upward.
**Young Cato**                              He is slain.
**Brutus**   O Julius Caesar, thou art mighty yet!
Thy spirit walks abroad, and turns our swords                              95
In our own proper entrails.°
**Young Cato**                    Brave Titinius!
Look where he have not crown'd dead Cassius.
**Brutus**   Are yet two Romans living such as these?
The last of all the Romans, fare thee well!
It is impossible that ever Rome                                             100
Should breed thy fellow. Friends, I owe more tears
To this dead man than you shall see me pay.
I shall find time, Cassius, I shall find time.
Come therefore, and to Thasos send his body:
His funerals shall not be in our camp,                                     105

---

**94–96. O Julius Caesar . . . proper entrails:** Brutus observes that Caesar, though dead, has such influence that he has forced the conspirators to kill themselves.

Lest it discomfort us. Lucilius, come;
And come, young Cato; let us to the field.
Labeo and Flavius, set our battles on.
'Tis three a clock; and, Romans, yet ere night
We shall try fortune in a second fight.                    110

*(Exeunt)*

## Scene 4

*As the battle rages, Cato is killed. Hoping to protect Brutus and
allow him to escape, Lucilius tells the enemy soldiers who capture
him that he is Brutus. Antony arrives and recognizes Lucilius.*

*Another part of the field. Enter* **Brutus, Messala, Young Cato,
Lucilius** *and* **Flavius**.

**Brutus**   Yet, countrymen, O, yet hold up your heads!

*(Exit)*

**Young Cato**   What bastard doth not? Who will go with me?
I will proclaim my name about the field.
I am the son of Marcus Cato, ho!
A foe to tyrants, and my country's friend.               5
I am the son of Marcus Cato, ho!

*(Enter* **Soldiers,** *and fight. Young Cato falls)*

**Lucilius**   And I am Brutus, Marcus Brutus, I!
Brutus, my country's friend; know me for Brutus!
O young and noble Cato, art thou down?
Why, now thou diest as bravely as Titinius,              10
And mayst be honour'd, being Cato's son.
**1st Soldier**   Yield, or thou diest.
**Lucilius**                               Only I yield to die:

There is so much that thou wilt kill me straight:
Kill Brutus, and be honour'd in his death.

**1st Soldier**   We must not. A noble prisoner!                              15

*(Enter **Antony**)*

**2nd Soldier**   Room, ho! Tell Antony, Brutus is ta'en.
**1st Soldier**   I'll tell the news. Here comes the general.
Brutus is ta'en, Brutus is ta'en, my lord.
**Antony**   Where is he?
**Lucilius**   Safe, Antony; Brutus is safe enough.                           20
I dare assure thee that no enemy
Shall ever take alive the noble Brutus.
The gods defend him from so great a shame!
When you do find him, or alive or dead,
He will be found like Brutus, like himself.                                   25
**Antony**   This is not Brutus, friend; but, I assure you,
A prize no less in worth. Keep this man safe;
Give him all kindness; I had rather have
Such men my friends than enemies. Go on,
And see where Brutus be alive or dead;                                        30
And bring us word unto Octavius's tent
How every thing is chanc'd.

*(Exeunt)*

## Scene 5

*The last survivors of the armies of Brutus and Cassius have been
driven onto a small hill. Brutus, knowing that defeat is at hand,
kills himself. The others flee. Octavius and Antony come upon
Brutus's body and acknowledge their respect for the man that they
have just defeated.*

*Another part of field. Enter* **Brutus, Dardanius, Clitus, Strato**
*and* **Volumnius**.

**Brutus**   Come, poor remains of friends, rest on this rock.

**Clitus**   Statilius show'd the torch-light; but, my lord,
  He came not back; he is or ta'en or slain.

**Brutus**   Sit thee down, Clitus. Slaying is the word;
  It is a deed in fashion. Hark thee, Clitus. *(Whispers)*     5

**Clitus**   What, I, my lord? No, not for all the world.

**Brutus**   Peace then. No words.

**Clitus**                                   I'll rather kill myself.

**Brutus**   Hark thee, Dardanius. *(Whispers)*

**Dardanius**                          Shall I do such a deed?

**Clitus**   O Dardanius!

**Dardanius**   O Clitus!     10

**Clitus**   What ill request did Brutus make to thee?

**Dardanius**   To kill him, Clitus. Look, he meditates.

**Clitus**   Now is that noble vessel full of grief,
  That it runs over even at his eyes.

**Brutus**   Come hither, good Volumnius: list a word.     15

**Volumnius**   What says my lord?

**Brutus**                                   Why, this, Volumnius:
  The ghost of Caesar hath appear'd to me
  Two several times by night: at Sardis once,
  And this last night, here in Philippi fields.
  I know my hour is come.

**Volumnius**                          Not so, my lord.     20

**Brutus**   Nay, I am sure it is, Volumnius.
  Thou seest the world, Volumnius, how it goes;
  Our enemies have beat us to the pit.
  It is more worthy to leap in ourselves
  Than tarry° till they push us. Good Volumnius,     25
  Thou know'st that we two went to school together:
  Even for that our love of old, I prithee
  Hold thou my sword-hilts, whilst I run on it.

25. **tarry**: wait.

**Volumnius**   That's not an office for a friend, my lord.

**Clitus**   Fly, fly, my lord, there is no tarrying here.                    30

**Brutus**   Farewell to you; and you; and you, Volumnius.
Strato, thou hast been all this while asleep;
Farewell to thee too, Strato. Countrymen,
My heart doth joy that yet in all my life
I found no man but he was true to me.                                         35
I shall have glory by this losing day
More than Octavius and Mark Antony
By this vile conquest shall attain unto.°
So fare you well at once; for Brutus's tongue
Hath almost ended his life's history.                                         40
Night hangs upon mine eyes; my bones would rest,
That have but labour'd to attain this hour.

*(Alarum. Cry within 'Fly, fly, fly!')*

**Clitus**   Fly, my lord, fly!

**Brutus**                           Hence! I will follow.

*(Exeunt **Clitus, Dardanius,** and **Volumnius**)*

I prithee, Strato, stay thou by thy lord.
Thou art a fellow of a good respect;                                          45
Thy life hath had some smatch of honour in it.
Hold then my sword, and turn away thy face,
While I do run upon it. Wilt thou, Strato?

**Strato**   Give me your hand first. Fare you well, my lord.

**Brutus**   Farewell, good Strato. Caesar, now be still;                     50
I kill'd not thee with half so good a will.

*(Dies)*

*(Alarum. Retreat. Enter **Antony, Octavius, Messala, Lucilius** and
the Army)*

---

**36–38. I shall . . . attain unto:** I will be better remembered in my loss than they will be in their victory.

**Octavius**   What man is that?

**Messala**   My master's man. Strato, where is thy master?

**Strato**   Free from the bondage you are in, Messala.
     The conquerors can but make a fire of him;               55
     For Brutus only overcame himself,
     And no man else hath honour by his death.

**Lucilius**   So Brutus should be found. I thank thee, Brutus,
     That thou hast prov'd Lucilius's saying° true.

**Octavius**   All that serv'd Brutus, I will entertain° them.         60
     Fellow, wilt thou bestow thy time with me?

**Strato**   Ay, if Messala will prefer me to you.

**Octavius**   Do so, good Messala.

**Messala**   How died my master, Strato?

**Strato**   I held the sword, and he did run on it.                65

**Messala**   Octavius, then take him to follow thee,
     That did the latest service to my master.

**Antony**   This was the noblest Roman of them all.
     All the conspirators save only he
     Did that they did in envy of great Caesar;          70
     He only, in a general honest thought
     And common good to all, made one of them.
     His life was gentle, and the elements
     So mix'd in him, that Nature might stand up
     And say to all the world, 'This was a man!'         75

**Octavius**   According to his virtue let us use him,
     With all respect and rites of burial.
     Within my tent his bones tonight shall lie,
     Most like a soldier, order'd honourably.
     So call the field to rest, and let's away,          80
     To part the glories of this happy day.

*(Exeunt omnes)*

---

**59. Lucilius's saying:** see Act 5, Scene 4, lines 21–22.    **60. entertain:** employ.

# Reviewing the Selection

Answer each of the following questions without looking back at the play.

*Recalling Facts*

1. During the night before the battle of Philippi, Brutus sees
   - ☐ a. the ghost of his father.
   - ☐ b. the ghost of Caesar.
   - ☐ c. Portia in a dream.
   - ☐ d. Cassius in a dream.

*Understanding Main Ideas*

2. In Act 4 Brutus and Cassius almost come to blows. The cause of their disagreement is that
   - ☐ a. Brutus wants to make peace with Antony and Octavius.
   - ☐ b. Cassius wants to attack Antony and Octavius without delay.
   - ☐ c. Brutus accuses Cassius of taking bribes.
   - ☐ d. Cassius accuses Brutus of being a coward.

*Placing Events in Order*

3. Brutus kills himself
   - ☐ a. before the battle begins.
   - ☐ b. when he learns that Cassius has killed himself.
   - ☐ c. before he hears of Portia's death.
   - ☐ d. when he realizes that his forces are near defeat.

*Finding Supporting Details*

4. Cassius kills himself because he
   - ☐ a. feels guilty about Caesar's murder.
   - ☐ b. knows that his forces will be defeated.
   - ☐ c. thinks his forces are beaten.
   - ☐ d. has lost his fortune and his honor.

*Tragedy and Theme*

5. "Then in my tent, Cassius, <u>enlarge</u> your griefs, / And I will give you audience." In this context *enlarge* means
   - ☐ a. describe.
   - ☐ b. exaggerate.
   - ☐ c. bury.
   - ☐ d. remove.

## Interpreting the Selection

Answer each of the following questions. You may look back at the play if necessary.

6. Antony and Octavius make a list of all the people they want to have killed. They want the people killed in order to
   - ☐ a. make Brutus and Cassius feel sorry about the deaths of their friends.
   - ☐ b. protect themselves against any threat to their power.
   - ☐ c. increase the number of senators in Rome.
   - ☐ d. win the favor of the Roman people.

7. Which of the following statements best describes the friendship between Cassius and Brutus after Caesar's death?
   - ☐ a. Their friendship is stronger than ever.
   - ☐ b. They both are tense and easily insulted.
   - ☐ c. They will never trust each other again.
   - ☐ d. Their friendship has ended.

8. Why do you think Shakespeare has Caesar's ghost appear toward the end of Act 4?
   ☐ a. to show that Caesar's spirit still lives
   ☐ b. to show that Caesar was a successful general
   ☐ c. to show how superstitious the Romans are
   ☐ d. to remind the audience that Brutus killed Caesar

9. During the battle there is some confusion between the forces of Cassius and Brutus because
   ☐ a. Cassius's soldiers betray him.
   ☐ b. Brutus surrenders.
   ☐ c. the two groups are wearing different uniforms.
   ☐ d. Cassius does not know that Brutus has ordered his soldiers to attack.

10. Brutus's last words are addressed to Caesar: "Caesar, now be still; / I kill'd not thee with half so good a will." By those lines, Brutus means that
    ☐ a. he now hates Caesar, although he once loved him.
    ☐ b. it was easier to kill Caesar than it is to kill himself.
    ☐ c. it is easier to kill himself than it was to kill Caesar.
    ☐ d. he does not feel responsible for the death of Caesar.

# Tragedy and Theme

The word *tragedy* is used often in everyday life. You have probably heard people say, "Isn't it a tragedy that she outlived him?" or, "It was a tragic accident." In those contexts the speakers mean that an event was very sad. It made them feel pity or compassion.

In literature tragedy has a broader meaning. First, a tragedy focuses on the behavior of one or more main characters. Second, it involves the struggle of a tragic hero or heroine to overcome a difficulty. Third, the struggle, which sometimes involves innocent people, results in the downfall—perhaps even the death—of the main character. The character's downfall may be caused by a mistake in judgment, unexpected outside forces, or a combination of both. In many tragedies the main character or characters gain understanding or awareness at the end.

In the tragedy *Julius Caesar*, Shakespeare develops several themes. The theme of a work is its underlying message or idea. The themes in *Julius Caesar* are not stated directly. Rather, they are implied, or suggested. You can discover the themes by thinking carefully about what you have read.

In this lesson you will analyze the ways in which *Julius Caesar* fits the definition of a tragedy. You will also learn how Shakespeare weaves several themes into the play.

# The Tragic Hero

If *Julius Caesar* is a tragedy, who is the main character, or tragic hero? Is it Caesar? After all, the play bears his name. Caesar is important, even though he dies at the beginning of Act 3. Yet Caesar is not the tragic hero. You never really get to know him. He is not struggling to overcome a problem that leads to his downfall.

Brutus is the central focus of the play. He is at the heart of the action. At the beginning of the play, he is fearful of Caesar's growing ambition, and Cassius tries to involve him in the murder plot. He reluctantly agrees and joins in the murder in Act 3. At the end of the play, Brutus dies because of his decision to join the conspiracy against Caesar.

*1. List the main actions that Brutus takes in the play. (Save the list to use in answering a later question.)*

In Shakespeare's time playwrights often wrote tragedies about rulers or other people belonging to the nobility. Like the ancient Greeks, who wrote the first tragedies, people in Elizabethan England believed that only someone in a high position could experience the strong emotions and suffer the terrible downfall of a tragic hero. Modern tragedies, however, are often about common people who suffer and fall because of some inner weakness in themselves or because of problems in society.

According to the traditional view, Brutus has the qualities of a tragic hero. He is a highly respected Roman noble. Everyone, including Cassius and Caesar, looks up to him. He is an honest man, a deep thinker, and a persuasive public speaker. As the tragic hero, he faces an extremely important decision.

*2. What decision must Brutus make? Why is it such an important decision? What reasons does he have for taking the course of action he chooses?*

In Acts 4 and 5 you see the results of Brutus's decision. Caesar is dead. Antony has won the sympathy of the Roman people. Brutus, Cassius, and the other conspirators have gathered their followers to battle Caesar's heir, Octavius, and Antony.

*3. Think about what happens after the death of Caesar. Make a list of all*

*the things that go wrong for Brutus in Act 4. Are those problems his fault?
Explain your answer.*

In the final part of the tragedy, Brutus kills himself. An important
part of tragedy is that the tragic character's destruction is partly a result
of his or her personality. Through some personal flaw or shortcoming,
the character falls from a high position and is destroyed.

4. *Think about what happens in Act 5. What event or events lead directly
to Brutus's death? Is Brutus at fault? Explain your answer.*

5. *Think about the list of Brutus's actions you made in answer to question 1. In what ways does Brutus's personality lead to his downfall?*

Brutus is not the only character in the play to die. Cassius and
others also die. Antony says of Brutus, "This was the noblest Roman of
them all." Part of the pity that the audience feels stems from the fact that
such a great man had to die. Despite his honesty and noble motives,
Brutus made mistakes. The consequence of those mistakes is death.

## Discovering the Themes

If someone asked you, What is *Julius Caesar* about? you might explain
the high points of the plot. Yet the play, like all of Shakespeare's work,
goes far beyond the simple story. It carries several underlying messages,
or themes, about life and the human condition.

Scholars have written many books about the themes treated in
Shakespeare's plays. The themes that follow are commonly discussed in
connection with *Julius Caesar*.

**Power.** A major theme of the play is the effect of power on people. As
the play begins, Caesar has won great political power, and his former
friends are suspicious of him.

Brutus has power, too. It comes from his reputation as an honorable
man. Cassius has the power to sway people. He can even influence
someone as moral as Brutus to join a murder plot. In Act 4 Antony gains

military power by joining forces with Octavius. Think about the effect of power on each of the main characters.

*6. How did power affect Caesar's view of himself? How does Brutus's power lead to his downfall? How is Antony changed by gaining military power?*

**Friendship.** A second theme in the play is the varying nature of friendship. The conspirators are all friends of Caesar's. On the day they murder him, Caesar greets them as his friends. Cassius wins Brutus over to the plot partly because they are friends. When Caesar dies, his last words express his shock that Brutus, his best friend, is among his killers. Antony's friendship with Caesar leads to the war that destroys Brutus and Cassius. Shortly before he kills himself, Brutus bids farewell to his friends.

*7. Reread lines 33 to 35 in Act 5, Scene 5. In your own words, explain what Brutus is saying about his life and friendship.*

*8. Skim the play to find at least one other reference to friendship. What do you think Shakespeare is saying about friendship in the reference you chose?*

**Principles versus Practical Goals.** A third theme in the play centers on the value of principles or ideals versus the value of practical goals. Two major characters in *Julius Caesar* are practical men. Cassius is a man who will compromise, flatter, and lie to get what he wants. He uses deceit (the false letters) to get Brutus to join the conspiracy against Caesar. Antony is also a practical man. After Caesar is killed, he flees, but then returns and pretends to support Caesar's murderers. Later when he and Octavius are in power, he condemns to death anyone who might stand in his way.

*9. What do the two practical characters achieve in the short term? What are the long-term results of their actions?*

Brutus, by contrast, is a man of principle. He will do nothing that he does not believe is honest. He is less capable of quick action than Cassius and Antony are. He examines questions from every angle. Once he makes a decision, he stands by it because he has considered it so carefully.

*10. Which approach do you think Shakespeare most admired—that of Brutus or that of Cassius and Antony? Explain your answer.*

## The Author's Purpose

A great work of literature such as *Julius Caesar* often raises more questions than it answers. Many people have debated what Shakespeare's purpose was in writing this play. How did he feel about his characters? Who are the heroes and who are the villains? There are no right answers to those questions. To discover the author's purpose, you must examine the characters and decide for yourself.

Consider Mark Antony. He is a loyal friend to Caesar. After Caesar's death, he risks his life to honor the fallen leader. He is a clever speaker, and he is generous in victory. After Brutus dies, Antony honors his memory.

Yet Shakespeare has also given Antony some dishonorable traits. He rouses the mob to violence against Caesar's murderers. He deceives Brutus and the other conspirators. Recall his soliloquy in front of Caesar's corpse (Act 3, Scene 1) when he promises to avenge the murder. That speech comes right after he shakes the bloodied hands of Caesar's murderers to show that he sides with them.

Antony is also a ruthless politician. At the beginning of Act 4, he sentences several former friends to death. When you add up all Antony's good and bad qualities, do you get a hero or a villain? The answer is that you can get either or both. Shakespeare did not intend to put Antony into a single category. What Shakespeare intended to do was to show that friendship can lead a good man to do some terrible things.

*11. In the play find at least two places in which Shakespeare presents Julius Caesar as a man the audience might admire. Then find at least two places in which he presents Caesar as a man the audience might dislike.*

While examining Shakespeare's purpose, you must think about the murder of Caesar. Caesar's assassination is the central event in the play. The first two acts prepare for the murder. The events that follow Act 3

result from the murder. How did Shakespeare feel about the assassination of Caesar?

Reread Act 5, Scene 3 (lines 45 and 46), where Cassius dies. His last
words are: "Caesar, thou art reveng'd, / Even with the sword that kill'd
thee." When Brutus kills himself in Act 5, Scene 5 (lines 50 and 51), his
last words are: "Caesar, now be still; / I kill'd not thee with half so good
a will."

*12. How are those two speeches similar? What might that similarity tell
you about Shakespeare's view of Caesar's assassination?*

## Questions for Thought and Discussion

The questions and activities that follow will help you explore *Julius
Caesar*, Acts 4 and 5, in more depth and at the same time develop your
critical thinking skills.

1. **Comparing.** What events or developments make Cassius decide to
   end his life? How is his suicide different from Brutus's suicide?

2. **Organizing a Debate.** Organize a debate around this question: Did
   Shakespeare approve of the assassination of Caesar? One side should
   take the affirmative. Those students should find evidence from the
   play to show that Shakespeare believed that the murder of Caesar was
   justified. The other side should take the negative. Those students
   should find evidence to support the view that Shakespeare felt that
   the assassination was wrong.

3. **Evaluating.** Do you think Brutus feels guilty about the killing of
   Caesar? Find evidence in Acts 4 and 5 to support your decision.

4. **Expressing an Opinion.** Why do you think Shakespeare's *Julius Caesar*
   is still popular today? Give reasons for your opinion.

## Writing About Literature

Several suggestions for writing projects follow. You may be asked to
complete one or more of these projects. If you have any questions about

how to begin a writing assignment, review Using the Writing Process, beginning on page 385.

1. **Writing a Eulogy.** In Act 4 you learn that Portia has killed herself. In Act 5 the chief conspirators, Cassius and Brutus, die by their own hands. Choose one of those characters and write a eulogy to be given orally. A eulogy is a speech in honor of someone who has died. For examples of this type of speech, study the eulogies that Brutus and Antony deliver in Act 3, Scene 2, after Caesar's death.

2. **Interpreting Shakespeare's Language.** Reread the speech that Antony makes when he finds Brutus's body (Act 5, Scene 5, lines 68 to 75). Make sure that you understand what he is saying. Then rewrite the speech in modern English.

3. **Relating Character and Theme.** Imagine that you could choose to play any part in a production of *Julius Caesar*. In a short paper explain what character you would choose to play and why you would want that part. Then explain how the character you have chosen relates to one of the play's themes discussed in this chapter.

4. **Reporting on Research.** Find out about the assassination of Julius Caesar as recorded in history. Then compare that information to the assassination of Caesar in Shakespeare's play. Suggest why you think Shakespeare may have made the changes he did.

# Four Short Plays

## The Devil and Daniel Webster
STEPHEN VINCENT BENÉT

*Conflict and Resolution*

## The Ugly Duckling
A. A. MILNE

*Parody and Humor*

## The Master Thief
PAUL SILLS

*Staging a Skit*

## A Marriage Proposal
ANTON CHEKHOV

*Farce and Satire*

*U*nlike *Julius Caesar*, which is a full-length play, the selections you will read in Unit Two are short, one-act plays. If you think of Shakespeare's play as similar to a novel, then the plays in this unit are similar to short stories. Like short stories, they are complete in themselves. Although one-act plays have plots, characters, and conflicts, those elements are compressed.

One-act plays are more compact than full-length plays, and they usually have fewer characters. You seldom find the minor characters that are common in a longer play. Short plays usually have a single main plot and do not contain subplots.

One-act plays are popular with small acting companies, which may put on a number of plays during a season. Amateur groups and schools often choose to produce short plays because they usually require simpler staging than full-length plays do. A good one-act play, however, can be just as effective in communicating its message to the audience as a full-length work. To be successful, any play, no matter what its length, must capture and sustain the audience's interest.

The four short plays in Unit Two succeed in capturing and sustaining the audience's interest because of their use of humor. The kinds of humor in each play differ. The first selection, *The Devil and Daniel Webster*, is a serious play about a serious subject. Yet the two title characters are clever men who try to outwit each other in a humorous way. *The Ugly Duckling* is a play that is designed to make the audience laugh. It ridicules a number of subjects, from fairy tales to royalty to marriage. Yet behind the laughter is a serious statement about how people relate to one another.

*The Master Thief*, which is a <u>skit</u>, or a comic sketch, and *A Marriage Proposal* are both amusing because of their situations and their characters. As you read the plays, think about how the playwrights combine elements of humor with a serious message. You should also imagine how each play might use costumes, scenery, and lighting, and how the actors might move around on the stage.

| Selection | *The Devil and Daniel Webster* |
| | STEPHEN VINCENT BENÉT |
| Lesson | *Conflict and Resolution* |

❖

## About the Selection

*The Devil and Daniel Webster* by Stephen Vincent Benét is a play that is based on a German legend. The legend concerns an ambitious scholar named Faust who made a bargain with the devil. He signed a contract in blood, promising his soul to the devil in exchange for youth, knowledge, and magical powers. The contract stated that at the end of a certain time, the devil would claim Faust's soul. The Faust legend has fascinated people for centuries. It has inspired plays, stories, novels, paintings, poems, as well as operas and symphonies.

Benét's play *The Devil and Daniel Webster* is a Faustian story set in the United States. The actions take place in Cross Corners, a small New Hampshire town, in 1841. The central character is an ambitious young man named Jabez Stone. Stone is a successful farmer and a rising politician.

The play begins during a wedding reception held for Jabez Stone and his bride, Mary. The young couple are very happy. Friends and neighbors have gathered to celebrate the marriage. The guests dance and gossip and wait for the arrival of Daniel Webster. As you can tell from the title, Webster has an important role in the play.

Daniel Webster was a real person. He was born in New Hampshire in 1782. He became a famous lawyer and a great politician. He represented New Hampshire in the House of Representatives and was later a United States senator from Massachusetts. He served as secretary of state twice and ran for president in 1836. By the time this play was written in 1938, Webster had become a folk hero. He was especially popular among New Englanders.

Daniel Webster was admired for his skill as a persuasive speaker. His stern, imposing presence and quick mind made him a respected figure both in the courtroom and in Congress. According to a New England saying, "Old Daniel Webster could probably out-argue the devil himself."

In Benét's play Webster does just that. During an unusual courtroom scene, with a man's soul at stake, Webster stands up to the devil. The trial adds a new twist to the Faust legend by giving the condemned soul a second chance.

Stephen Vincent Benét is well known for writing both poetry and prose. Benét was born in Bethlehem, Pennsylvania, in 1898. As a child, he moved frequently because his father, an army officer, was transferred to various posts. Those early experiences may have aroused Benét's interest in the folklore and history of the United States.

As a young man, Benét wrote and published *John Brown's Body*, a long narrative poem about the Civil War. In 1928 he won a Pulitzer Prize for the poem. Besides writing many poems, Benét published a number of short stories. Among them was "The Devil and Daniel Webster." Benét later made the story into the one-act play that you will read. The story has also been made into an opera and a movie.

When you start reading the play, you will notice that it differs from *Julius Caesar* in many ways. Benét gives more background information than Shakespeare did. Benét also includes more stage directions. Stage directions are any information that is intended for the director, the actors, or the readers of a play. Stage directions are separate from the dialogue and are often printed in *italics*. Benét lets you know how the characters sound. He tells you, for example, that a character whispers or looks embarrassed or laughs. In Shakespeare's play you had to decide for yourself how each character looked and sounded.

## Lesson Preview

The lesson that follows *The Devil and Daniel Webster* focuses on conflict in the play. As you learned in Chapter 1, a conflict is a struggle or tension between opposing forces that is central to the plot of a play.

Conflict is an essential part of any play. It provides the action for the plot, interest for the audience, and reasons for the characters to behave in certain ways.

The questions that follow will help you recognize the elements of conflict in *The Devil and Daniel Webster.* As you read the play, think about how you would answer these questions.

**1** What is the most important conflict in the play? Are there minor conflicts? What are they? How do they relate to the major conflict?

**2** When do you first become aware of a conflict? What makes you aware of it?

**3** Who are the main characters in the play? How is each character involved in the major conflict?

**4** What are the possible outcomes of the conflict? What is the actual outcome?

## Vocabulary

Here are some difficult words that appear in the selection that follows. Study the words and their definitions, as well as the sentences that show how the words are used. This will help you get the most from your reading.

**feigned** not real; false. *The child's feigned illness was just an excuse to stay home from school.*

**assent** agreement. *During the meeting the mayor gave his assent to the council's excellent proposal.*

**knell** the sound of a bell, especially when rung slowly for a death, a funeral, or a disaster. *Before the funeral, the church bell rang a slow knell.*

**abominable** causing disgust or hatred. *No family should be forced to live in these abominable housing conditions.*

# The Devil and Daniel Webster

STEPHEN VINCENT BENÉT

## Characters

Jabez Stone
Mary Stone
Daniel Webster
Mr. Scratch
The Fiddler
Justice Hathorne
Justice Hathorne's Clerk
King Philip
Teach
Walter Butler
Simon Girty
Dale
Men and Women of
    Cross Corners,
    New Hampshire

## Scene—Jabez Stone's Farmhouse
## Time—1841

*The scene is the main room of* **Jabez Stone's** *New Hampshire farmhouse in 1841, a big, comfortable room that hasn't yet developed the stuffiness of a front parlor. A door leads to the kitchen, another door to the outside. Windows, in center, show a glimpse of summer landscape. Most of the furniture has been cleared away for the dance which follows the wedding of* **Jabez** *and* **Mary Stone,** *but there is a settle or bench by the fireplace, a table with some wedding presents upon it,* *at least three chairs by the table, and a cider barrel on which the* **Fiddler** *sits, in front of the table. Near the table there is a cupboard where there are glasses and a jug. There is a clock.*

*A country wedding has been in progress—the wedding of* **Jabez** *and* **Mary Stone.** *He is a husky young farmer, around twenty-eight or thirty. The bride is in her early twenties. He is dressed in stiff store clothes but not ridiculously—they are of good quality and he looks important. The bride is in a simple white or cream wedding dress and may carry a small, stiff bouquet of country flowers.*

*Now the wedding is over and the guests are dancing. The* **Fiddler** *is perched on the cider barrel. He plays and calls square-dance figures. The guests include the recognizable types of a small New England town—doctor, lawyer, storekeeper, old maid, schoolteacher, farmer, etc. There is an air of prosperity and hearty country mirth about the whole affair.*

*At rise,* **Jabez** *and* **Mary** *are up left center, receiving the congratulations of a few last guests, who talk to them and pass on to the dance. The others are dancing. There is a buzz of conversation that follows the tune of the dance music.*

**First Woman**   Right nice wedding.

**First Man**   Handsome couple.

**Second Woman**   *(passing through crowd with dish of oyster stew)* Oysters for supper!

**Second Man**   *(passing cake)* And layer cake—layer cake—

**An Old Man**   *(hobbling toward cider barrel)* Makes me feel young again! Oh, by jingo!

**An Old Woman**   *(pursuing him)* Henry, Henry, you've been drinking cider!

**Fiddler**   Set to your partners! Dosy-do!

**Women**   Mary and Jabez.

**Men**   Jabez and Mary.

**A Woman**   Where's the State Senator?

**A Man**   Where's the lucky bride?

*(With cries of "Mary—Jabez—strike it up, fiddler—make room for the bride and groom," the* **Crowd** *drags* **Mary** *and* **Jabez***, pleased but embarrassed, into the center of the room, and* **Mary** *and* **Jabez** *do a little solo dance, while the* **Crowd** *claps, applauds, and makes various remarks.)*

**A Man**   Handsome steppers!

**A Woman**   She's pretty as a picture.

**A Second Man**   Cut your pigeon wing,[1] Jabez!

**The Old Man**   Young again, young again, that's the way I feel! *(He tries to cut a pigeon wing himself.)*

**The Old Woman**   Henry, Henry, careful of your rheumatiz!

**A Third Woman**   Makes me feel all teary, seeing them so happy.

*(The solo dance ends, the music stops for a moment.)*

**The Old Man**   *(gossiping to a neighbor)* Wonder where he got it all. Stones was always poor.

**His Neighbor**   Ain't poor now. Makes you wonder just a mite.

**A Third Man**   Don't begrudge it to him—but I wonder where he got it.

**The Old Man**   *(starting to whisper)* Let me tell you something—

**The Old Woman**   *(quickly)* Henry, Henry, don't you start to gossip. *(She drags him away.)*

**Fiddler**   *(cutting in)* Set to your partners! Scratch for corn!

*(The dance resumes, but as it does so, the* **Crowd** *chants back and forth.)*

**Women**   Gossip's got a sharp tooth.

**Men**   Gossip's got a mean tooth.

**Women**   She's a lucky woman. They're a lucky pair.

**Men**   That's true as gospel. But I wonder where he got it.

---

1. **pigeon wing:** a step in folk dancing.

**Women**  Money, land, and riches.

**Men**  Just came out of nowhere.

**Women and Men**  *(together)* Wonder where he got it all. But that's his business.

**Fiddler**  Left and right—grand chain!

*(The dance rises to a pitch of ecstasy with the final figure. The fiddle squeaks and stops. The dancers mop their brows.)*

**First Man**  Whew! Ain't danced like that since I was kneehigh to a grasshopper!

**Second Man**  Play us "The Portland Fancy," fiddler!

**Third Man**  No, wait a minute, neighbor. Let's hear from the happy pair! Hey, Jabez!

**Fourth Man**  Let's hear from the State Senator!

*(They crowd around **Jabez** and push him up on the settle.)*

**Old Man**  Might as well. It's the last time he'll have the last word!

**Old Woman**  Now, Henry Banks, you ought to be ashamed of yourself!

**Old Man**  Told you so, Jabez!

**The Crowd**  Speech!

**Jabez**  *(embarrassed)* Neighbors, friends—I'm not much of a speaker, spite of your 'lecting me to State Senate—

**The Crowd**  That's the ticket, Jabez. Smart man, Jabez. I voted for ye. Go ahead, Senator, you're doing fine.

**Jabez**  But we're certainly glad to have you here—me and Mary. And we want to thank you for coming and—

**A Voice**  Vote the Whig ticket!

**Another Voice**  Hurray for Daniel Webster!

**Jabez**  And I'm glad Hi Foster said that, for those are my sentiments, too. Mr. Webster has promised to honor us with his presence here tonight.

**The Crowd**  Hurray for Dan'l! Hurray for the greatest man in the U.S.!

**Jabez**  And when he comes, I know we'll give him a real New Hampshire welcome.

**The Crowd**   Sure we will—Webster forever—and to hell with Henry Clay![2]

**Jabez**   And meanwhile—well, there's Mary and me *(takes her hand)* and, if you folks don't have a good time, well, we won't feel right about getting married at all. Because I know I've been lucky—and I hope she feels that way, too. And, well, we're going to be happy or bust a trace![3] *(He wipes his brow to terrific applause. He and **Mary** look at each other.)*

**A Woman**   *(in kitchen doorway)* Come and get the cider, folks!

*(The **Crowd** begins to drift away—a few to the kitchen, a few toward the door that leads to the outside. They furnish a shifting background to the next little scene, where **Mary** and **Jabez** are left alone by the fireplace.)*

**Jabez**   Mary.

**Mary**   Mr. Stone.

**Jabez**   Mary.

**Mary**   My husband.

**Jabez**   That's a big word, husband.

**Mary**   It's a good word.

**Jabez**   Are you happy, Mary?

**Mary**   Yes. So happy I'm afraid.

**Jabez**   Afraid?

**Mary**   I suppose it happens to every girl—just for a minute. It's like spring turning into summer. You want it to be summer. But the spring was sweet. *(Dismissing the mood.)* I'm sorry. Forgive me. It just came and went, like something cold. As if we'd been too lucky.

**Jabez**   We can't be too lucky, Mary. Not you and me.

**Mary**   *(rather mischievously)* If you say so, Mr. Stone. But you don't even know what sort of housekeeper I am. And Aunt Hepsy says—

---

2. **Henry Clay:** an American politician and rival of Daniel Webster in Congress for many years. **3. trace:** a strap used to connect an animal's harness to the vehicle it is pulling.

**Jabez**  Bother your Aunt Hepsy! There's just you and me and that's all that matters in the world.

**Mary**  And you don't know something else—

**Jabez**  What's that?

**Mary**  How proud I am of you. Ever since I was a little girl. Ever since you carried my books. Oh, I'm sorry for women who can't be proud of their men. It must be a lonely feeling.

**Jabez**  *(uncomfortably)* A man can't always be proud of everything, Mary. There's some things a man does, or might do, when he has to make his way.

**Mary**  *(laughing)* I know—terrible things—like being the best farmer in the county and the best State Senator—

**Jabez**  *(quietly)* And a few things besides. But you remember one thing, Mary, whatever happens. It was all for you. And nothing's going to happen. Because he hasn't come yet—and he would have come if it was wrong.

**Mary**  But it's wonderful to have Mr. Webster come to us.

**Jabez**  I wasn't thinking about Mr. Webster. *(He takes both her hands.)* Mary, I've got something to tell you. I should have told you before, but I couldn't seem to bear it. Only, now that it's all right, I can. Ten years ago—

**A Voice**  *(from off stage)* Dan'l! Dan'l Webster!

*(**Jabez** drops **Mary's** hands and looks around. The **Crowd** begins to mill and gather toward the door. Others rush in from the kitchen.)*

**Another Voice**  Black Dan'l! He's come!
**Another Voice**  Three cheers for the greatest man in the U.S.!
**Another Voice**  Three cheers for Daniel Webster!

*(And, to the cheering and applause of the **Crowd**, **Daniel Webster** enters and stands for a moment upstage, in the familiar pose, his head thrown back, his attitude leonine.[4] He stops the cheering of the **Crowd** with a gesture.)*

---

4. **leonine:** like a lion.

**Webster**  Neighbors, old friends—it does me good to hear you. But don't cheer me—I'm not running for President this summer. *(A laugh from the* **Crowd**.*)* I'm here on a better errand—to pay my humble respects to a most charming lady and her very fortunate spouse.

*(There is a twang of a fiddle string breaking.)*

**Fiddler**  'Tarnation! Busted a string!
**A Voice**  He's always bustin' strings.

*(***Webster*** *blinks at the interruption but goes on.)*

**Webster**  We're proud of State Senator Stone in these parts—we know what he's done. Ten years ago he started out with a patch of land that was mostly rocks and mortgages and now—well, you've only to look around you. I don't know that I've ever seen a likelier farm, not even at Marshfield, and I hope, before I die, I'll have the privilege of shaking his hand as Governor of this state. I don't know how he's done it—I couldn't have done it myself. But I know this— Jabez Stone wears no man's collar. *(At this statement there is a discordant squeak from the fiddle and* **Jabez** *looks embarrassed.* **Webster** *knits his brows.)* And what's more, if I know Jabez, he never will. But I didn't come here to talk politics—I came to kiss the bride. *(He does so amid great applause. He shakes hands with* **Jabez**.*)* Congratulations, Stone— you're a lucky man. And now, if our friend in the corner will give us a tune on his fiddle—

*(The* **Crowd** *presses forward to meet the great man. He shakes hands with several.)*

**A Man**  Remember me, Mr. Webster? Saw ye up at the State House at Concord.
**Another Man**  Glad to see ye, Mr. Webster. I voted for ye ten times.

*(***Webster*** *receives their homage politely, but his mind is still on music.)*

**Webster** *(a trifle irritated)* I said, if our friend in the corner would give us a tune on his fiddle—

**Fiddler** *(passionately, flinging the fiddle down)* Hell's delight—excuse me, Mr. Webster. But the very devil's got into that fiddle of mine. She was doing all right up to just a minute ago. But now I've tuned her and tuned her and she won't play a note I want.

*(And, at this point, **Mr. Scratch** makes his appearance. He has entered, unobserved, and mixed with the **Crowd** while all eyes were upon **Daniel Webster**. He is, of course, the devil—a New England devil, dressed like a rather shabby attorney but with something just a little wrong in clothes and appearance. For one thing, he wears black gloves on his hands. He carries a large black tin box, like a botanist's collecting box, under one arm. Now he slips through the **Crowd** and taps the **Fiddler** on the shoulder.)*

**Scratch** *(insinuatingly)* Maybe you need some rosin[5] on your bow, fiddler?

**Fiddler** Maybe I do and maybe I don't. *(Turns and confronts the stranger.)* But who are you? I don't remember seeing you before.

**Scratch** Oh, I'm just a friend—a humble friend of the bridegroom's. *(He walks toward **Jabez**. Apologetically.)* I'm afraid I came in the wrong way, Mr. Stone. You've improved the place so much since I last saw it that I hardly knew the front door. But, I assure you, I came as fast as I could.

**Jabez** *(obviously shocked)* It—it doesn't matter. *(With a great effort.)* Mary—Mr. Webster—this is a—a friend of mine from Boston—a legal friend. I didn't expect him today but—

**Scratch** Oh, my dear Mr. Stone—an occasion like this—I wouldn't miss it for the world. *(He bows.)* Charmed, Mrs. Stone. Delighted, Mr. Webster. But—don't let me break up the merriment of the meeting. *(He turns back toward the table and the **Fiddler**.)*

**Fiddler** *(with a grudge, to **Scratch**)* Boston lawyer, eh?

---

5. **rosin:** a hard, yellowish substance used on violin bows to keep them from slipping.

**Scratch**  You might call me that.

**Fiddler**  *(tapping the tin box with his bow)* And what have you got in that big box of yours? Law papers?

**Scratch**  Oh, curiosities for the most part. I'm a collector, too.

**Fiddler**  Don't hold much with Boston curiosities, myself. And you know about fiddling, too, do you? Know all about it?

**Scratch**  Oh—*(A deprecatory shrug.)*

**Fiddler**  Don't shrug your shoulders at me—I ain't no Frenchman. Telling me I needed more rosin!

**Mary**  *(trying to stop the quarrel)* Isaac, please—

**Fiddler**  Sorry, Mary—Mrs. Stone. But I been playing the fiddle at Cross Corners weddings for twenty-five years. And now here comes a stranger from Boston and tells me I need more rosin!

**Scratch**  But, my good friend—

**Fiddler**  Rosin, indeed! Here—play it yourself then and see what you can make of it! *(He thrusts the fiddle at **Scratch**. The latter stiffens, slowly lays his black collecting box on the table, and takes the fiddle.)*

**Scratch**  *(with feigned embarrassment)* But really, I— *(He bows toward **Jabez**.)* Shall I, Mr. Senator?

*(**Jabez** makes a helpless gesture of assent.)*

**Mary**  *(to **Jabez**)* Mr. Stone, Mr. Stone—are you ill?

**Jabez**  No—no—but I feel—it's hot—

**Webster**  *(chuckling)* Don't you fret, Mrs. Stone. I've got the right medicine for him. *(He pulls a flask from his pocket.)* Ten-year-old Medford, Stone. I buy it by the keg down at Marshfield. Here— *(He tries to give some of the rum to **Jabez**.)*

**Jabez**  No— *(He turns.)* Mary—Mr. Webster— *(But he cannot explain. With a burst.)* Oh, let him play—let him play! Don't you see he's bound to? Don't you see there's nothing we can do?

*(A rustle of discomfort among the guests. **Scratch** draws the bow across the fiddle in a horrible discord.)*

**Fiddler** *(triumphantly)* I told you so, stranger. The devil's in that fiddle!

**Scratch** I'm afraid it needs special tuning. *(Draws the bow in a second discord.)* There, that's better. *(Grinning.)* And now for this happy—this very happy occasion—in tribute to the bride and groom—I'll play something appropriate—a song of young love—

**Mary** Oh, Jabez, Mr. Webster—stop him! Do you see his hands? He's playing with gloves on his hands.

*(**Webster** starts forward, but, even as he does so, **Scratch** begins to play and all freeze as **Scratch** goes on with the extremely inappropriate song that follows. At first his manner is oily and mocking. It is not till he reaches the line "The devil took the words away" that he really becomes terrifying and the **Crowd** starts to be afraid.)*

**Scratch** *(accompanying himself fantastically)*

> Young William was a thriving boy.
> (Listen to my doleful tale.)
> Young Mary Clark was all his joy.
> (Listen to my doleful tale.)
>
> He swore he'd love her all his life.
> She swore she'd be his loving wife.
>
> But William found a gambler's den
> And drank with livery-stable men.
>
> He played the cards, he played the dice.
> He would not listen to advice.
>
> And when in church he tried to pray,
> The devil took the words away.

*(**Scratch**, still playing, starts to march across the stage.)*

The devil got him by the toe,
And so, alas, he had to go.

"Young Mary Clark, young Mary Clark,
I now must go into the dark."

*(These last two verses have been directed at* **Jabez.** **Scratch** *continues, now turning on* **Mary.**)

Young Mary lay upon her bed.
"Alas, my Will-i-am is dead."

He came to her a bleeding ghost—

*(He rushes at* **Mary** *but* **Webster** *stands between them.)*

**Webster**  Stop! Stop! You miserable wretch, can't you see that you're frightening Mrs. Stone? *(He wrenches the fiddle out of* **Scratch's** *hands and tosses it aside.)* And now, sir—out of this house!

**Scratch**  *(facing him)* You're a bold man, Mr. Webster. Too bold for your own good, perhaps. And anyhow, it wasn't my fiddle. It belonged to— *(He wheels and sees the* **Fiddler** *tampering with the collecting box that has been left on the table.)* Idiot! What are you doing with my collecting box? *(He rushes for the* **Fiddler** *and chases him around the table, but the* **Fiddler** *is just one jump ahead.)*

**Fiddler**  Boston lawyer, eh? Well, I don't think so. I think you've got something in that box of yours you're afraid to show. And, by jingo— *(He throws open the lid of the box. The lights wink and there is a clap of thunder. All eyes stare upward. Something has flown out of the box. But what?* **Fiddler,** *with relief.)* Why, 'tain't nothing but a moth.

**Mary**  A white moth—a flying thing.

**Webster**  A common moth—*Telea polyphemus*[6]—

**The Crowd**  A moth—just a moth—a moth—

**Fiddler**  *(terrified)* But it ain't. It ain't no common moth! I seen it! And

---

6. *Telea polyphemus:* the Latin scientific name for a moth.

it's got a death's head on it! *(He strikes at the invisible object with his bow to drive it away.)*

**Voice of the Moth**   Help me, neighbors! Help me!

**Webster**   What's that? It wails like a lost soul.

**Mary**   A lost soul.

**The Crowd**   A lost soul—lost—in darkness—in the darkness.

**Voice of the Moth**   Help me, neighbors!

**Fiddler**   It sounds like Miser Stevens.

**Jabez**   Miser Stevens!

**The Crowd**   The miser—Miser Stevens—a lost soul—lost.

**Fiddler**   *(frantically)* It sounds like Miser Stevens—and you had him in your box. But it can't be. He ain't dead.

**Jabez**   He ain't dead—I tell you he ain't dead! He was just as spry and mean as a woodchuck Tuesday.

**The Crowd**   Miser Stevens—soul of Miser Stevens—but he ain't dead.

**Scratch**   *(dominating them)* Listen!

*(A bell off stage begins to toll a knell, slowly, solemnly.)*

**Mary**   The bell—the church bell—the bell that rang at my wedding.

**Webster**   The church bell—the passing bell.

**Jabez**   The funeral bell.

**The Crowd**   The bell—the passing bell—Miser Stevens—dead.

**Voice of the Moth**   Help me, neighbors, help me! I sold my soul to the devil. But I'm not the first or the last. Help me. Help Jabez Stone!

**Scratch**   Ah, would you! *(He catches the moth in his red bandanna, stuffs it back into his collecting box, and shuts the lid with a snap.)*

**Voice of the Moth**   *(fading)* Lost—lost forever, forever. Lost, like Jabez Stone.

*(The **Crowd** turns on **Jabez**. They read his secret in his face.)*

**The Crowd**   Jabez Stone—Jabez Stone—answer us—answer us.

**Mary**   Tell them, dear—answer them—you are good—you are brave— you are innocent.

*(But the **Crowd** is all pointing hands and horrified eyes.)*

**The Crowd**   Jabez Stone—Jabez Stone. Who's your friend in black, Jabez Stone? *(They point to **Scratch**.)*

**Webster**   Answer them, Mr. State Senator.

**The Crowd**   Jabez Stone—Jabez Stone. Where did you get your money, Jabez Stone?

*(**Scratch** grins and taps his collecting box. **Jabez** cannot speak.)*

**Jabez**   I—I— *(He stops.)*

**The Crowd**   Jabez Stone—Jabez Stone. What was the price you paid for it, Jabez Stone?

**Jabez**   *(looking around wildly)* Help me, neighbors! Help me!

*(This cracks the built-up tension and sends the **Crowd** over the edge into fanaticism.)*

**A Woman's Voice**   *(high and hysterical)* He's sold his soul to the devil! *(She points to **Jabez**.)*

**Other Voices**   To the devil!

**The Crowd**   He's sold his soul to the devil! The devil himself! The devil's playing the fiddle! The devil's come for his own!

**Jabez**   *(appealing)* But, neighbors—I didn't know—I didn't mean—oh, help me!

**The Crowd**   *(inexorably)* He's sold his soul to the devil!

**Scratch**   *(grinning)* To the devil!

**The Crowd**   He's sold his soul to the devil! There's no help left for him, neighbors! Run, hide, hurry, before we're caught! He's a lost soul—Jabez Stone—he's the devil's own! Run, hide, hasten! *(They stream across the stage like a flurry of bats, the cannier picking up the wedding presents they have given to take along with them.)*

*(**Mr. Scratch** drives them out into the night, fiddle in hand, and follows them. **Jabez** and **Mary** are left with **Webster**. **Jabez** has sunk*

*into a chair, beaten, with his head in his hands.* **Mary** *is trying to comfort him.* **Webster** *looks at them for a moment and shakes his head sadly. As he crosses to exit to the porch, his hand drops for a moment on* **Jabez'** *shoulder, but* **Jabez** *makes no sign.* **Webster** *exits.* **Jabez** *lifts his head.)*


**Mary**   *(comforting him)* My dear—my dear—

**Jabez**   I—it's all true, Mary. All true. You must hurry.

**Mary**   Hurry?

**Jabez**   Hurry after them—back to the village—back to your folks. Mr. Webster will take you—you'll be safe with Mr. Webster. You see, it's all true and he'll be back in a minute. *(With a shudder.)* The other one. *(He groans.)* I've got until twelve o'clock. That's the contract. But there isn't much time.

**Mary**   Are you telling me to run away from you, Mr. Stone?

**Jabez**   You don't understand, Mary. It's true.

**Mary**   We made some promises to each other. Maybe you've forgotten them. But I haven't. I said, it's for better or worse. It's for better or worse. I said, in sickness or in health. Well, that covers the ground, Mr. Stone.

**Jabez**   But, Mary, you must. I command you.

**Mary**   "For thy people shall be my people and thy God my God." *(Quietly.)* That was Ruth, in the Book. I always liked the name of Ruth—always liked the thought of her. I always thought—I'll call a child Ruth, sometime. I guess that was just a girl's notion. *(She breaks.)* But, oh, Jabez—why?

**Jabez**   It started years ago, Mary. I guess I was a youngster then—guess I must have been. A youngster with a lot of ambitions and no way in the world to get there. I wanted city clothes and a big white house. I wanted to be State Senator and have people look up to me. But all I got on the farm was a crop of stones. You could work all day and all night but that was all you got.

**Mary** *(softly)* It was pretty, that hill farm, Jabez. You could look all the way across the valley.

**Jabez** Pretty? It was fever and ague[7]—it was stones and blight. If I had a horse, he got colic. If I planted garden truck, the woodchucks ate it. I'd lie awake nights and try to figure out a way to get somewhere —but there wasn't any way. And all the time you were growing up, in the town. I couldn't ask you to marry me and take you to a place like that.

**Mary** Do you think it's the place makes the difference to a woman? I'd—I'd have kept your house. I'd have stroked the cat and fed the chickens and seen you wiped your shoes on the mat. I wouldn't have asked for more. Oh, Jabez—why didn't you tell me?

**Jabez** It happened before I could. Just an average day—you know—just an average day. But there was a mean east wind and a mean small rain. Well, I was plowing, and the share[8] broke clean off on a rock where there hadn't been any rock the day before. I didn't have money for a new one—I didn't have money to get it mended. So I said it and I said loud, "I'll sell my soul for about two cents," I said. *(He stops.* **Mary** *stares at him.)* Well, that's all there is to it, I guess. He came along that afternoon—that fellow from Boston—and the dog looked at him and ran away. Well, I had to make it more than two cents, but he was agreeable to that. So I pricked my thumb with a pin and signed the paper. It felt hot when you touched it, that paper. I keep remembering that. *(He pauses.)* And it's all come true and he's kept his part of the bargain. I got the riches and I've married you. And, oh, God almighty, what shall I do?

**Mary** Let us run away! Let us creep and hide!

**Jabez** You can't run away from the devil—I've seen his horses. Miser Stevens tried to run away.

**Mary** Let us pray—let us pray to the God of Mercy that He redeem us.

**Jabez** I can't pray, Mary. The words just burn in my heart.

---

7. **ague:** a chill or fit of shivering.   8. **share:** refers to a plowshare—the cutting blade of a plow.

**Mary**   I won't let you go! I won't! There must be someone who could help us. I'll get the judge and the squire—

**Jabez**   Who'll take a case against old Scratch? Who'll face the devil himself and do him brown? There isn't a lawyer in the world who'd dare do that.

*(**Webster** appears in the doorway.)*

**Webster**   Good evening, neighbors. Did you say something about lawyers—

**Mary**   Mr. Webster!

**Jabez**   Dan'l Webster! But I thought—

**Webster**   You'll excuse me for leaving you for a moment. I was just taking a stroll on the porch, in the cool of the evening. Fine summer evening, too.

**Jabez**   Well, it might be, I guess, but that kind of depends on the circumstances.

**Webster**   Hm. Yes. I happened to overhear a little of your conversation. I gather you're in trouble, neighbor Stone.

**Jabez**   Sore trouble.

**Webster**   *(delicately)* Sort of law case, I understand.

**Jabez**   You might call it that, Mr. Webster. Kind of a mortgage case, in a way.

**Mary**   Oh, Jabez!

**Webster**   Mortgage case. Well, I don't generally plead now, except before the Supreme Court, but this case of yours presents some very unusual features and I never deserted a neighbor in trouble yet. So, if I can be of any assistance—

**Mary**   Oh, Mr. Webster, will you help him?

**Jabez**   It's a terrible lot to ask you. But—well, you see, there's Mary. And, if you could see your way to it—

**Webster**   I will.

**Mary**   *(weeping with relief)* Oh, Mr. Webster!

**Webster**   There, there, Mrs. Stone. After all, if two New Hampshire men aren't a match for the devil, we might as well give the country back to the Indians. When is he coming, Jabez?

**Jabez**   Twelve o'clock. The time's getting late.

**Webster**   Then I'd better refresh my memory. The—er—mortgage was for a definite term of years?

**Jabez**   Ten years.

**Webster**   And it falls due—?

**Jabez**   Tonight. Oh, I can't see how I came to be such a fool!

**Webster**   No use crying over spilt milk, Stone. We've got to get you out of it now. But tell me one thing. Did you sign this precious document of your own free will?

**Jabez**   Yes, it was my own free will. I can't deny that.

**Webster**   Hm, that's a trifle unfortunate. But we'll see.

**Mary**   Oh, Mr. Webster, can you save him? Can you?

**Webster**   I shall do my best, madam. That's all you can ever say till you see what the jury looks like.

**Mary**   But even you, Mr. Webster— Oh, I know you're Secretary of State. I know you're a great man. I know you've done wonderful things. But it's different—fighting the devil!

**Webster**   *(towering)* I've fought John C. Calhoun,[9] madam. And I've fought Henry Clay. And, by the great shade of Andrew Jackson, I'd fight ten thousand devils to save a New Hampshire man!

**Jabez**   You hear, Mary?

**Mary**   Yes. And I trust Mr. Webster. But—oh, there must be some way that I can help!

**Webster**   There is one, madam, and a hard one. As Mr. Stone's counsel, I must formally request your withdrawal.

**Mary**   No.

**Webster**   Madam, think for a moment. You cannot help Mr. Stone. Since you are his wife, your testimony would be prejudiced. And frankly,

---

**9. John C. Calhoun:** an American politician and defender of the interests of the South against those of the North. Calhoun, Clay, and Webster were longtime rivals in Congress. Each was an outstanding speaker.

madam, in a very few moments this is going to be no place for a lady.

**Mary** But I can't—I can't leave him. I can't bear it!

**Jabez** You must go, Mary. You must.

**Webster** Pray, madam—you can help us with your prayers. Are the prayers of the innocent unavailing?

**Mary** Oh, I'll pray—I'll pray. But a woman's more than a praying machine, whatever men think. And how do I know?

**Webster** Trust me, Mrs. Stone.

**Mary** *(turns to go, and, with one hand on* **Jabez'** *shoulder, as she moves to the door, says the following prayer)*

Now may there be a blessing and a light betwixt thee and me forever.

For, as Ruth unto Naomi, so do I cleave unto thee.

Set me as a seal upon thy heart, as a seal upon thine arm, for love
is strong as death.

Many waters cannot quench love, neither can the floods drown it.

As Ruth unto Naomi, so do I cleave unto thee.

The Lord watch between thee and me when we are absent, one from
the other.

Amen. Amen. *(She goes out.)*

**Webster** Amen.

**Jabez** Thank you, Mr. Webster. She ought to go. But I couldn't have made her do it.

**Webster** Well, Stone, I know ladies—and I wouldn't be surprised if she's still got her ear to the keyhole. But she's best out of this night's business. How long have we got to wait?

**Jabez** *(beginning to be terrified again)* Not long—not long.

**Webster** Then I'll just get out the jug, with your permission, Stone. Somehow or other, waiting's wonderfully shorter with a jug. *(He crosses to the cupboard, gets out jug and glasses, pours himself a drink.)* Ten-year-old Medford. There's nothing like it. I saw an inchworm take a drop of it once, and he stood right up on his hind legs and bit a bee. Come, try a nip.

**Jabez**   There's no joy in it for me.

**Webster**   Oh, come, man, come! Just because you've sold your soul to the devil, that needn't make you a teetotaler. *(He laughs and passes the jug to* **Jabez***, who tries to pour from it. But at that moment the clock whirs and begins to strike the three-quarters, and* **Jabez** *spills the liquor.)*

**Jabez**   Oh, God!

**Webster**   Never mind. It's a nervous feeling, waiting for a trial to begin. I remember my first case—

**Jabez**   'Tain't that. *(He turns to* **Webster***.)* Mr. Webster—Mr. Webster— for God's sake harness your horses and get away from this place as fast as you can!

**Webster**   *(placidly)* You've brought me a long way, neighbor, to tell me you don't like my company.

**Jabez**   I've brought you the devil's own way. I can see it all now. He's after both of us—him and his damn collecting box! Well, he can have me if he likes. I don't say I relish it, but I made the bargain. But you're the whole United States! He can't get you, Mr. Webster— he mustn't get you!

**Webster**   I'm obliged to you, neighbor Stone. It's kindly thought of. But there's a jug on the table and a case in hand. And I never left a jug or a case half finished in my life. *(There is a knock at the door.* **Jabez** *gives a cry.)* Ah, I thought your clock was a trifle slow, neighbor Stone. Come in!

*(***Scratch*** enters from the night.)*

**Scratch**   Mr. Webster! This *is* a pleasure!

**Webster**   Attorney of record for Jabez Stone. Might I ask your name?

**Scratch**   I've gone by a good many. Perhaps Scratch will do for the evening. I'm often called that in these regions. May I? *(He sits at the table and pours a drink from the jug. The liquor steams as it pours into the glass while* **Jabez** *watches, terrified.* **Scratch** *grins, toasting* **Webster** *and* **Jabez** *silently in the liquor. Then he becomes businesslike. To* **Webster***.)* And now I call upon you, as a law-abiding citizen, to assist me in taking possession of my property.

**Webster**  Not so fast, Mr. Scratch. Produce your evidence, If you have it.

**Scratch**  *(takes out a black pocketbook and examines papers)* Slattery—Stanley—Stone. *(Takes out a deed.)* There, Mr. Webster. All open and aboveboard and in due and legal form. Our firm has its reputation to consider—we deal only in the one way.

**Webster**  *(taking deed and looking it over)* Hm. This appears—I say it appears—to be properly drawn. But, of course, we contest the signature. *(Tosses it back, contemptuously.)*

**Scratch**  *(suddenly turning on **Jabez** and shooting a finger at him)* Is that your signature?

**Jabez**  *(wearily)* You know damn well it is.

**Webster**  *(angrily)* Keep quiet, Stone. *(To **Scratch**.)* But that is a minor matter. This precious document isn't worth the paper it's written on. The law permits no traffic in human flesh.

**Scratch**  Oh, my dear Mr. Webster! Courts in every state in the Union have held that human flesh is property and recoverable. Read your Fugitive Slave Act.[10] Or shall I cite Brander versus McRae?[11]

**Webster**  But, in the case of the State of Maryland versus Four Barrels of Bourbon—

**Scratch**  That was overruled, as you know, sir. North Carolina versus Jenkins and Co.

**Webster**  *(unwillingly)* You seem to have an excellent acquaintance with the law, sir.

**Scratch**  Sir, that is no fault of mine. Where I come from we have always gotten the pick of the bar.

**Webster**  *(changing his note, heartily)* Well, come now, sir. There's no need to make hay and oats of a trifling matter when we're both sensible men. Surely we can settle this little difficulty out of court. My client

---

10. **Fugitive Slave Act:** a federal law that required escaped slaves to be returned to their owners.
11. **Brander versus McRae:** a court case involving slavery. In this dialogue between Scratch and Webster, Benét shows them talking as two lawyers might speak. Each mentions law cases that favor his own argument.

is quite prepared to offer a compromise. (**Scratch** *smiles.*) A very substantial compromise. (**Scratch** *smiles more broadly, slowly shaking his head.*) Hang it, man, we offer ten thousand dollars! (**Scratch** *signs No.*) Twenty thousand—thirty—name your figure! I'll raise it if I have to mortgage Marshfield!

**Scratch**  Quite useless, Mr. Webster. There is only one thing I want from you—the execution of my contract.

**Webster**  But this is absurd. Mr. Stone is now a State Senator. The property has greatly increased in value!

**Scratch**  The principle of *caveat emptor*[12] still holds, Mr. Webster. (*He yawns and looks at the clock.*) And now, if you have no further arguments to adduce, I'm rather pressed for time— (*He rises briskly as if to take* **Jabez** *into custody.*)

**Webster**  (*thundering*) Pressed or not, you shall not have this man. Mr. Stone is an American citizen and no American citizen may be forced into the service of a foreign prince. We fought England for that, in 'twelve,[13] and we'll fight all hell for it again!

**Scratch**  Foreign? And who calls me a foreigner?

**Webster**  Well, I never yet heard of the dev—of your claiming American citizenship.

**Scratch**  And who with better right? When the first wrong was done to the first Indian, I was there. When the first slaver put out for the Congo, I stood on her deck. Am I not in your books and stories and beliefs, from the first settlements on? Am I not spoken of still in every church in New England? 'Tis true the North claims me for a Southerner and the South for a Northerner, but I am neither. I am merely an honest American like yourself—and of the best descent— for, to tell the truth, Mr. Webster, though I don't like to boast of it, my name is older in the country than yours.

**Webster**  Aha! Then I stand on the Constitution! I demand a trial for my client!

---

12. *caveat emptor:* a Latin phrase meaning "Let the buyer beware."  13. 'twelve: refers to the War of 1812, in which the United States fought Great Britain.

**Scratch**   The case is hardly one for an ordinary jury—and indeed, the lateness of the hour—

**Webster**   Let it be any court you choose, so it is an American judge and an American jury. Let it be the quick or the dead, I'll abide the issue.

**Scratch**   The quick or the dead! You have said it. *(He points his finger at the place where the* **Jury** *is to appear. There is a clap of thunder and a flash of light. The stage blacks out completely. All that can be seen is the face of* **Scratch***, lit with a ghastly green light, as he recites the invocation that summons the* **Jury***. As, one by one, the important* **Jurymen** *are mentioned, they appear.)*

> I summon the jury Mr. Webster demands.
> From churchyard mold and gallows grave,
> Brimstone pit and burning gulf,
> I summon them!
> Dastard, liar, scoundrel, knave,
> I summon them! Appear!
> There's Simon Girty,[14] the renegade,
> The haunter of the forest glade,
> Who joined with Indian and wolf
> To hunt the pioneer.
> The stains upon his hunting shirt
> Are not the blood of the deer.
> There's Walter Butler,[15] the loyalist,
> Who carried a firebrand in his fist
> Of massacre and shame.
> King Philip's[16] eye is wild and bright.
> They slew him in the great Swamp Fight,
> But still, with terror and affright,
> The land recalls his name.

---

14. **Simon Girty:** an American frontiersman who switched sides to join the British during the American Revolution. Girty led Indian war parties against American settlers and encouraged the torture of prisoners.   15. **Walter Butler:** a Loyalist—supporter of Britain during the American Revolution. He raided settlements in New York.   16. **King Philip:** chief of the Wampanoag Indians. His real name was Metacom. King Philip's War (1675–1676) involved bloody battles between Indians and colonists.

Blackbeard Teach,[17] the pirate fell,
Smeet the strangler, hot from hell,
Dale,[18] who broke men on the wheel,
Morton,[19] of the tarnished steel—
I summon them, I summon them
From their tormented flame!
Quick or dead, quick or dead,
Broken heart and bitter head,
True Americans, each one,
Traitor and disloyal son,
Cankered earth and twisted tree,
Outcasts of eternity,
Twelve great sinners, tried and true,
For the work they are to do!
I summon them, I summon them!
Appear, appear, appear!

*(The* **Jury** *has now taken its place in the box,* **Walter Butler** *in the place of foreman. They are eerily lit and so made up as to suggest the unearthly. They sit stiffly in their box. At first, when one moves, all move, in stylized gestures. It is not till the end of* **Webster's** *speech that they begin to show any trace of humanity. They speak rhythmically, and, at first, in low, eerie voices.)*

**Jabez** *(seeing them, horrified)* A jury of the dead!
**Jury** Of the dead!
**Jabez** A jury of the damned!
**Jury** Of the damned!
**Scratch** Are you content with the jury, Mr. Webster?

---

**17. Blackbeard Teach:** Edward Teach, a British pirate who terrorized the North Atlantic from 1716 to 1718. **18. Sir Thomas Dale:** the stern ruler of the Virginia colony. He was known for his harsh penalties and strict discipline. **19. Thomas Morton:** an English fur trader and adventurer. He settled in Massachusetts in 1624. He came into conflict with his Puritan neighbors for loose living and selling arms to the Indians.

**Webster** Quite content. Though I miss General Arnold[20] from the company.

**Scratch** Benedict Arnold is engaged upon other business. Ah, you asked for a justice, I believe. *(He points his finger and* **Justice Hathorne**,[21] *a tall, lean, terrifying Puritan, appears, followed by his* **Clerk***.)* Justice Hathorne is a jurist of experience. He presided at the Salem witch trials. There were others who repented of the business later. But not he, not he!

**Hathorne** Repent of such notable wonders and undertakings? Nay, hang them, hang them all! *(He takes his place on the bench.)*

*(The* **Clerk**, *an ominous little man with clawlike hands, takes his place. The room has now been transformed into a courtroom.)*

**Clerk** *(in a gabble of ritual)* Oyes, oyes, oyes.[22] All ye who have business with this honorable court of special session this night, step forward!

**Hathorne** *(with gavel)* Call the first case.

**Clerk** The World, the Flesh, and the Devil versus Jabez Stone.

**Hathorne** Who appears for the plaintiff?

**Scratch** I, Your Honor.

**Hathorne** And for the defendant?

**Webster** I.

**Jury** The case—the case—he'll have little luck with this case.

**Hathorne** The case will proceed.

**Webster** Your Honor, I move to dismiss this case on the grounds of improper jurisdiction.

**Hathorne** Motion denied.

**Webster** On the grounds of insufficient evidence.

**Hathorne** Motion denied.

**Jury** Motion denied—denied. Motion denied.

**Webster** I will take an exception.

---

**20. Benedict Arnold:** the brilliant revolutionary general who turned traitor and joined the British.
**21. Justice Hathorne:** the judge who presided over the Salem witch trials. He sentenced a number of people to death by hanging. **22. oyes:** hear ye! The word is repeated three times at the start of a day's court session to get everyone's attention.

**Hathorne** There are no exceptions in this court.

**Jury** No exceptions—no exceptions in this court. It's a bad case, Daniel Webster—a losing case.

**Webster** Your Honor—

**Hathorne** The prosecution will proceed—

**Scratch** Your Honor—gentlemen of the jury. This is a plain, straightforward case. It need not detain us long.

**Jury** Detain us long—it will not detain us long.

**Scratch** It concerns one thing alone—the transference, barter, and sale of a certain piece of property, to wit, his soul, by Jabez Stone, farmer, of Cross Corners, New Hampshire. That transference, barter, or sale is attested by a deed. I offer that deed in evidence and mark it Exhibit A.

**Webster** I object.

**Hathorne** Objection denied. Mark it Exhibit A.

*(**Scratch** hands the deed—an ominous and impressive document—to the **Clerk**, who hands it to **Hathorne**. **Hathorne** hands it back to the **Clerk**, who stamps it. All very fast and with mechanical gestures.)*

**Jury** Exhibit A—mark it Exhibit A. *(**Scratch** takes the deed from the **Clerk** and offers it to the **Jury**, who pass it rapidly among them, hardly looking at it, and hand it back to **Scratch**.)* We know the deed—the deed—it burns in our fingers—we do not have to see the deed. It's a losing case.

**Scratch** It offers incontestable evidence of the truth of the prosecution's claim. I shall now call Jabez Stone to the witness stand.

**Jury** *(hungrily)* Jabez Stone to the witness stand—Jabez Stone. He's a fine, fat fellow, Jabez Stone. He'll fry like a batter cake, once we get him where we want him.

**Webster** Your Honor, I move that this jury be discharged for flagrant and open bias!

**Hathorne** Motion denied.

**Webster** Exception.

**Hathorne**   Exception denied.

**Jury**   His motion's always denied. He thinks himself smart and clever—lawyer Webster. But his motion's always denied.

**Webster**   Your Honor! *(He chokes with anger.)*

**Clerk**   *(advancing)* Jabez Stone to the witness stand!

**Jury**   Jabez Stone—Jabez Stone.

*(**Webster** gives **Jabez** an encouraging pat on the back, and **Jabez** takes his place on the witness stand, very scared.)*

**Clerk**   *(offering a black book)* Do you solemnly swear—testify—so help you—and it's no good, for we don't care what you testify?

**Jabez**   I do.

**Scratch**   What's your name?

**Jabez**   Jabez Stone.

**Scratch**   Occupation?

**Jabez**   Farmer.

**Scratch**   Residence?

**Jabez**   Cross Corners, New Hampshire.

*(These three questions are very fast and mechanical on the part of **Scratch**. He is absolutely sure of victory and just going through a form.)*

**Jury**   A farmer—he'll farm in hell—we'll see that he farms in hell.

**Scratch**   Now, Jabez Stone, answer me. You'd better, you know. You haven't got a chance, and there'll be a cooler place by the fire for you.

**Webster**   I protest! This is intimidation! This mocks all justice!

**Hathorne**   The protest is irrelevant, incompetent, and immaterial. We have our own justice. The protest is denied.

**Jury**   Irrelevant, incompetent, and immaterial—we have our own justice—oho, Daniel Webster! *(The **Jury's** eyes fix upon **Webster** for an instant, hungrily.)*

**Scratch**   Did you or did you not sign this document?

**Jabez**   Oh, I signed it! You know I signed it. And if I have to go to hell for it, I'll go!

*(A sigh sweeps over the **Jury**.)*

**Jury**   One of us—one of us now—we'll save a place by the fire for you, Jabez Stone.

**Scratch**   The prosecution rests.

**Hathorne**   Remove the prisoner.

**Webster**   But I wish to cross-examine—I wish to prove—

**Hathorne**   There will be no cross-examination. We have our own justice. You may speak, if you like. But be brief.

**Jury**   Brief—be very brief—we're weary of earth—incompetent, irrelevant, and immaterial—they say he's a smart man, Webster, but he's lost his case tonight—be very brief—we have our own justice here.

*(**Webster** stares around him like a baited bull. He can't find words.)*

**Mary's Voice**   *(from off stage)* Set me as a seal upon thy heart, as a seal upon thine arm, for love is strong as death—

**Jury**   *(loudly)* A seal!—ha, ha—a burning seal!

**Mary's Voice**   Love is strong—

**Jury**   *(drowning her out)* Death is stronger than love. Set the seal upon Daniel Webster—the burning seal of the lost. Make him one of us— one of the damned—one with Jabez Stone!

*(The **Jury's** eyes all fix upon **Webster**. The **Clerk** advances as if to take him into custody. But **Webster** silences them all with a great gesture.)*

**Webster**   Be still!

I was going to thunder and roar. I shall not do that.

I was going to denounce and defy. I shall not do that.

You have judged this man already with your abominable justice. See
    that you defend it. For I shall not speak of this man.

You are demons now, but once you were men. I shall speak to every
    one of you.

Of common things I speak, of small things and common.

The freshness of morning to the young, the taste of food to the
    hungry, the day's toil, the rest by the fire, the quiet sleep.

These are good things.

But without freedom they sicken, without freedom they are nothing.

Freedom is the bread and the morning and the risen sun.

It was for freedom we came in the boats and the ships. It was for freedom we came.

It has been a long journey, a hard one, a bitter one.

But, out of the wrong and the right, the sufferings and the starvations, there is a new thing, a free thing.

The traitors in their treachery, the wise in their wisdom, the valiant in their courage—all, all have played a part.

It may not be denied in hell nor shall hell prevail against it.

Have you forgotten this? *(He turns to the **Jury**.)* Have you forgotten the forest?

**Girty**    *(as in a dream)* The forest, the rustle of the forest, the free forest.

**Webster**    *(to King Philip)* Have you forgotten your lost nation?

**King Philip**    My lost nation—my fires in the wood—my warriors.

**Webster**    *(to **Teach**)* Have you forgotten the sea and the way of ships?

**Teach**    The sea—and the swift ships sailing—the blue sea.

**Jury**    Forgotten—remembered—forgotten yet remembered.

**Webster**    You were men once. Have you forgotten?

**Jury**    We were men once. We have not thought of it nor remembered. But we were men.

**Webster**    Now here is this man with good and evil in his heart.

Do you know him? He is your brother. Will you take the law of the oppressor and bind him down?

It is not for him that I speak. It is for all of you.

There is sadness in being a man but it is a proud thing, too.

There is failure and despair on the journey—the endless journey of mankind.

We are tricked and trapped—we stumble into the pit—but, out of the pit, we rise again.

No demon that was ever foaled can know the inwardness of that— only men—bewildered men.

They have broken freedom with their hands and cast her out from the nations—yet shall she live while man lives.

She shall live in the blood and the heart—she shall live in the earth of this country—she shall not be broken.

When the whips of the oppressors are broken and their names forgotten and destroyed,

I see you, mighty, shining, liberty, liberty! I see free men walking and talking under a free star.

God save the United States and the men who have made her free. The defense rests.

**Jury** *(exultantly)* We were men—we were free—we were men—we have not forgotten—our children—our children shall follow and be free.

**Hathorne** *(rapping with gavel)* The jury will retire to consider its verdict.

**Butler** *(rising)* There is no need. The jury has heard Mr. Webster. We find for the defendant, Jabez Stone!

**Jury** Not guilty!

**Scratch** *(in a screech, rushing forward)* But, Your Honor—

*(But even as he does so, there is a flash and a thunderclap, the stage blacks out again, and when the lights come on, **Judge** and **Jury** are gone. The yellow light of dawn lights the windows.)*

**Jabez** They're gone and it's morning—Mary, Mary!

**Mary** *(in doorway)* My love—my dear. *(She rushes to him.)*

*(Meanwhile **Scratch** has been collecting his papers and is trying to sneak out. But **Webster** catches him.)*

**Webster** Just a minute, Mr. Scratch. I'll have that paper first, if you please. *(He takes the deed and tears it.)* And now, sir, I'll have *you!*

**Scratch** Come, come, Mr. Webster. This sort of thing is ridic—ouch— is ridiculous. If you're worried about the costs of the case, naturally I'd be glad to pay.

**Webster** And so you shall! First of all, you'll promise and covenant never to bother Jabez Stone or any other New Hampshire man from now till doomsday. For any hell we want to raise in this state we can raise ourselves, without any help from you.

**Scratch**   Ouch! Well, they never did run very big to the barrel but—ouch—I agree!

**Webster**   See you keep to the bargain! And then—well, I've got a ram named Goliath. He can butt through an iron door. I'd like to turn you loose in his field and see what he could do to you. (**Scratch** *trembles.*) But that would be hard on the ram. So we'll just call in the neighbors and give you a shivaree.

**Scratch**   Mr. Webster, please—oh—

**Webster**   Neighbors! Neighbors! Come in and see what a long-barreled, slab-sided, lantern-jawed, fortunetelling note-shaver I've got by the scruff of the neck! Bring on your kettles and your pans! (*A noise and murmur outside.*) Bring on your muskets and your flails!

**Jabez**   We'll drive him out of New Hampshire!

**Mary**   We'll drive old Scratch away!

(*The* **Crowd** *rushes in, with muskets, flails, brooms, etc. They pursue* **Scratch** *around the stage, chanting.*)

**The Crowd**   We'll drive him out of New Hampshire!
We'll drive old Scratch away!
Forever and a day, boys,
Forever and a day!

(*They finally catch* **Scratch** *between two of them and fling him out of the door bodily.*)

**A Man**   Three cheers for Dan'l Webster!

**Another Man**   Three cheers for Daniel Webster! He's licked the devil!

**Webster**   (*moving to center stage, and joining* **Jabez'** *hands and* **Mary's**) And whom God hath joined let no man put asunder. (*He kisses* **Mary** *and turns, dusting his hands.*) Well, that job's done. I hope there's pie for breakfast, neighbor Stone.

(*Some of the women, dancing, bring in pies from the kitchen.*)

# Reviewing the Selection

Answer each of the following questions without looking back at the play.

*Recalling Facts*

1. In *The Devil and Daniel Webster*, the devil is called
   □ a. Jabez.
   □ b. Mr. Hathorne.
   □ c. Miser Stevens.
   □ d. Scratch.

*Understanding Main Ideas*

2. Daniel Webster finally persuades the jury to find Jabez not guilty by
   □ a. showing that Jabez is a simple, honest farmer.
   □ b. speaking to them about freedom.
   □ c. telling them Jabez did not understand the contract.
   □ d. offering them money.

*Placing Events in Order*

3. Before Scratch appears, Jabez
   □ a. tells the townspeople that he has sold his soul to the devil.
   □ b. tries, but fails, to tell Mary of his deal with the devil.
   □ c. asks Mr. Webster to defend him against the devil.
   □ d. has forgotten that the devil is coming for him.

4. When Scratch arrives at the wedding, Benét lets the audience know who Scratch really is. Each of the following details lets you know that Scratch is the devil *except* that he
   - ☐ a. wears black gloves.
   - ☐ b. carries a mysterious black tin box.
   - ☐ c. is nice to Mary.
   - ☐ d. upsets the fiddler.

5. Scratch says, "There is only one thing I want from you—the <u>execution</u> of my contract." In this context *execution* means
   - ☐ a. hanging.
   - ☐ b. carrying out.
   - ☐ c. return.
   - ☐ d. destruction.

## Interpreting the Selection

Answer each of the following questions. You may look back at the play if necessary.

6. Which of the following statements about Mary Stone is probably true?
   - ☐ a. Mary thought Jabez should honor his bargain with Scratch.
   - ☐ b. Mary was disgusted with Jabez for selling his soul to the devil.
   - ☐ c. Mary liked Jabez even when he was poor.
   - ☐ d. Mary married Jabez because he was rich.

7. When Scratch summons the members of the jury, he chooses twelve
   ☐ a. famous criminals and sinners.
   ☐ b. heroes who helped the cause of freedom.
   ☐ c. townspeople and friends of Jabez Stone.
   ☐ d. lawyers who had opposed Daniel Webster in the past.

8. What does Benét mean when he has Scratch say, "I am merely an honest American like yourself—and of the best descent—for, to tell the truth, Mr. Webster, though I don't like to boast of it, my name is older in the country than yours"?
   ☐ a. Evil has always existed.
   ☐ b. The devil is not always evil.
   ☐ c. The devil is not as bad as he is pictured.
   ☐ d. Scratch is not really the devil.

9. Early in the play, Benét gives several hints that something bad is going to happen. Which of the following lines gives such a clue?
   ☐ a. **Fiddler**   Set to your partners! Dosy-do!
   ☐ b. **Mary**   But it's wonderful to have Mr. Webster come to us.
   ☐ c. **A Woman**   She's pretty as a picture.
   ☐ d. **Jabez**   But you remember one thing, Mary, whatever happens. It was all for you.

10. Jabez sold his soul to the devil for all of the following reasons *except* that he
    ☐ a. wanted to be state senator.
    ☐ b. was ambitious.
    ☐ c. was an evil person.
    ☐ d. was frustrated with being poor.

# Conflict and Resolution

Conflict is at the heart of all drama. As you have learned, conflict is a struggle or tension between opposing forces. In a story or a play, conflict provides motives, or reasons, for people to behave in certain ways.

Often a story or a play has more than one conflict. In *Julius Caesar*, for example, you studied the conflict between the conspirators and Caesar. You also examined the struggle that Brutus experienced within himself. Those struggles shaped the action of the play. They also helped to explain the behavior of certain characters.

Everyday life is full of conflicts. A war between nations is a conflict. The struggle between a drowning person and the sea is another example of a conflict. Imagine the conflict between two students running for class president.

The conflict in *The Devil and Daniel Webster* moves along the action of the plot. It causes the characters to behave in certain ways. The conflict also leads to a resolution—the outcome or the conclusion of the play.

In this lesson you will study the different kinds of conflict in *The Devil and Daniel Webster* and learn how Stephen Vincent Benét resolves those conflicts. You will also examine the elements of suspense in the play. Suspense helps to build the important conflicts and to interest the audience in the resolution of the play.

## External and Internal Conflicts

You will usually find more than one conflict in a work of literature. The conflicts in a story or a play can be external or internal. In *The Devil and Daniel Webster*, Jabez Stone faces both an external and an internal conflict.

**External Conflict.** An <u>external conflict</u> is a struggle between a person and an outside force. The four kinds of external conflict are (1) conflict between people, (2) conflict between a person and society, (3) conflict between groups, and (4) conflict between a person and the forces of nature.

In Benét's play the main external conflict is between Jabez Stone and Scratch. The entire play revolves around that conflict. Scratch claims Jabez's soul as payment for the gifts he gave to Jabez. Jabez, however, does not want to fulfill his part of the bargain.

*1. For most of the play, who appears to have the upper hand in the main conflict? What information supports your answer?*

There is another important external conflict in the play. It centers on the battle between Daniel Webster and Scratch. Their conflict takes place in a courtroom. In that conflict the prosecution and the defense present their views to a judge and jury. Yet the courtroom conflict in this play is different from the conflict in typical trials.

*2. How does the courtroom conflict between Daniel Webster and Scratch differ from most courtroom conflicts? At the beginning of the conflict, who appears most likely to win? Why?*

**Internal Conflict.** The second kind of conflict in the play is internal conflict. An internal conflict takes place entirely within a person's mind. It usually involves a clash of emotions or a struggle within the character's conscience. An internal conflict, for example, can arise from a decision that a person must make.

*3. Before the play begins, Jabez Stone faces an internal conflict when he makes his bargain with the devil. What struggle within himself do you think Jabez faces? Why does he make his final decision?*

When the play begins, Jabez is faced with another internal conflict: whether or not to tell Mary about his bargain with Scratch. He wants to tell her, but he is understandably reluctant to do so. Just as he is about to speak, he is interrupted by the arrival of Daniel Webster.

*4. Imagine that you are in Jabez's situation. Would you tell Mary about the bargain with Scratch? Why or why not?*

Benét shows Jabez's internal conflict through the play's dialogue. If you were seeing the play, you might learn through the actions of the actor playing Jabez that Jabez was experiencing an inner conflict. The actor might express tension through his voice or his movements. He might pace the stage nervously and look pale and frightened.

*5. Review the dialogue between Jabez and Mary just before Daniel Webster appears. Try speaking Jabez's lines. Then describe how you would say them onstage and what movements you might use.*

## Foreshadowing and Suspense

In *The Devil and Daniel Webster,* as in many other plays, the author does not reveal the conflict right away. Instead, Benét slowly builds the suspense by giving you hints about later events in the play.

Benét begins the play by describing the setting—the time and the place of the action of a story. He also introduces the characters. You learn that the play is set at a wedding party in a New Hampshire farmhouse. Several neighbors speak about the young couple, Jabez and Mary Stone.

At this point in the play, Benét begins to hint at the conflict. Foreshadowing is the use of hints, clues, or signs to suggest events that are going to happen later on in the play. Foreshadowing is a device used by many writers to build suspense. Benét uses foreshadowing to arouse your curiosity and to keep your interest. By hinting at the conflict early in the play, he makes you wonder what is going to happen.

In the dialogue Benét foreshadows the conflict that Jabez Stone faces. Read the dialogue between the old man, his neighbor, and a third man.

**The Old Man**   *(gossiping to a neighbor)* Wonder where he got it all. Stones was always poor.
**His Neighbor**   Ain't poor now. Makes you wonder just a mite.
**A Third Man**   Don't begrudge it to him—but I wonder where he got it.

*6. What does that dialogue suggest? Read on until the fiddler says, "Left and right—grand chain!" How does the gossiping among Jabez's neighbors foreshadow events to come?*

Another instance of foreshadowing occurs in the scene between

Jabez and Mary when they are left alone by the fireplace. They are happy, but Mary has a sense of uneasiness—"As if we'd been too lucky," she says. Her uneasiness foreshadows events that will soon take place—events that show that Mary and Jabez are, indeed, unnaturally lucky.

*7. Skim the first half of the play. Find two other examples of fore-shadowing. Explain how each example foreshadows something that happens later in the play.*

## Conflict and Suspense

Scratch is central to the conflict in the play. When Scratch first appears onstage, the audience knows right away that he is an unusual and evil character. If you are reading the play, you know he is the devil because Benét tells you that in his stage directions. If you are seeing a performance of the play, you will notice *"something just a little wrong in clothes and appearance."* His black gloves and his black box suggest something ominous, or threatening. Thus, the devil's appearance builds suspense.

At first, Scratch pretends he is an insignificant guest. He tells the fiddler, "Oh, I'm just a friend—a humble friend of the bridegroom's." Yet the audience senses that Scratch is far more than that. His appearance means trouble for the young bridegroom. The problem foreshadowed earlier now has to be faced.

Scratch's arrival affects the wedding guests. Although they do not know or recognize the devil, they sense his evil character. The fiddler resents Scratch's telling him how to play his fiddle. When Scratch plays a discordant note and sings an offensive song, the guests become uncomfortable. When the fiddler opens Scratch's mysterious black box and releases the lost soul of Miser Stevens, the guests are shocked and horrified. They realize then who Scratch is. They soon learn why he has come to Jabez's wedding.

Scratch's character and behavior make the guests fear and dislike him. His character also makes the audience feel sympathy for Jabez and Mary. You do not want Mary to lose her husband. You hope that Jabez will not be taken away by the devil. By involving the audience in the conflict and by arousing sympathy for the young couple, Benét heightens the tension and suspense.

*8. Think of the conflict in the courtroom between Daniel Webster and Scratch. How does Benét make the audience feel sympathy for Webster?*

In drama suspense is closely connected to the outcome of the conflict. The suspense in *The Devil and Daniel Webster* comes from the uncertainty over what will happen to Jabez. Will he have to go with Scratch? Can Daniel Webster successfully defend Jabez? Will the jury even listen to Webster, or is the jury simply a tool of the devil? All those questions must be resolved before the play ends.

## Symbols and Conflict

The conflict in *The Devil and Daniel Webster* concerns ideas as well as individuals. The main characters can be seen as symbols of those ideas. A symbol is an image, an object, or a person that stands for something other or more important than itself. For example, a dove is a symbol for peace. Arrows or guns often symbolize war. What might the main characters in this play stand for?

Jabez Stone is a young man in trouble because of his ambitions. He wants to be a prosperous farmer, he wants to become a successful politician, and he wants to marry Mary. In a moment of weakness, he promises his soul to the devil in exchange for the fulfillment of his desires. Jabez is a symbol of human weakness and ambition. When Webster talks to the jury, he points to Jabez as a "man with good and evil in his heart." Like all humans, Jabez has both good and bad sides to his character.

Scratch is another character who has symbolic importance. As the devil, he represents evil. He can also be seen as symbolic of something else. Benét introduces Scratch as a "Boston lawyer." To the people in a small New England town, a Boston lawyer might symbolize certain ideas.

*9. What do you think Scratch the lawyer might symbolize?*

The third main character, Daniel Webster, also has symbolic importance. Benét has deliberately chosen a historical character to defend Jabez against the devil. If you read Webster's speech to the jury, you can tell that he stands for freedom, democracy, and the rights of the individual. Webster symbolizes the ideals of the United States and its Constitution.

*10. Look at the characters who make up the jury and reread the footnotes about them. In the play each jury member is described as a sinner. What sins do they symbolize?*

## Resolution

The conflicts in *The Devil and Daniel Webster* move the play toward its resolution. Jabez's internal conflict about whether or not to tell Mary about his bargain is resolved when Scratch appears. The central conflict over Jabez's soul is not resolved, however, until the jury gives its verdict.

As the conflict draws to a climax, Benét increases the suspense. He introduces an unsympathetic judge and jury. Both are the tools of the devil. Each time Webster tries to defend Jabez, the judge and jury reject his efforts. Webster appears to be helpless against the forces of evil, and it seems certain that the jury will convict Jabez.

Then Webster takes the floor. Imagine how the great speaker might stand on the stage as he gets ready to address the jury. Webster makes a passionate appeal to the members of the jury. Even though they are criminals and sinners, he speaks to them as men who once enjoyed freedom. "Have you forgotten this?" he asks each member.

Webster's speech succeeds. The jury is swept up by the idea of freedom. The sinners reject the devil and turn down evil in favor of freedom. The climax leads the play toward its conclusion. At the end of the play, Benét resolves the conflicts between Jabez and Scratch, between Webster and Scratch, and between good and evil. The devil is forced to give up Jabez's contract and is driven from New Hampshire by Jabez's neighbors.

*11. Imagine how the resolution might be staged. Describe the movements and voices of Scratch, Webster, and Jabez's neighbors.*

## Questions for Thought and Discussion

The questions and activities that follow will help you explore *The Devil and Daniel Webster* in more depth and at the same time develop your critical thinking skills.

1. **Expressing an Opinion.** If you had been on the jury hearing Jabez's case, how would you have voted? Give reasons for your opinion.

2. **Identifying the Author's Purpose.** Webster demands a jury trial but lets Scratch choose the jurors. What types of people does Scratch pick for the jury? Why do you think Benét has Scratch choose those people?

3. **Understanding Symbols.** Find at least three ways in which Scratch represents evil. What character in the play stands for good? Find evidence in the play to show how that character represents good.

4. **Comparing.** Think about the conflicts in *Julius Caesar* and in *The Devil and Daniel Webster*. How important is the external conflict in each play? How important is the internal conflict in each?

## Writing About Literature

Several suggestions for writing projects follow. You may be asked to complete one or more of these projects. If you have any questions about how to begin a writing assignment, review Using the Writing Process, beginning on page 385.

1. **Describing a Situation.** *The Devil and Daniel Webster* is an imaginary story. Yet the situation that Jabez faced is not so far from reality. He was tempted by an easy and immediate solution to a problem. Later he had to deal with the consequences of his decision. Imagine a real-life situation in which a person is tempted as Jabez was. Describe the situation and its results. Then tell how the experience is similar to that of Jabez Stone in *The Devil and Daniel Webster*.

2. **Reporting on Research.** Using library sources, find out more about one of the historical characters or events mentioned in the play. For example, you might research Daniel Webster, Henry Clay, or the Fugitive Slave Act. Write a brief report explaining the importance of the person or event in the history of the United States.

3. **Staging a Scene.** Choose a scene or an incident in the play that you would enjoy staging. Prepare notes on how you would stage the scene. Be sure to describe the scenery and the costumes. Describe the placement of the characters onstage, the lighting, and the way you would have the different characters say their lines.

| | |
|---|---|
| **Selection** | *The Ugly Duckling* |
| | A. A. Milne |
| **Lesson** | *Parody and Humor* |

## About the Selection

When you were a child, you probably read or heard many fairy tales. "Cinderella," "Snow White and the Seven Dwarfs," and "Sleeping Beauty" are just a few of the best-known fairy tales. Many fairy tales describe imaginary kingdoms. The main characters are often a king and a queen or a prince and a princess. The plot might involve a courageous prince fighting a dragon to rescue a beautiful princess.

In *The Ugly Duckling* A. A. Milne relies on your knowledge of the typical characters and plots of fairy tales. In fact, Milne has taken the title of his play from a Hans Christian Andersen fairy tale called "The Ugly Duckling." Andersen was a nineteenth-century Danish writer whose fairy tales became popular around the world.

In Andersen's fairy tale a brood of ducklings are hatched, and one is different from all the others. The duckling is ugly. Because of its appearance, other ducklings and even other animals mock it and treat it cruelly.

The duckling is forced to leave the brood. It suffers terribly and almost dies of cold and starvation. Eventually, the ugly duckling grows into a beautiful, graceful swan. It had not looked like the other ducklings because it was not a duck at all. When it meets the animals that had once mocked it, the swan is admired by them. At the end of the story, the swan is thankful for having "gone through so much suffering, for it made him appreciate his present happiness and the loveliness of everything about him all the more."

Andersen's tale makes a point about two kinds of beauty: outward beauty, or good looks, and inner beauty—qualities such as kindness and goodness. By choosing the title *The Ugly Duckling* for his play, Milne is offering a clue to the play's theme.

Milne's play is about a princess who is considered plain and unattractive by her parents, the king and queen. Because of the princess's appearance, none of the local princes want to marry her. Her parents are frustrated because they cannot find a husband for their daughter. Finally, the king and queen think of a plan that they hope will solve their problem.

The play is full of humor, as you will see. The playwright has the characters act and speak seriously. The audience, however, knows that he does not want them to take the characters seriously.

Alan Alexander Milne, better known as A. A. Milne, was born in London, England, in 1882. After graduating from Cambridge University, he went to work for a newspaper. Milne began writing plays during World War I. He became well known as the author of plays, novels, short stories, and humorous essays.

Milne is best remembered as the author of *Winnie-the-Pooh*. Since the first book about Pooh was published in 1926, the stories of Christopher Robin and his teddy bear, Pooh, have been read by many children. Milne did not like being known for writing those children's books. He preferred to be recognized for his other writing.

## Lesson Preview

The lesson that follows *The Ugly Duckling* focuses on parody and humor. Parody is a kind of humorous writing in which a writer imitates another, more serious piece of literature. *The Ugly Duckling*, however, also carries a serious message.

The questions that follow will help you identify the various elements of humor in the play. As you read, think about how you would answer these questions.

**1** When do you realize that the play is imitating fairy tales? What clues lead you to this realization?

**2** Who are the main characters? What are they like? Why are they humorous?

**3** How is the plot similar to fairy-tale plots? How is it different?

**4** How does the dialogue make the play humorous?

**5** What do you think is the message of Milne's play?

## Vocabulary

Here are some difficult words that appear in the selection that follows. Study the words and their definitions, as well as the sentences that show how the words are used. This will help you get the most from your reading.

**posterity** the people of future times; descendants. *Posterity will have many environmental problems to solve.*

**tactfully** with delicacy and diplomacy. *The mediator handled the difficult situation tactfully, without angering any of the parties involved.*

**monotonous** tiresome because of sameness or repetition. *Many students fell asleep during the monotonous lecture.*

**predecessor** a person who has held a job or an office before another. *My predecessor left this job because she was offered a better position.*

**doggedness** persistence; stubbornness. *Although George was not a good violinist, his doggedness and desire to improve earned him a seat in the school orchestra.*

**surreptitiously** secretly; stealthily. *Because I hated peas, I surreptitiously pushed them under the table for the dog.*

**waft** to transport lightly as if by wind or waves. *The spring breeze will waft fresh air into this stuffy room.*

# The Ugly Duckling

A. A. MILNE

## Characters

The King
The Queen
The Princess Camilla
The Chancellor
Dulcibella
Prince Simon
Carlo

*The* **Scene** *is the Throne Room of the Palace; a room of many doors, or, if preferred, curtain openings: simply furnished with three thrones for Their Majesties and Her Royal Highness the* **Princess Camilla**—*in other words, with three handsome chairs. At each side is a long seat; reserved, as it might be, for His Majesty's Council (if any), but useful, as today, for other purposes. The* **King** *is asleep on his throne with a handkerchief over his face. He is a king of any country from any storybook, in whatever costume you please. But he should be wearing his crown.*

**A Voice** *(announcing)* His Excellency the Chancellor! *(The* **Chancellor,** *an elderly man in horn-rimmed spectacles, enters, bowing. The* **King** *wakes up with a start and removes the handkerchief from his face.)*

**King** *(with simple dignity)* I was thinking.

**Chancellor** *(bowing)* Never, Your Majesty, was greater need for thought than now.

**King** That's what I was thinking. *(He struggles into a more dignified position.)* Well, what is it? More trouble?

**Chancellor**   What we might call the old trouble, Your Majesty.

**King**   It's what I was saying last night to the Queen. "Uneasy lies the head that wears a crown," was how I put it.

**Chancellor**   A profound and original thought, which may well go down to posterity.

**King**   You mean it may go down well with posterity. I hope so. Remind me to tell you some time of another little thing I said to Her Majesty: something about a fierce light beating on a throne. Posterity would like that, too. Well, what is it?

**Chancellor**   It is in the matter of Her Royal Highness' wedding.

**King**   Oh . . . yes.

**Chancellor**   As Your Majesty is aware, the young Prince Simon arrives today to seek Her Royal Highness' hand in marriage. He has been traveling in distant lands and, as I understand, has not—er—has not——

**King**   You mean he hasn't heard anything.

**Chancellor**   It's a little difficult to put this tactfully, Your Majesty.

**King**   Do your best, and I will tell you afterwards how you got on.

**Chancellor**   Let me put it this way. The Prince Simon will naturally assume that Her Royal Highness has the customary—so customary as to be, in my own poor opinion, slightly monotonous—has what one might call the inevitable—so inevitable as to be, in my opinion again, almost mechanical—will assume, that she has the, as *I* think of it, faultily faultless, icily regular, splendidly——

**King**   What you are trying to say in the fewest words possible is that my daughter is not beautiful.

**Chancellor**   Her beauty is certainly elusive,[1] Your Majesty.

**King**   It is. It has eluded you, it has eluded me, it has eluded everybody who has seen her. It even eluded the Court Painter. His last words were, "Well, I did my best." His successor is now painting the view across the water-meadows from the West Turret. He says that his doctor has advised him to keep to landscape.

---

**1. elusive:** hard to grasp.

**Chancellor**   It is unfortunate, Your Majesty, but there it is. One just cannot understand how it can have occurred.

**King**   You don't think she takes after *me*, at all? You don't detect a likeness?

**Chancellor**   Most certainly not, Your Majesty.

**King**   Good. . . . Your predecessor did.

**Chancellor**   I have often wondered what happened to my predecessor.

**King**   Well, now you know. *(There is a short silence.)*

**Chancellor**   Looking at the bright side, although Her Royal Highness is not, strictly speaking, beautiful——

**King**   Not, truthfully speaking, beautiful——

**Chancellor**   Yet she has great beauty of character.

**King**   My dear Chancellor, we are not considering Her Royal Highness' character, but her chances of getting married. You observe that there is a distinction.

**Chancellor**   Yes, Your Majesty.

**King**   Looking at it from the suitor's point of view. If a girl is beautiful, it is easy to assume that she has, tucked away inside her, an equally beautiful character. But it is impossible to assume that an unattractive girl, however elevated in character, has, tucked away inside her, an equally beautiful face. That is, so to speak, not where you want it—tucked away.

**Chancellor**   Quite so, Your Majesty.

**King**   This doesn't, of course, alter the fact that the Princess Camilla is quite the nicest person in the Kingdom.

**Chancellor**   *(enthusiastically)* She is indeed, Your Majesty. *(Hurriedly.)* With the exception, I need hardly say, of Your Majesty—and Her Majesty.

**King**   Your exceptions are tolerated for their loyalty and condemned for their extreme fatuity.[2]

**Chancellor**   Thank you, Your Majesty.

**King**   As an adjective for your King, the word "nice" is ill-chosen. As an adjective for Her Majesty, it is—ill-chosen. *(At which moment* **Her**

---

2. **fatuity:** stupidity.

**Majesty** *comes in. The* **King** *rises. The* **Chancellor** *puts himself at right angles.)*

**Queen** *(briskly)* Ah. Talking about Camilla? *(She sits down.)*

**King** *(returning to his throne)* As always, my dear, you are right.

**Queen** *(to* **Chancellor***)* This fellow, Simon——What's he like?

**Chancellor** Nobody has seen him, Your Majesty.

**Queen** How old is he?

**Chancellor** Five-and-twenty, I understand.

**Queen** In twenty-five years he must have been seen by somebody.

**King** *(to the* **Chancellor***)* Just a fleeting glimpse.

**Chancellor** I meant, Your Majesty, that no detailed report of him has reached this country, save that he has the usual personal advantages and qualities expected of a Prince, and has been traveling in distant and dangerous lands.

**Queen** Ah! Nothing gone wrong with his eyes? Sunstroke or anything?

**Chancellor** Not that I am aware of, Your Majesty. At the same time, as I was venturing to say to His Majesty, Her Royal Highness' character and disposition are so outstandingly——

**Queen** Stuff and nonsense. You remember what happened when we had the Tournament of Love last year.

**Chancellor** I was not myself present, Your Majesty. I had not then the honor of—I was abroad, and never heard the full story.

**Queen** No; it was the other fool. They all rode up to Camilla to pay their homage[3]—it was the first time they had seen her. The heralds blew their trumpets, and announced that she would marry whichever Prince was left master of the field when all but one had been unhorsed. The trumpets were blown again, they charged enthusiastically into the fight, and—— *(The* **King** *looks nonchalantly at the ceiling and whistles a few bars.)*—don't do that.

**King** I'm sorry, my dear.

**Queen** *(to* **Chancellor***)* And what happened? They all simultaneously fell off their horses and assumed a position of defeat.

---

3. **homage:** respect.

*Parody and Humor*

**King**   One of them was not quite so quick as the others. I was very quick. I proclaimed him the victor.

**Queen**   At the Feast of Betrothal held that night——

**King**   We were all very quick.

**Queen**   The Chancellor announced that by the laws of the country the successful suitor had to pass a further test. He had to give the correct answer to a riddle.

**Chancellor**   Such undoubtedly is the fact, Your Majesty.

**King**   There are times for announcing facts, and times for looking at things in a broadminded way. Please remember that, Chancellor.

**Chancellor**   Yes, Your Majesty.

**Queen**   I invented the riddle myself. Quite an easy one. What is it which has four legs and barks like a dog? The answer is, "A dog."

**King**   *(to* **Chancellor***)* You see that?

**Chancellor**   Yes, Your Majesty.

**King**   It isn't difficult.

**Queen**   He, however, seemed to find it so. He said an eagle. Then he said a serpent; a very high mountain with slippery sides; two peacocks; a moonlit night; the day after tomorrow——

**King**   Nobody could accuse him of not trying.

**Queen**   *I* did.

**King**   I *should* have said that nobody could fail to recognize in his attitude an appearance of doggedness.

**Queen**   Finally he said. "Death." I nudged the King——

**King**   Accepting the word "nudge" for the moment, I rubbed my ankle with one hand, clapped him on the shoulder with the other, and congratulated him on the correct answer. He disappeared under the table, and, personally, I never saw him again.

**Queen**   His body was found in the moat next morning.

**Chancellor**   But what was he doing in the moat, Your Majesty?

**King**   Bobbing about. Try not to ask needless questions.

**Chancellor**   It all seems so strange.

**Queen**   What does?

**Chancellor** That Her Royal Highness, alone of all the Princesses one has ever heard of, should lack that invariable attribute of Royalty, supreme beauty.

**Queen** *(to the* **King***)* That was your Great-Aunt Malkin. She came to the christening. You know what she said.

**King** It was cryptic.[4] Great-Aunt Malkin's besetting weakness. She came to *my* christening—she was one hundred and one then, and that was fifty-one years ago. *(To the* **Chancellor.***)* How old would that make her?

**Chancellor** One hundred and fifty-two, Your Majesty.

**King** *(after a thought)* About that, yes. She promised me that when I grew up I should have all the happiness which my wife deserved. It struck me at the time—well, when I say "at the time," I was only a week old—but it did strike me as soon as anything could strike me—I mean of that nature—well, work it out for yourself, Chancellor. It opens up a most interesting field of speculation. Though naturally I have not liked to go into it all deeply with Her Majesty.

**Queen** I never heard anything less cryptic. She was wishing you extreme happiness.

**King** I don't think she was *wishing* me anything. However.

**Chancellor** *(to the* **Queen***)* But what, Your Majesty, did she wish Her Royal Highness?

**Queen** Her other godmother—on my side—had promised her the dazzling beauty for which all the women in my family are famous—— *(She pauses, and the* **King** *snaps his fingers surreptitiously in the direction of the* **Chancellor.***)*

**Chancellor** *(hurriedly)* Indeed, yes, Your Majesty. *(The* **King** *relaxes.)*

**Queen** And Great-Aunt Malkin said—*(to the* **King***)*—what were the words?

**King**
> I give you with this kiss
> A wedding-day surprise.
> Where ignorance is bliss
> 'Tis folly to be wise.

---

4. **cryptic:** mysterious.

I thought the last two lines rather neat. But what it *meant*——

**Queen**   We can all see what it meant. She was given beauty—and where is it? Great-Aunt Malkin took it away from her. The wedding-day surprise is that there will never be a wedding day.

**King**   Young men being what they are, my dear, it would be much more surprising if there *were* a wedding day. So how——*(The* **Princess** *comes in. She is young, happy, healthy, but not beautiful. Or let us say that by some trick of make-up or arrangement of hair she seems plain to us: unlike the* **Princess** *of the storybooks.)*

**Princess**   *(to the* **King***)* Hallo, darling! *(Seeing the others.)* Oh, I say! Affairs of state? Sorry.

**King**   *(holding out his hand)* Don't go, Camilla. *(She takes his hand.)*

**Chancellor**   Shall I withdraw, Your Majesty?

**Queen**   You are aware, Camilla, that Prince Simon arrives today?

**Princess**   He has arrived. They're just letting down the drawbridge.

**King**   *(jumping up)* Arrived! I must——

**Princess**   Darling, you know what the drawbridge is like. It takes at *least* half an hour to let it down.

**King**   *(sitting down)* It wants oil. *(To the* **Chancellor.***)* Have *you* been grudging it oil?

**Princess**   It wants a new drawbridge, darling.

**Chancellor**   Have I Your Majesty's permission——

**King**   Yes, yes. *(The* **Chancellor** *bows and goes out.)*

**Queen**   You've told him, of course? It's the only chance.

**King**   Er—no. I was just going to, when——

**Queen**   Then I'd better. *(She goes to the door.)* You can explain to the girl; I'll have her sent to you. You've told Camilla?

**King**   Er—no. I was just going to, when——

**Queen**   Then you'd better tell her now.

**King**   My dear, are you sure——

**Queen**   It's the only chance left. *(Dramatically to heaven.)* My daughter! *(She goes out. There is a little silence when she is gone.)*

**King**   Camilla, I want to talk seriously to you about marriage.

**Princess**   Yes, father.

**King**  It is time that you learnt some of the facts of life.

**Princess**  Yes, father.

**King**  Now the great fact about marriage is that once you're married you live happy ever after. All our history books affirm this.

**Princess**  And your own experience too, darling.

**King**  *(with dignity)* Let us confine ourselves to history for the moment.

**Princess**  Yes, father.

**King**  Of course, there *may* be an exception here and there, which, as it were, proves the rule; just as—oh, well, never mind.

**Princess**  *(smiling)* Go on, darling. You were going to say that an exception here and there proves the rule that all princesses are beautiful.

**King**  Well—leave that for the moment. The point is that it doesn't matter *how* you marry, or *who* you marry, as long as you *get* married. Because you'll be happy ever after in any case. Do you follow me so far?

**Princess**  Yes, father.

**King**  Well, your mother and I have a little plan——

**Princess**  Was that it, going out of the door just now?

**King**  Er—yes. It concerns your waiting-maid.

**Princess**  Darling, I have several.

**King**  Only one that leaps to the eye, so to speak. The one with the—well, with everything.

**Princess**  Dulcibella?

**King**  That's the one. It is our little plan that at the first meeting she should pass herself off as the Princess—a harmless ruse,[5] of which you will find frequent record in the history books—and allure Prince Simon to his—that is to say, bring him up to the——In other words, the wedding will take place immediately afterwards, and as quietly as possible—well, naturally in view of the fact that your Aunt Malkin is one hundred and fifty-two; and since you will be wearing the family bridal veil—which is no doubt how the custom arose—the surprise after the ceremony will be his. Are you following me at all? Your attention seems to be wandering.

---

**5. ruse:** trick.

**Princess**   I was wondering why you needed to tell me.

**King**   Just a precautionary measure, in case you happened to meet the Prince or his attendant before the ceremony; in which case, of course, you would pass yourself off as the maid——

**Princess**   A harmless ruse, of which, also, you will find frequent record in the history books.

**King**   Exactly. But the occasion need not arise.

**A Voice**   *(announcing)* The woman, Dulcibella!

**King**   Ah! *(To the **Princess**.)* Now, Camilla, if you will just retire to your own apartments, I will come to you there when we are ready for the actual ceremony. *(He leads her out as he is talking: and as he returns calls out.)* Come in, my dear! (**Dulcibella** *comes in. She is beautiful, but dumb.)* Now don't be frightened, there is nothing to be frightened about. Has Her Majesty told you what you have to do?

**Dulcibella**   Y-yes, Your Majesty.

**King**   Well now, let's see how well you can do it. You are sitting here, we will say. *(He leads her to a seat.)* Now imagine that I am Prince Simon. *(He curls his moustache and puts his stomach in. She giggles.)* You are the beautiful Princess Camilla whom he has never seen. *(She giggles again.)* This is a serious moment in your life, and you will find that a giggle will not be helpful. *(He goes to the door.)* I am announced: "His Royal Highness Prince Simon!" That's me being announced. Remember what I said about giggling. You should have a far-away look upon the face. *(She does her best.)* Farther away than that. *(She tries again.)* No, that's too far. You are sitting there, thinking beautiful thoughts—in maiden meditation, fancy-free, as I remember saying to Her Majesty once . . . speaking of somebody else . . . fancy-free, but with the mouth definitely shut—that's better. I advance and fall upon one knee. *(He does so.)* You extend your hand graciously—*graciously;* you're not trying to push him in the face—that's better, and I raise it to my lips—so—and I kiss it—*(he kisses it warmly)*—no, perhaps not so ardently as that, more like this *(he kisses it again)*, and I say, "Your Royal Highness, this is the most—er——Your Royal Highness, I shall ever be—no—Your Royal Highness, it is the proudest——" Well, the point is that *he* will say it, and it will be something complimentary, and then he will take your hand in both of his, and press it to his heart. *(He does so.)* And then—what do *you* say?

**Dulcibella**   Coo![6]

**King**   No, *not* Coo.

**Dulcibella**   Never had anyone do *that* to me before.

**King**   That also strikes the wrong note. What you want to say is, "Oh, Prince Simon!" . . . Say it.

**Dulcibella**   *(loudly)* Oh, Prince Simon!

**King**   No, no. You don't need to shout until he has said "What?" two or three times. Always consider the possibility that he *isn't* deaf. Softly, and giving the words a dying fall, letting them play around his head like a flight of doves.

**Dulcibella**   *(still a little overloud)* O-o-o-o-h, Prinsimon!

**King**   Keep the idea in your mind of a flight of *doves* rather than a flight of panic-stricken elephants, and you will be all right. Now I'm going to get up, and you must, as it were, *waft* me into a seat by your side. *(She starts wafting.) Not* rescuing a drowning man, that's another idea altogether, useful at times, but at the moment inappropriate. Wafting. Prince Simon will put the necessary muscles into play—all you require to do is to indicate by a gracious movement of the hand the seat you require him to take. Now! *(He gets up, a little stiffly, and sits next to her.)* That was better. Well, here we are. Now, I think you give me a look: something, let us say, halfway between the breathless adoration of a nun and the voluptuous[7] abandonment of a woman of the world; with an undertone of regal dignity, touched, as it were, with good comradeship. Now try that. *(She gives him a vacant look of bewilderment.)* Frankly, that didn't quite get it. There was just a little something missing. An absence, as it were, of all the qualities I asked for, and in their place an odd resemblance to an unsatisfied fish.

---

**6. Coo:** a British expression of surprise.   **7. voluptuous:** suggesting sensual pleasure and delights.

*Parody and Humor*

Let us try to get at it another way. Dulcibella, have you a young man of your own?

**Dulcibella** *(eagerly, seizing his hand)* Oo, yes, he's ever so smart, he's an archer, well not as you might say a real archer, he works in the armory, but old Bottlenose, *you* know who I mean, the Captain of the Guard, says the very next man they ever has to shoot, my Eg shall take his place, knowing Father and how it is with Eg and me, and me being maid to Her Royal Highness and can't marry me till he's a real soldier, but ever so loving, and funny like, the things he says, I said to him once, "Eg," I said——

**King** *(getting up)* I rather fancy, Dulcibella, that if you think of Eg all the time, *say* as little as possible, and, when thinking of Eg, see that the mouth is not more than partially open, you will do very well. I will show you where you are to sit and wait for His Royal Highness. *(He leads her out. On the way he is saying.)* Now remember—*waft—waft*—not *hoick.* (**Prince Simon** *wanders in from the back unannounced. He is a very ordinary-looking young man in rather dusty clothes. He gives a deep sigh of relief as he sinks into the* **King's** *throne. . . .* **Camilla***, a new and strangely beautiful* **Camilla***, comes in.)*

**Princess** *(surprised)* Well!

**Prince** Oh, hallo!

**Princess** Ought you?

**Prince** *(getting up)* Do sit down, won't you?

**Princess** Who are you, and how did you get here?

**Prince** Well, that's rather a long story. Couldn't we sit down? You could sit here if you liked, but it isn't very comfortable.

**Princess** That is the King's Throne.

**Prince** Oh, is that what it is?

**Princess** Thrones are not meant to be comfortable.

**Prince** Well, I don't know if they're meant to be, but they certainly aren't.

**Princess** Why are you sitting on the King's Throne, and who are you?

**Prince** My name is Carlo.

**Princess** Mine is Dulcibella.

**Prince**   Good. And now couldn't we sit down?

**Princess**   *(sitting down on the long seat to the left of the throne and, as it were, wafting him to a place next to her)* You may sit here, if you like. Why are you so tired? *(He sits down.)*

**Prince**   I've been taking very strenuous exercise.

**Princess**   Is that part of the long story?

**Prince**   It is.

**Princess**   *(settling herself)* I love stories.

**Prince**   This isn't a story really. You see, I'm attendant on Prince Simon, who is visiting here.

**Princess**   Oh? I'm attendant on Her Royal Highness.

**Prince**   Then you know what he's here for.

**Princess**   Yes.

**Prince**   She's very beautiful, I hear.

**Princess**   Did you hear that? Where have you been lately?

**Prince**   Traveling in distant lands—with Prince Simon.

**Princess**   Ah! All the same, I don't understand. Is Prince Simon in the Palace now? The drawbridge *can't* be down yet!

**Prince**   I don't suppose it is. *And* what a noise it makes coming down!

**Princess**   Isn't it terrible?

**Prince**   I couldn't stand it any more. I just had to get away. That's why I'm here.

**Princess**   But how?

**Prince**   Well, there's only one way, isn't there? That beech tree, and then a swing and a grab for the battlements, and don't ask me to remember it all—— *(He shudders.)*

**Princess**   You mean you came across the moat by that beech tree?

**Prince**   Yes. I got so tired of hanging about.

**Princess**   But it's terribly dangerous!

**Prince**   That's why I'm so exhausted. Nervous shock. *(He lies back and breathes loudly.)*

**Princess**   Of course, it's different for *me*.

**Prince**   *(sitting up)* Say that again. I must have got it wrong.

**Princess**  It's different for me, because I'm used to it. Besides, I'm so much lighter.

**Prince**  You don't mean that *you*——

**Princess**  Oh yes, often.

**Prince**  And I thought I was a brave man! At least, I didn't until five minutes ago, and now I don't again.

**Princess**  Oh, but you are! And I think it's wonderful to do it straight off the first time.

**Prince**  Well, *you* did.

**Princess**  Oh no, not the first time. When I was a child.

**Prince**  You mean that you crashed?

**Princess**  Well, you only fall into the moat.

**Prince**  Only! Can you *swim?*

**Princess**  Of course.

**Prince**  So you swam to the castle walls, and yelled for help, and they fished you out and walloped you. And next day you tried again. Well, if *that* isn't pluck——

**Princess**  Of course I didn't. I swam back, and did it at once; I mean I tried again at once. It wasn't until the third time that I actually did it. You see, I was afraid I might lose my nerve.

**Prince**  Afraid she might lose her nerve!

**Princess**  There's a way of getting over from this side, too; a tree grows out from the wall and you jump into another tree—I don't think it's quite so easy.

**Prince**  Not quite so easy. Good. You must show me.

**Princess**  Oh, I will.

**Prince**  Perhaps it might be as well if you taught me how to swim first. I've often heard about swimming, but never——

**Princess**  You can't swim?

**Prince**  No. Don't look so surprised. There are a lot of other things which I can't do. I'll tell you about them as soon as you have a couple of years to spare.

**Princess**  You can't swim and yet you crossed by the beech tree! And you're *ever* so much heavier than I am! Now who's brave?

**Prince**   *(getting up)* You keep talking about how light you are. I must see if there's anything in it. Stand up! *(She stands obediently and he picks her up.)* You're right, Dulcibella. I could hold you here forever. *(Looking at her.)* You're very lovely. Do you know how lovely you are?

**Princess**   Yes. *(She laughs suddenly and happily.)*

**Prince**   Why do you laugh?

**Princess**   Aren't you tired of holding me?

**Prince**   Frankly, yes. I exaggerated when I said I could hold you forever. When you've been hanging by the arms for ten minutes over a very deep moat, wondering if it's too late to learn how to swim—*(he puts her down)*—what I meant was that I should *like* to hold you forever. Why did you laugh?

**Princess**   Oh, well, it was a little private joke of mine.

**Prince**   If it comes to that, I've got a private joke too. Let's exchange them.

**Princess**   Mine's very private. One other woman in the whole world knows, and that's all.

**Prince**   Mine's just as private. One other man knows, and that's all.

**Princess**   What fun. I love secrets. . . . Well, here's mine. When I was born, one of my godmothers promised that I should be very beautiful.

**Prince**   How right she was.

**Princess**   But the other one said this:

> I give you with this kiss
> A wedding-day surprise.
> Where ignorance is bliss
> 'Tis folly to be wise.

And nobody knew what it meant. And I grew up very plain. And then, when I was about ten, I met my godmother in the forest one day. It was my tenth birthday. Nobody knows this—except you.

**Prince**   Except us.

**Princess**   Except us. And she told me what her gift meant. It meant that I *was* beautiful—but everybody else was to go on being ignorant, and thinking me plain, until my wedding-day. Because, she said, she didn't want me to grow up spoilt and wilful and vain, as I should have done if everybody had always been saying how beautiful I was; and the best thing in the world, she said, was to be quite sure of yourself, but not to expect admiration from other people. So ever since then my mirror has told me I'm beautiful, and everybody else thinks me ugly, and I get a lot of fun out of it.

**Prince**   Well, seeing that Dulcibella is the result, I can only say that your godmother was very, very wise.

**Princess**   And now tell me *your* secret.

**Prince**   It isn't such a pretty one. You see, Prince Simon was going to woo Princess Camilla, and he'd heard that she was beautiful and haughty and imperious—all *you* would have been if your godmother hadn't been so wise. And being a very ordinary-looking fellow himself, he was afraid she wouldn't think much of him, so he suggested to one of his attendants, a man called Carlo, of extremely attractive appearance, that *he* should pretend to be the Prince, and win the Princess' hand; and then at the last moment they would change places——

**Princess**   How would they do that?

**Prince**   The Prince was going to have been married in full armor—with his visor down.

**Princess**   *(laughing happily)* Oh, what fun!

**Prince**   Neat, isn't it?

**Princess**   *(laughing)* Oh, very . . . very . . . very.

**Prince**   Neat, but not so terribly *funny.* Why do you keep laughing?

**Princess**   Well, that's another secret.

**Prince**   If it comes to that, *I've* got another one up my sleeve. Shall we exchange again?

**Princess**   All right. You go first this time.

**Prince**   Very well. . . . I am not Carlo. *(Standing up and speaking dramatically.)* I am Simon!—ow! *(He sits down and rubs his leg violently.)*

**Princess**   *(alarmed)* What is it?

**Prince**   Cramp. *(In a mild voice, still rubbing.)* I was saying that I was Prince Simon.

**Princess**   Shall I rub it for you? *(She rubs.)*

**Prince**   *(still hopefully)* I am Simon.

**Princess**   Is that better?

**Prince**   *(despairingly)* I am Simon.

**Princess**   I know.

**Prince**   How did you know?

**Princess**   Well, you told me.

**Prince**   But oughtn't you to swoon[8] or something?

**Princess**   Why? History records many similar ruses.

**Prince**   *(amazed)* Is that so? I've never read history. I thought I was being profoundly original.

**Princess**   Oh, no! Now I'll tell you *my* secret. For reasons very much like your own the Princess Camilla, who is held to be extremely plain, feared to meet Prince Simon. Is the drawbridge down yet?

**Prince**   Do your people give a faint, surprised cheer every time it gets down?

**Princess**   Naturally.

**Prince**   Then it came down about three minutes ago.

**Princess**   Ah! Then at this very moment your man Carlo is declaring his passionate love for my maid, Dulcibella. That, I think, is funny. *(So does the* **Prince***. He laughs heartily.)* Dulcibella, by the way, is in love with a man she calls Eg, so I hope Carlo isn't getting carried away.

**Prince**   Carlo is married to a girl he calls "the little woman," so Eg has nothing to fear.

**Princess**   By the way, I don't know if you heard, but I said, or as good as said, that I am the Princess Camilla.

**Prince**   I wasn't surprised. History, of course, of which I read a great deal, records many similar ruses.

**Princess**   *(laughing)* Simon!

**Prince**   *(laughing)* Camilla! *(He stands up.)* May I try holding you again? *(She nods. He takes her in his arms and kisses her.)* Sweetheart!

**Princess**   You see, when you lifted me up before, you said, "You're very

---

8. **swoon:** faint.

lovely," and my godmother said that the first person to whom I would seem lovely was the man I should marry; so I knew then that you were Simon and I should marry you.

**Prince**   I knew directly I saw you that I should marry you, even if you were Dulcibella. By the way, which of you *am* I marrying?

**Princess**   When she lifts her veil, it will be Camilla. *(Voices are heard outside.)* Until then it will be Dulcibella.

**Prince**   *(in a whisper)* Then good-bye, Camilla, until you lift your veil.

**Princess**   Good-bye, Simon, until you raise your visor. *(The **King** and **Queen** come in arm-in-arm, followed by **Carlo** and **Dulcibella**, also arm-in-arm. The **Chancellor** precedes them, walking backwards, at a loyal angle.)*

**Prince**   *(supporting the **Chancellor** as an accident seems inevitable)* Careful! *(The **Chancellor** turns indignantly round.)*

**King**   Who and what is this? More accurately who and what are all these?

**Carlo**   My attendant, Carlo, Your Majesty. He will, with Your Majesty's permission, prepare me for the ceremony. *(The **Prince** bows.)*

**King**   Of course, of course!

**Queen**   *(to **Dulcibella**)* Your maid, Dulcibella, is it not, my love? *(**Dulcibella** nods violently.)* I thought so. *(To **Carlo**.)* She will prepare Her Royal Highness. *(The **Princess** curtsies.)*

**King**   Ah, yes. *Most* important.

**Princess**   *(curtsying)* I beg pardon, Your Majesty, if I've done wrong, but I found the gentleman wandering——

**King**   *(crossing to her)* Quite right, my dear, quite right. *(He pinches her cheek, and takes advantage of this kingly gesture to say in a loud whisper.)* We've pulled it off! *(They sit down; the **King** and **Queen** on their thrones, **Dulcibella** on the **Princess'** throne. **Carlo** stands behind **Dulcibella**, the **Chancellor** on the R. of the **Queen**, and the **Prince** and **Princess** behind the long seat on the left.)*

**Chancellor**   *(consulting documents)* H'r'm! Have I Your Majesty's authority to put the final test to His Royal Highness?

**Queen**   *(whispering to **King**)* Is this safe?

**King**   *(whispering)* Perfectly, my dear. I told him the answer a minute ago. *(Over his shoulder to* **Carlo.***)* Don't forget. *Dog. (Aloud.)* Proceed, Your Excellency. It is my desire that the affairs of my country should ever be conducted in a strictly constitutional manner.

**Chancellor**   *(oratorically)* By the constitution of the country, a suitor to Her Royal Highness' hand cannot be deemed successful until he has given the correct answer to a riddle. *(Conversationally.)* The last suitor answered incorrectly, and thus failed to win his bride.

**King**   By a coincidence he fell into the moat.

**Chancellor**   *(to* **Carlo***)* I have now to ask Your Royal Highness if you are prepared for the ordeal?

**Carlo**   *(cheerfully)* Absolutely.

**Chancellor**   I may mention, as a matter, possibly, of some slight historical interest to our visitor, that by the constitution of the country the same riddle is not allowed to be asked on two successive occasions.

**King**   *(startled)* What's that?

**Chancellor**   This one, it is interesting to recall, was propounded exactly a century ago, and we must take it as a fortunate omen that it was well and truly solved.

**King**   *(to* **Queen***)* I may want my sword directly.

**Chancellor**   The riddle is this. What is it which has four legs and mews like a cat?

**Carlo**   *(promptly)* A dog.

**King**   *(still more promptly)* Bravo, bravo! *(He claps loudly and nudges the* **Queen***, who claps too.)*

**Chancellor**   *(peering at his documents)* According to the records of the occasion to which I referred, the correct answer would seem to be——

**Princess**   *(to* **Prince***)* Say something, quick!

**Chancellor**   —not dog, but——

**Prince**   Your Majesty, have I permission to speak? Naturally His Royal Highness could not think of justifying himself on such an occasion, but I think that with Your Majesty's gracious permission, I could——

**King**   Certainly, certainly.

*Parody and Humor*

**Prince**   In our country, we have an animal to which we have given the name "dog," or, in the local dialect of the more mountainous districts, "doggie." It sits by the fireside and purrs.

**Carlo**   That's right. It purrs like anything.

**Prince**   When it needs milk, which is its staple food, it mews.

**Carlo**   *(enthusiastically)* Mews like nobody's business.

**Prince**   It also has four legs.

**Carlo**   One at each corner.

**Prince**   In some countries, I understand, this animal is called a "cat." In one distant country to which His Royal Highness and I penetrated it was called by the very curious name of "hippopotamus."

**Carlo**   That's right. *(To the **Prince**.)* Do you remember that ginger-colored hippopotamus which used to climb on to my shoulder and lick my ear?

**Prince**   I shall never forget it, sir. *(To the **King**.)* So you see, Your Majesty——

**King**   Thank you. I think that makes it perfectly clear. *(Firmly to the **Chancellor**.)* You are about to agree?

**Chancellor**   Undoubtedly, Your Majesty. May I be the first to congratulate His Royal Highness on solving the riddle so accurately?

**King**   You may be the first to see that all is in order for an immediate wedding.

**Chancellor**   Thank you, Your Majesty. *(He bows and withdraws. The **King** rises, as do the **Queen** and **Dulcibella**.)*

**King**   *(to **Carlo**)* Doubtless, Prince Simon, you will wish to retire and prepare yourself for the ceremony.

**Carlo**   Thank you, sir.

**Prince**   Have I Your Majesty's permission to attend His Royal Highness? It is the custom of his country for Princes of the royal blood to be married in full armor, a matter which requires a certain adjustment——

**King**   Of course, of course. *(**Carlo** bows to the **King** and **Queen** and goes out. As the **Prince** is about to follow, the **King** stops him.)* Young man, you have a quality of quickness which I admire. It is my pleasure to reward it in any way which commends itself to you.

**Prince**  Your Majesty is ever gracious. May I ask for my reward *after* the ceremony? *(He catches the eye of the* **Princess***, and they give each other a secret smile.)*

**King**  Certainly. *(The* **Prince** *bows and goes out. To* **Dulcibella***.)* Now, young woman, make yourself scarce. You've done your work excellently, and we will see that you and your—what was his name?

**Dulcibella**  Eg, Your Majesty.

**King**  —that you and your Eg are not forgotten.

**Dulcibella**  Coo! *(She curtsies and goes out.)*

**Princess**  *(calling)* Wait for me, Dulcibella!

**King**  *(to* **Queen***)* Well, my dear, we may congratulate ourselves. As I remember saying to somebody once, "You have not lost a daughter, you have gained a son." How does he strike you?

**Queen**  Stupid.

**King**  They made a very handsome pair, I thought, he and Dulcibella.

**Queen**  Both stupid.

**King**  I said nothing about stupidity. What I *said* was that they were both extremely handsome. That is the important thing. *(Struck by a sudden idea.)* Or isn't it?

**Queen**  What do you think of Prince Simon, Camilla?

**Princess**  I adore him. We shall be so happy together.

**King**  Well, of course you will. I told you so. Happy ever after.

**Queen**  Run along now and get ready.

**Princess**  Yes, mother. *(She throws a kiss to them and goes out.)*

**King**  *(anxiously)* My dear, have we been wrong about Camilla all this time? It seemed to me that she wasn't looking *quite* so plain as usual just now. Did *you* notice anything?

**Queen**  *(carelessly)* Just the excitement of the marriage.

**King**  *(relieved)* Ah, yes, that would account for it.

**Curtain**

# Reviewing the Selection

Answer each of the following questions without looking back at the play.

*Recalling Facts* ·

1. At the beginning of the play, the audience learns that Camilla is
   - ☐ a. likable but plain.
   - ☐ b. beautiful and spoiled.
   - ☐ c. plain and willful.
   - ☐ d. unhappy with her life.

*Understanding Main Ideas*

2. Which of the following statements best summarizes the main idea of the play?
   - ☐ a. Every woman deserves to have a happy marriage.
   - ☐ b. Inner beauty is more important than physical appearance.
   - ☐ c. Good health is more important than good looks.
   - ☐ d. If you are patient, you will find true love.

*Placing Events in Order*

3. Princess Camilla learns that she is beautiful
   - ☐ a. when she is a child.
   - ☐ b. after Prince Simon arrives.
   - ☐ c. at the Tournament of Love.
   - ☐ d. on her wedding day.

*Finding Supporting Details*

4. The Prince intends to disguise himself at the wedding by wearing
   - ☐ a. Carlo's hunting clothes.
   - ☐ b. a hood.
   - ☐ c. a suit of armor.
   - ☐ d. the Chancellor's spectacles.

5. The King says, "All our history books <u>affirm</u>
   this." In this context *affirm* means
   ☐ a. support.
   ☐ b. contradict.
   ☐ c. omit.
   ☐ d. argue constantly.

## Interpreting the Selection

Answer each of the following questions. You may look back at the play
if necessary.

6. What are Camilla's feelings about finding
   a husband?
   ☐ a. She is not at all worried about finding
          a husband.
   ☐ b. She is afraid that she will never
          get married.
   ☐ c. She would rather not be married.
   ☐ d. She knows that she is too plain to win
          a husband.

7. In this play most of the characters are
   ☐ a. able to see their own strengths
          and weaknesses.
   ☐ b. silly and shallow.
   ☐ c. highly intelligent.
   ☐ d. brave and strong.

8. In *The Ugly Duckling* A. A. Milne makes all of the following points *except*

☐ a. believe in yourself.

☐ b. people can make life more complicated than it has to be.

☐ c. only beautiful people can hope to live happily ever after.

☐ d. beauty is in the eye of the beholder.

*Analyzing*
*the Evidence*

9. Which character truly understands Great-Aunt Malkin's verse?

☐ a. the King

☐ b. the Queen

☐ c. the Princess

☐ d. the Chancellor

*Drawing*
*Conclusions*

10. What conclusion can you draw about the Chancellor?

☐ a. He is the power behind the throne.

☐ b. He wants the Princess to have a happy marriage.

☐ c. He will say anything to please the King.

☐ d. He does not like the Princess.

# *Parody and Humor*

As you read *The Ugly Duckling*, did you find yourself laughing at some of the dialogue or events in the play? Milne wrote this play as a <u>comedy</u>—a play that causes laughter and ends happily.

Comedy differs from tragedy in many ways. In a tragedy the main character is involved in a heroic struggle of some kind. In *Julius Caesar*, you will recall, Brutus had to decide whether to join the conspirators in the murder of Caesar. He carefully analyzed his motives and he expected others to do the same. In a comedy the main characters are usually more concerned with everyday matters than they are with noble ideals. Tragedies end disastrously with the downfall of the main character. Comedies end happily.

*The Ugly Duckling* is a particular kind of comedy known as a parody. Parody is a kind of humorous writing that imitates another, more serious piece of literature. In this play Milne humorously imitates traditional fairy tales. As you will learn in this lesson, the playwright uses various techniques to achieve his goals.

## Stage Directions and Setting

As soon as you read the stage directions for the opening scene of *The Ugly Duckling*, you realize that the play is going to be humorous. In the directions a playwright can establish the <u>mood</u>—the general feeling or atmosphere of a play. Milne, for example, tells you that the King is asleep with his handkerchief over his face. That image of a king is just the opposite of the usual picture of a dignified ruler. Milne then tells you: *"He is a king of any country from any storybook, in whatever costume you please."*

    *1. What mood do you think those stage directions establish?*

    Milne says the setting is any storybook country. He lets you picture the setting, but he assumes that you will imagine the kind of place described in fairy tales. That brief direction asks you to remember all the fairy tales you have ever heard. Such memories are important to the rest of the play, in which Milne makes fun of almost everything about traditional fairy tales.

    Throughout the play, Milne includes stage directions. Many of those directions add to the humor. Usually, they ridicule the behavior of a character. While the Queen is telling the Chancellor about the Tournament of Love, for example, the King *"looks nonchalantly at the ceiling and whistles a few bars."* He apologizes when the Queen reprimands him, but his actions suggest a husband who is bored by his wife's stories.

    *2. Skim the play to find at least two other stage directions that are humorous. Explain what is funny about each direction.*

## Parody and Character

Milne's parody is effective because the characters are funny. Milne uses characters who are stereotypes. A <u>stereotype</u> is a stock character who matches a fixed idea held by a number of people. A stereotype conforms to a certain pattern and lacks individuality. In the play, as in many fairy tales, there is a king, a queen, a princess, and a prince who wants to marry the princess. There are minor characters, such as the Chancellor, the Princess's maid, Dulcibella, and the Prince's attendant, Carlo. You hear about the King's Great-Aunt Malkin. Like the good and evil godmothers in many fairy tales, she has played her part before the story begins.

    Think about the various characters in *The Ugly Duckling*. Each matches a certain type of fairy-tale character. But at the same time, each is slightly different from those familiar storybook figures. The humor of the characters depends on this difference. Milne uses his characters to parody, or humorously imitate, traditional stereotypes.

As you read in Chapter 1, you can learn a lot about characters through their words and actions. The first characters you meet in this play are the King and the Chancellor. The King, who has been asleep on his throne, rouses himself and makes a hasty attempt to look dignified. Somewhat defensively, he tells the Chancellor that he has been thinking. The Chancellor is a cautious man. He supports anything the King says and flatters the King constantly.

*3. How is the King in Milne's play different from a storybook king? Give two examples of words or actions of the King that are different from what is expected of a storybook ruler.*

*4. What makes the Chancellor a humorous character?*

**The Hero and the Heroine.** The hero or the heroine is always the main character in a play or story. In fairy tales the hero is often a handsome prince who rescues a princess from danger. He is usually courageous, intelligent, and honorable. The princess is beautiful and clever. Milne, however, has changed those traditional stereotypes.

Early in the play, you learn that the Princess Camilla is not beautiful. Her plainness upsets her parents because they cannot find a prince to marry her. Yet the Princess is a delightful person. She is natural, friendly, and unspoiled by her position as the King and Queen's only child.

Look at the Princess's first appearance onstage. She comes into the room as the King, the Queen, and the Chancellor are talking:

**Princess** *(to the King)* Hallo, darling! *(Seeing the others.)* Oh, I say! Affairs of state? Sorry.

*5. What do those lines tell you about the Princess? As the plot develops, what else do you learn about the character of the Princess?*

Just as the Princess does not behave like a traditional fairy-tale princess, Prince Simon does not behave like a fairy-tale prince. He has little self-confidence and is fearful about meeting the Princess.

*6. Review the scene in which the Prince first appears. What do you learn about his character in that scene?*

*7. In your own words, briefly describe how Princess Camilla and Prince Simon are different from the stereotypes of traditional fairy-tale princesses and princes. Explain how this contrast is amusing.*

**The Minor Characters.** Even the minor characters are parodies of stereotypical storybook characters. They have the same roles in this play as they do in most fairy tales, but Milne makes fun of their behavior and attitudes.

Dulcibella, for example, is different from the servants in most fairy tales. Usually, servants in fairy tales simply do what they are told, and you learn little about them. In *The Ugly Duckling* Dulcibella behaves more like a real person. You learn that she is not very smart. She can barely follow the King's instructions. She is in love with Eg, a lowly worker in the palace armory.

*8. Choose one of the minor characters: Dulcibella, Carlo, or the Chancellor. Give evidence from the play to show how Milne uses the character to make fun of some aspect of fairy tales.*

## Parody and Plot

Another way in which Milne parodies fairy tales is through the plot of *The Ugly Duckling.* The action in the play centers on the need to find a husband for Princess Camilla. Think about the standard plots in fairy tales that are concerned with the marriage of a princess.

*9. Make a list of some of the ordeals, or tests, a prince has to face in traditional fairy tales before he can marry the princess. In* The Ugly Duckling *have any princes been tested to see if they are worthy of Princess Camilla? Explain your answer.*

**The Conflict.** In most fairy tales about a prince seeking to marry a princess, the main conflict centers on the test or tests which the prince must pass. Such tests involve dangerous struggles that are meant to measure the prince's worthiness. In Milne's parody, however, the tests of worthiness are absurd and are a minor element in the play. In *The Ugly Duckling* the main conflict develops from the idea that Princess Camilla is plain and will never get a husband. Because of her plainness, none of the eligible princes wants to marry her. Even her parents think that she will never marry.

The conflict ridicules the emphasis on beauty. Everyone agrees that the Princess "is quite the nicest person in the Kingdom." Yet to the King, the Queen, and the Chancellor, her character is less important than her appearance.

Irony is an important element of the conflict in *The Ugly Duckling*. Irony, you will recall, is the contrast between appearance and reality or between what is expected and what actually happens. The irony in the conflict points out that responsible and important people often have silly values. By emphasizing physical beauty, the King and Queen have overlooked the Princess's true beauty—her niceness.

The conflict in *The Ugly Duckling* is due, in part, to Great-Aunt Malkin's actions. Yet she has probably kept the Princess from being influenced by her parents' stupidity. Great-Aunt Malkin saw how silly the King and Queen were, so she made sure that Princess Camilla would be sensible and reasonable. She also made sure that the Princess would marry a husband who would love her for who she really was.

*10. Compare the action of Great-Aunt Malkin to the actions of godmothers in traditional fairy tales. How are they similar? How are they different?*

**The Resolution.** Like the resolutions in most fairy tales, the resolution of *The Ugly Duckling* contains a happy ending. Various characters adopt disguises—"a harmless ruse, of which you will find frequent record in the history books." While the King is coaching Dulcibella for her part, the Prince and Princess meet in an ordinary way. They exchange confidences. Although they fall in love in storybook fashion, their court-ship is not romantic.

*11. Reread the scene in which the Prince and the Princess reveal their true* identities to each other. *What is unusual about their revelations when compared with the conversations between princes and princesses in storybook romances?*

In the last scene the King and Queen are pleased with themselves. They think they have cleverly tricked the Prince into marrying their daughter. The audience and the young couple know otherwise. In the last scene Milne uses dramatic irony. You have information or an understanding of events that some of the characters do not have. Unlike the King and Queen, you really know why Prince Simon is marrying Camilla.

Another example of dramatic irony is contained in the dialogue at the end of the play.

*12. Reread the dialogue after Dulcibella curtsies and goes offstage. Explain the dramatic irony in the final scene of the play.*

## Dialogue and Humor

In comedy much of the humor is expressed through the dialogue. Milne uses various methods to create humor in the dialogue. For example, he exposes the King's silliness by having the King speak in clichés. A cliché is an expression or an idea that has become stale from overuse. In the opening scene the King uses a cliché when he describes his state of mind to the Chancellor.

> **King**   It's what I was saying last night to the Queen. "Uneasy
>    lies the head that wears a crown," was how I put it.

Both the King and the Chancellor seem to think that the King's thought is original, but the audience knows that it is not. The quotation is a famous line from Shakespeare's play *King Henry IV, Part 2.*

Circumlocution is another technique of humor that Milne employs in his play. Circumlocution is an indirect way of saying something. It often involves using many more words than necessary to express an idea. The Chancellor frequently uses circumlocution to express himself.

Instead of directly stating his opinion, he often says much more than he needs to say.

*13. Find an example of the Chancellor's circumlocution.*

In the dialogue Milne occasionally uses puns. A <u>pun</u> is a play on words that have similar sounds but very different meanings. Reread the scene on page 208 in which the Queen tells about the riddle she invented for the Prince at the Feast of Betrothal. The correct answer was "a dog," but the Prince kept coming up with other answers. The King's comment about the incident contains a pun:

**King**   Nobody could accuse him of not trying.
**Queen**   *I* did.
**King**   I *should* have said that nobody could fail to recognize in
        his attitude an appearance of doggedness.

Punning is often called "the lowest form of humor." Milne uses it deliberately to show the King's silliness.

*14. Find three examples of humorous dialogue. Explain why each example is amusing.*

## Questions for Thought and Discussion

The questions and activities that follow will help you explore *The Ugly Duckling* in more depth and at the same time develop your critical thinking skills.

1. **Identifying the Theme.** What do you think is the theme, or underlying message, of *The Ugly Duckling?* Use evidence from the play to support your view.

2. **Evaluating.** Princess Camilla's godmother told her that "the best thing in the world . . . was to be quite sure of yourself, but not to expect admiration from other people." Do you agree with that idea? Use examples from real life to support your opinion.

3. **Analyzing Character.** Which character in the play do you find most humorous? Why? Which character do you think A. A. Milne liked the best? Why?

4. **Developing a Scene.** Divide the class into small groups. Each group should choose an incident from the play to present to the rest of the class. You can choose an actual scene from the play or a scene that is described, such as the Tournament of Love or Princess Camilla's encounter at age ten with Great-Aunt Malkin. Practice your scene so that the humor is effective.

## Writing About Literature

Several suggestions for writing projects follow. You may be asked to complete one or more of these projects. If you have any questions about how to begin a writing assignment, review Using the Writing Process, beginning on page 385.

1. **Writing a Review.** Imagine that you have seen a performance of *The Ugly Duckling*. Write a review of the play for your school newspaper. In your review evaluate the main ideas of the play, but try not to reveal the whole plot.

2. **Creating Dialogue.** Think about what might happen after the end of *The Ugly Duckling*. Imagine the scene that might take place between any two characters, such as the King and the Queen, Dulcibella and Eg, or the Prince and the Princess. Write a short dialogue for the two characters.

3. **Comparing.** Read Hans Christian Andersen's fairy tale "The Ugly Duckling." Then compare the main character in that story to Princess Camilla in A. A. Milne's play. How are they similar? How are they different?

| Selection | ***The Master Thief*** |
| | PAUL SILLS |
| Lesson | *Staging a Skit* |

## About the Selection

*The Master Thief* is a skit, or a brief comic sketch. Like *The Ugly Duckling*, *The Master Thief* is based on a fairy tale. But Sills's purpose in adapting a traditional story for a stage performance is different from A. A. Milne's purpose.

As you learned, Milne chose to use only the title and basic theme of the ugly duckling story. He then wrote a play that parodied the typical characters and plots of traditional fairy tales. By contrast, Paul Sills wanted to dramatize a fairy tale while remaining true to the original story. He tried to preserve the simplicity and wonder of the fairy tale. But he did make certain changes. He made those changes to show that traditional fairy tales still have something to say to modern readers.

*The Master Thief* tells the story of a clever and resourceful young man. Although the young man is a thief, he robs only the rich. You will notice that in the play the characters sing a song called "Dear Landlord." The song was written by Bob Dylan in the 1960s; it was not part of the original fairy tale. When you read the lyrics of the song, think about why Sills included it in the play.

*The Master Thief* was published in a collection of one-act plays that were performed together under the title *Story Theatre*. Story Theatre was also the name of the traveling theater company that staged those plays.

Story Theatre was founded in New York in 1970. The company began as an improvisational group. That is, the performers invented plots and created dialogue onstage. Some of the plays in *Story Theatre* were written and staged at the same time. The plays were later made into a series of half-hour television productions.

Most of the fairy tales in *Story Theatre* came from Aesop, a Greek slave who died about 560 B.C. Aesop is famous for his fables, which are stories that contain a moral. "The Tortoise and the Hare" and "The Fox and the Grapes" are two of his best-known fables. Other tales in *Story Theatre* were adapted from the German fairy tales collected in the nineteenth century by Jacob and Wilhelm Grimm. Paul Sills selected a group of those fairy tales and adapted them for stage performances.

## Lesson Preview

The lesson that follows *The Master Thief* focuses on staging a play. When a play is being prepared for production, the director has to make hundreds of decisions about the play's physical presentation. What should the stage look like? What kind of scenery should be used? Should the actors wear costumes? What kind of costumes are appropriate?

As you have learned, some playwrights include stage directions in their scripts. Paul Sills, for example, includes many stage directions in *The Master Thief*.

*The Master Thief* is a comedy, so its staging should help focus the audience's attention on the humor. The questions that follow will help you think about the kinds of staging decisions that must be made. As you read, think about how you would answer these questions.

**1** Read the explanation of the abbreviations on page 255. What kinds of directions does Sills give the actors? Why do you think he gives those directions?

**2** How is *The Master Thief* different from the other plays you have read so far? What is unusual about the dialogue?

**3** Who are the main characters? Which are humorous characters? Why?

**4** What is humorous about the plot of the play?

**5** Why do you think Sills included verses from the Bob Dylan song "Dear Landlord" at various points in the play?

## Vocabulary

Here are some difficult words that appear in the selection that follows. Study the words and their definitions, as well as the sentences that show how the words are used. This will help you get the most from your reading.

**contrive**  bring about; manage. *How did you contrive to get into the building without using a key?*

**tottering**  staggering unsteadily. *The baby was tottering back and forth between its mother and father.*

**reproach**  accuse; express displeasure with. *George's mother should reproach him for his sloppy manners.*

**ruckus**  noisy confusion; disturbance. *The fox caused a great ruckus in the henhouse.*

# *The Master Thief*

PAUL SILLS

## Characters

Old Man
Wife
Master Thief
Count
First Soldier
Second Soldier
Third Soldier
Countess
Parson
Clerk

*(Music: "Dear Landlord")*

*(**Old Man** enters U. R., meets **Wife** U. C., crosses D. to D. C. **Wife** enters U. L., meets **Old Man** U. C., crosses D. to D. C.)*

**Old Man**   One day an old man

**Wife**   . . . and his wife were standing in front of their miserable house resting awhile from their work. When suddenly, a splendid carriage pulled by six black horses came driving up,

*(**Master Thief** enters D. L., crosses to R. of C. **Old Man** and **Wife** go to L. of **Master Thief**.)*

**Master Thief**   . . . and a richly dressed man descended.

*(Pause)*

**Old Man**   What do you want?

**Master Thief**   I want nothing but to enjoy for once a simple peasant meal. Cook for me some potatoes, in the way you always have them, and I will sit and dine with you.

**Old Man**   You are a count, or a prince, or perhaps even a duke; but fine gentlemen often have such fancies, you shall have your wish.

**Wife**   And the old woman went into the kitchen, to prepare the dish. *(Exits* **L. Old Man** *leads* **Master Thief D.***, kneels* **D. C.***)*

**Old Man**   And the old man led him into the garden where he began to tie up young trees to stakes he had driven into the ground.

[The **Old Man** took a young tree, put it in a hole, drove in a post beside it, and when he had shoveled in some earth and had trampled it firmly down, he tied the stem of the tree above, below and in the middle, fast[1] to the post by a rope of straw.]

**Master Thief**   *(Crosses* **D. L.***)* Have you no children who could help you with your work?

**Old Man**   No. 'Tis true I had a son once, sharp, knowing, full of bad tricks; he ran off and I have not heard of him since.

**Master Thief**   What of this old twisted tree here? Why don't you tie it to a stake so that it too might grow straight like these others?

**Old Man**   *(Crosses* **D. L.** *to old tree, back to* **D. C.***, kneels)* Sir, you speak according to your knowledge, but it is easy to see that you know nothing of gardening. It's too late for that old tree. You have to start with the young.

**Master Thief**   Perhaps that is how it was with your son. If you had trained him while he was young perhaps he would not have run away.

**Old Man**   I don't know, perhaps.

**Master Thief**   *(Pushes* **Old Man D. R.***)* Would you know him if you were to see him again?

**Old Man**   Not by his face.

---

1. **fast:** securely.

**Master Thief**   No! Well, how then?

**Old Man**   I don't know. He had a mark about him.

**Master Thief**   A mark? What sort of a mark?

**Old Man**   A birthmark.

**Master Thief**   Where was it?

**Old Man**   On his neck.

**Master Thief**   What did it look like?

**Old Man**   In the shape of a bean.

**Master Thief and Old Man**   A bean?

[The **Thief** then pulled his collar open and showed the **Old Man** his neck.]

**Old Man**   Yes, yes, that's it.

[Then the **Old Man** realized who the **Stranger** really was and, putting his arms around him, said:]

You are my son? Where have you been? (**Master Thief** *kneels* **D. C.**, *ties tree to stake*.) How could you be my son, to live in such wealth and luxury? What have you done to contrive this?

**Master Thief**   I have become a thief. (**Old Man** *steps* **U**.) But I am no common criminal, I am a master thief. I steal only from the rich.

**Old Man**   A thief is still a thief. (*Crosses* **D. C.** *to* **U. R.** *of* **Master Thief**.) If your godfather the count up there in the castle hears of this, he will not hold you fondly as he did when he baptized you. He will hang you from the nearest halter.[2]

**Master Thief**   Be easy, Father. I've learned my trade well. I am going to see him this evening.

(**Old Man** *leads* **Master Thief** **U. L. Wife** *enters* **L**., *meets* **Master Thief** **C**. *They embrace*.)

**Old Man**   And so the old man took him to his mother,

**Wife**   . . . and when she heard that he was her son, she wept for joy,

2. **halter:** rope.

**Master Thief**  . . . but when he told her that he had become a thief,

**Wife**  *(Crosses* **D. L.***)* . . . a second stream flowed down her face. "Still, he is my son, and my eyes have beheld him once more." (**Wife** *and* **Old Man** *exit* L.*)* And they went in to fetch the wretched food which he had not eaten in so long.

**Master Thief**  That night the master thief rode to see the count. *(Gallops counterclockwise twice, ties horse* **U. R.***, crosses* **C.***, enters, crosses* **D. R.***)*

*(Music)*
*Dear Landlord, please don't put a price on my soul,*
*My burden is heavy, my dreams are beyond control,*
*When that steamboat whistle blows,*
*I'm going to give you all that I've got to give,*
*And hope that you receive it well,*
*Depending on the way you feel that you live.*

(**Count** *enters* **U. L.***, crosses to* **Master Thief***, shakes hands* **C.***)*

**Count**  The count received him civilly,[3] for he took him for a distinguished man.

**Master Thief**  But when the stranger revealed himself,

**Count**  *(Crosses* **D. R.***, gets glasses of wine.)* . . . the count turned pale and was silent for some time. *(Gives* **Master Thief** *glass.)* You are my godson, and therefore mercy shall take the place of justice. Since you pride yourself on being a thief, I will put your art to the proof, but if you do not stand the test, you must marry the rope maker's daughter,[4] and the croaking of the raven will be your music on the occasion. *(***Count** *and* **Master Thief** *click glasses.)*

**Master Thief**  Lord count, think of three tasks as difficult as you like, and if I do not perform them all, do with me what you will.

**Count**  You shall steal the horse I keep for my own riding from out of the stable; you shall steal the sheet from beneath the bodies of my wife and myself while we are asleep, without our observing it, and

---

3. **civilly:** politely.  4. **marry the rope maker's daughter:** die by hanging.

*Staging a Skit*

the wedding ring of my wife as well: and you shall steal from out of the church, the parson and the clerk. Mark what I am saying, for your life depends on it. *(Exits L.)*

**Master Thief** *(Crosses D. L. to step.)* That night the master thief put on the garments of an old woman. Onto his face he painted the wrinkles of age. Into a cask of old Hungarian wine, he mixed a powerful sleeping potion and putting the cask on his back, with slow and tottering steps, *(Crosses U. to U. C. **Three Soldiers** enter U. R., leading horse to U. C.)* he made his way to the courtyard of the count.

[In the courtyard, **Three Soldiers** were guarding the horse.]

**First Soldier**   Halt! Who goes there? It's only an old woman. What have you got in your cask, old mother?

**Master Thief**   A cask of fine wine.

**First Soldier**   Well, let's have some.

**Master Thief**   I live by trade, for money and kind words I am quite ready to let you have a glass.

**First Soldier**   Well, here's some money then.

**Second Soldier**   Me, too.

**Third Soldier**   I'm afraid that I'll have to trade you for what I'm sure is a long-awaited kiss. *(Kisses the "old woman.")*

**Master Thief**   Ho, ho! A double portion for you, my son. *(**All Three Soldiers** drink the wine that the thief gave them.)* What duties do you perform for our lord, the count?

**First Soldier**   *(Takes horse from U. C., circles R. to C.)* We guard the count's horse.

[The **Soldiers** brought the horse down.]

One man held the bridle,

**Third Soldier**   . . . another held the tail

**Second Soldier**   . . . and the third sat on the horse's back.

**Third Soldier**   And very soon

**Second Soldier**   . . . they all

**First Soldier**  . . . fell asleep.

**Master Thief**  The master thief took a piece of rope and placed it in the hand of the man holding the bridle, a wisp of straw went into the hand of the man holding the tail, but what of the man on top of the horse?

*(Crosses* L. *for winch.[5] After three lifts, takes horse, exits* U. R.*)*

[Then he had a good idea. He unbuckled the girths of the saddle, tied a couple of ropes which were hanging to a ring on the wall fast to the saddle, and drew the sleeping **Rider** up into the air on it. Then he twisted the rope around the posts and made it fast. He soon unloosed the horse from the chain.]

And silently led the horse out of the courtyard. *(A cock crows.)*

**Count**  *(Enters* D. L.*)* The next morning, the count entered his courtyard. The horse! The horse!

**Second Soldier**  Get me down from here! Help!

*(***Master Thief*** enters* U. R., *riding horse. He cuts down* **Second Soldier,** *circles counterclockwise to* R.*)*

[The **Master Thief** rode into the courtyard on the **Count's** horse and cut the **Soldier** down from the saddle. The **Soldiers** quickly left the courtyard muttering . . .]

**Soldiers**  *(Ad lib.)*[6] We were tricked. . . . Witchcraft, it was witchcraft . . . that old woman did it. . . . *(Exit* U. R. **Count** *takes the horse.)*

**Count**  Neatly done, I must say, but I trust things will not go so well for you the second time. Remember the sheet and the ring, *(Mounts horse, exits* U. L.*)* and I warn you that if you come before me as a thief, I will handle you as I would a thief.

---

5. **winch:** a machine with a crank used for lifting heavy objects.  6. *ad lib:* an abbreviation for the Latin phrase *ad libitum,* meaning "as one pleases." In the theater, it means the actors can make up appropriate words or gestures as they go along.

[The **Count** rode off on his horse.]

**Master Thief**  *(Circles to* **C.***)* That night the master thief made his way to the gallows.[7] There he cut down the body of a poor sinner who was hanging from a halter, and carried the *(Crosses* **D. L.** *to* **D. L.** *pit.)* corpse to the count's castle. He set up a ladder against the count's bedroom window and with the corpse on his back began to climb.

*(***Count*** and* **Countess** *enter* **U. L.***, cross* **C.***)*

**Countess**  Inside the castle, the countess was preparing for bed. She clasped the hand with the wedding ring tightly together. Husband, do you think the thief will come?

**Count**  Yes. All the doors are locked and bolted. *(Crosses* **D. L.***, opens window, returns* **U. C.***)* If he comes in through this window, *(***Count** *opens window* **D. C.***)* I will shoot the thief.

*(The* **Count** *and* **Countess** *go to bed.)*

**Master Thief**  The master thief lifted the corpse higher and higher until the head showed at the window.

[The **Count**, who was watching in his bed, fired a pistol at him and immediately the **Master Thief** let the body fall down, and hid himself in one corner.]

**Count**  I have shot the thief.
**Countess**  Are you sure?
**Count**  Yes, he's lying there dead. I must go down and bury him.
**Countess**  No, husband, please send the guards. I'm afraid to stay alone.
**Count**  Stay here and remain calm, my dear.
**Countess**  You always say that.

[The **Master Thief** saw distinctly how the **Count** got out of the

---

7. **gallows:** a wooden framework with a rope, used for hanging people.

window onto the ladder, came down and carried the dead body into the garden.]

**Master Thief**   As he descended the ladder, the master thief entered the dimly-lit corridor disguised as the count himself.

**Countess**   Husband?

[The **Thief** then stole nimbly out of his corner and climbed up the ladder straight into the **Countess'** bedroom. And in the **Count's** voice he said . . . ]

**Master Thief**   Remain calm, my dear.

**Countess**   What of the thief?

**Master Thief**   I've shot my own godson. (**Countess** *goes to him, the* **Thief** *hides his face from her.*)

**Countess**   Don't feel sad, dear. *(They embrace).*

**Master Thief**   I feel better now. But I must give him a proper burial. Give me the sheet so that I might wind his body in it.

**Countess**   You mustn't reproach yourself.

**Master Thief**   I don't.

[The **Countess** took the sheet off the bed, and she and the **Thief** folded it together.]

*(Starts to exit* **D. L.** *)* Ah, wife, I have a fit of magnanimity[8] upon me. The thief so much wanted the ring, give it to me so that I may bury it with his body.

**Countess**   She would not disobey her husband, so unwillingly she drew the ring from her finger and gave it to him. (**Master Thief** *exits* **D. L.**)

[The **Thief** made off with both of these items. The **Count** returned through the window.]

(**Count** *enters from* **D. L.** *pit, cross* **R.** *of* **C.**)

**Count**   Dear wife!

---

8. **magnanimity:** extreme generosity.

**Countess**  What!

**Count**  The sheet! Where is the sheet?

*(The **Thief** returns with the sheet and the ring. He puts the sheet back on the bed and after teasing the **Countess** a bit gives the ring back to her.)*

*(Music)*
*Dear Landlord, please hear these words that I speak.*
*I know you've suffered much,*
*In this you are not so unique.*
*All of us at times have tried too hard,*
*Too long, too fast and too much,*
*And all of us have filled our lives up with things,*
*We can see, but we just cannot touch.*

**Count**  *(Crosses* D. L. *to* **Master Thief***.)* Are you a wizard? Who has snatched you from out of the grave from which I myself have laid you? (**Master Thief** *crosses* U. L.) But you have not reached the end yet, you still have a third task to perform. Do not forget the parson and the clerk, and if you do not succeed in that, then all is of no use.

*(**Count** takes **Countess**, exits* U. R. *As they exit she calls back to the* **Thief***.)*

**Countess**  You did well.

**Master Thief**  *(Crosses* D. C., *kneels.)* That night, the master thief made his way to the churchyard. He carried a large sack from which he withdrew several large land crabs. On the backs of these curious creatures he had melted pieces of wax candle. Lighting each candle, he allowed them to scurry about in and among the gravestones. As the clock in the tower struck twelve, (**Master Thief** *crosses* U. L.) he entered the church and climbed the steps of the pulpit. "Hearken, hearken, the end of all things is come, judgment is nigh. Hearken."

*(**Parson** and **Clerk** enter* U. R., *cross* D.)*

**Parson**   The parson

**Clerk**   . . . and the clerk

**Parson**   . . . were the first to hear.

**Master Thief**   I am St. Peter. (**Clerk** *starts to exit* U.R., *but* **Parson** *pulls him* D. C.) I am he who opens and shuts the gates of Heaven. (**Master Thief** *crosses* D. L.) Look about you in the courtyard, see the souls of the departed, how they wander to and fro in search of their bones.

**Parson**   Something very strange is going on in the churchyard.

**Master Thief**   If you would join me this night in Paradise, come, climb into this sack.

**Clerk**   Parson, I think we should take advantage of this incredible opportunity.

**Master Thief**   Come, climb into this sack. (**Parson** *and* **Clerk** *get into position to tumble from* D. L. *They quickly get into the sack.*) The master thief closed up the mouth of the sack and pulled it down the church steps. (**Master Thief** *leads* **Parson** *and* **Clerk** R. *to* D. R. *and* U. *to* U. R., *then* L. *to* U. C.)

**Clerk**   Why is it so bumpy?

**Master Thief**   We are going over the mountains.

**Parson**   Why is it so wet?

**Master Thief**   We are going through rain clouds.

**Clerk**   Why do I feel so sick?

**Master Thief**   Because you're a sinner. And finally into the pigeon coop of the count. (***Flapping Noises** and **Coos**.*)

[The **Count** entered the pigeon coop and the thief slit open the sack.]

(**Count** *enters from* D. R., *crosses* U. C., R. *of* **Parson** *and* **Clerk**.)

**Count**   The count, hearing a ruckus in his pigeon coop, went to investigate.

**Parson**   Why, Your Grace, you made it too!

*(**Parson** shakes hands with **Count**. **Parson** and **Clerk** exit **D. L.**
**Master Thief** lets pigeon fly at **L**. **Count** receives it, lets it go **D. C.**)*

*(Music)*
*Dear landlord, please don't dismiss my case,*
*I'm not about to argue, not about to move to no other place.*
*Each of us has his own special gift,*
*You know that was meant to be true,*
*And if you don't underestimate me,*
*I won't underestimate you.*

**Count**   You are an arch-thief and you have won your wager. You have escaped with a whole skin, but see that you leave my land at once, for, if you ever set foot on it again, you can count on your elevation to the gallows. *(Exits **L**.)*

**Master Thief**   *(Mounts horse **D. C.**, rides counterclockwise to **U. R.**, exits.)* The master thief took leave of that country, went forth into the wide, wide world, and no one has ever heard of him since.

*(Music)*
*And if you don't underestimate me,*
*I won't underestimate you.*

# Reviewing the Selection

Answer each of the following questions without looking back at the play.

*Recalling Facts*

1. The master thief is the count's
   - ☐ a. brother.
   - ☐ b. godson.
   - ☐ c. son.
   - ☐ d. father.

*Understanding Main Ideas*

2. Which of the following statements from the play best expresses the main idea?
   - ☐ a. "A thief is still a thief."
   - ☐ b. "If you don't underestimate me, I won't underestimate you."
   - ☐ c. "If you had trained him while he was young perhaps he would not have run away."
   - ☐ d. "If you would join me this night in Paradise, come, climb into this sack."

*Placing Events in Order*

3. What is the third task the master thief has to accomplish?
   - ☐ a. steal from his parents
   - ☐ b. steal the count's horse
   - ☐ c. find a bedsheet in the church
   - ☐ d. steal the parson and the clerk

*Finding Supporting Details*

4. The master thief tells his parents that he has returned home to
   - ☐ a. reform his ways.
   - ☐ b. taste simple peasant food again.
   - ☐ c. show them how successful he is.
   - ☐ d. win the count's forgiveness.

5. "The count received him civilly, for he took
   him for a <u>distinguished</u> man." In this context
   *distinguished* means
   ☐ a. important.
   ☐ b. rude.
   ☐ c. handsome.
   ☐ d. friendly.

## Interpreting the Selection

Answer each of the following questions. You may look back at the play
if necessary.

6. The count believes that the tasks he gives
   the master thief
   ☐ a. will make the thief become an
         honest man.
   ☐ b. will keep the thief from the gallows.
   ☐ c. are impossible to accomplish.
   ☐ d. are fair punishment for the crimes the
         thief has committed.

7. Which of the following adjectives best
   describes the master thief?
   ☐ a. thoughtful
   ☐ b. selfish
   ☐ c. resourceful
   ☐ d. uneducated

8. The author of *The Master Thief* probably wants you to
   - ☐ a. dislike the thief.
   - ☐ b. think of the count as the hero of the play.
   - ☐ c. feel sorry for the parson and the clerk.
   - ☐ d. see more than one side to the master thief's character.

9. Which of the following motives seems to be important to the parson?
   - ☐ a. saving souls
   - ☐ b. getting to heaven
   - ☐ c. helping the poor
   - ☐ d. punishing criminals

10. After reading this play, you can conclude that the master thief
    - ☐ a. does not enjoy his profession.
    - ☐ b. wishes he could live like a peasant again.
    - ☐ c. believes he will go to heaven.
    - ☐ d. will continue in his life of crime.

# Staging a Skit

Like *The Ugly Duckling,* Paul Sills's *The Master Thief* is a comedy. Both plays provoke laughter and end happily. Both plays also use traditional fairy tales as their starting points. *The Ugly Duckling,* however, is written as a parody. The play humorously imitates a certain kind of fairy tale.

*The Master Thief* is a skit. Skits are often performed by amateur, or nonprofessional actors. Schools, clubs, and other organizations some-times stage skits as part of an evening's entertainment. Because a skit is brief, it must accomplish its purpose in a short time. As a result, the staging of a skit is important to its success.

In this lesson you will study the elements of staging. You will learn how Paul Sills combines staging with narration and dialogue to develop the play's humor. You will also examine the kinds of irony that contribute to the humor of *The Master Thief.*

## Elements of Staging

The staging of any kind of play influences the audience's reaction to the play. Staging involves many important decisions. It includes deciding exactly what will happen on the stage when each line is spoken. Staging determines what the lighting, scenery, and costumes will be like. It determines how the actors will stand or move as they deliver their lines, and how they will enter and leave the stage.

Some playwrights give detailed staging notes. Others give very few. If you think back to *Julius Caesar,* you may remember that Shakespeare included only a few stage directions. He told you when someone entered, when someone exited, and when someone died. Modern playwrights usually include more stage directions. Many decisions, however, are still left to the director.

**Entrances, Exits, and Movement Onstage.** Paul Sills includes many stage directions in *The Master Thief.* The most common are notes for the actors' entrances, exits, and movements about the stage. To tell the actors about those movements, he uses certain standard abbreviations: U. for upstage, the area farthest from the audience; D. for downstage, the area closest to the audience; L. for left; R. for right; and C. for center. The following illustration will help you to picture the various parts of the stage:

| Upstage Right<br>(U.R.) | Upstage Center<br>(U.C.) | Upstage Left<br>(U.L.) |
|---|---|---|
| Right<br>(R.) | Center<br>(C.) | Left<br>(L.) |
| Downstage Right<br>(D.R.) | Downstage Center<br>(D.C.) | Downstage Left<br>(D.L.) |

The Audience

The directions may seem confusing at first, but they really are very simple once you become familiar with the abbreviations. They are as important to actors and directors as traffic signals are to drivers.

*1. Read the first set of stage directions at the beginning of* The Master Thief. *Write them out, replacing the abbreviations with the actual words. Then draw a sketch of the stage and use dotted lines to show the movements of the old man and his wife.*

This play contains many more stage directions than the other plays in this book do. Why does Sills choose to detail the movements of each character? As you have read, Sills was part of Story Theatre, a traveling theater company that developed and staged its own plays. Sills studied the improvised scenes and wrote them in their final form. He was closely involved with the development and staging of each play, so he included the directions that worked well when his company performed the play.

Sills had another reason for including so many stage directions. *The Master Thief* is a humorous skit, and the actions of the characters contribute to the humor. When you read the play, it is important for you to picture the way in which the characters move about the stage. Sometimes an actor's movements reinforce the dialogue. For example, a line in the play says that the thief rode. As that line is spoken, the thief gallops about the stage pretending to be on a horse.

*2. Find two examples of stage directions that contribute to the humor of the play. Explain what you think is funny about each direction.*

**Scenery, Sound, Costumes, and Makeup.** A director can choose to stage a play with elaborate scenery or with none at all. In *The Master Thief* the action of the play occurs in several different settings. Yet because this is a skit performed with a small budget, the play would probably not have elaborate scenery. Sills does not describe any scenery because Story Theatre did not use any.

*3. Make a list of each scene described in the play. Do you think scenery would be necessary for any or all of them? Explain how you might suggest each scene without using elaborate scenery.*

Sills gives directions for some sound effects, costumes, and makeup. Those elements of staging are extremely useful. They inform the audience about the setting as well as tell you about the characters.

*4. Find at least one example each of stage directions concerning sound, costumes, and makeup. What purpose does each direction serve?*

**Props.** Another element of staging involves the props—any movable articles, other than costumes and scenery, used in a play. The word *props* is a shortened version of *properties*. A full-length play might use many props. Items such as a newspaper, a pistol, a briefcase, an overcoat, or a bouquet of flowers are props. Because Story Theatre did not use any scenery, the actors relied on simple props to suggest various settings.

   5. *Skim* The Master Thief *and list at least eight props used in the play.*

   6. *Review your list of props. What purpose do you think the props serve?*

## Narration and Dialogue

*The Master Thief* is written in a different way from plays such as *Julius Caesar* and *The Devil and Daniel Webster.* When writing and staging his work, Paul Sills experimented with new ways of presenting information. In *The Master Thief* he combined methods of both playwriting and storytelling.

In the plays you read in earlier chapters, the action is constructed around dialogue. Shakespeare, for example, lets you know everything that happens in *Julius Caesar* through the words of his characters. Sills, however, uses both dialogue and narration. Narration is the kind of writing which gives the events and actions of the story. Narration is seldom found in plays because the characters themselves tell the story through the dialogue. By using narration, Sills deliberately blurs the line between storytelling and playwriting.

**Vantage Point.** Read the beginning of *The Master Thief.* In that scene the characters enter and begin to speak. You expect them to address one another. Instead, the old man and his wife start to tell a story as though they are not involved in it. They tell the story from an outside vantage point, or viewpoint. That is, the characters tell the story as though they are standing outside the events. They speak of their own characters as "he" or "she." They do not use the words "I" or "me." They are soon joined by the master thief. He, too, uses an outside vantage point.

In the opening narrative the three characters use narration to give you the background to the story. Then they begin to speak to one another as you expect characters to do in a play. The play continues to alternate between narration and dialogue.

*7. How can you tell when the characters are using narration? What kind of information do they give you through the narration?*

**Staging the Narration.** In addition to having the characters narrate part of the plot, Sills uses another experimental technique. He includes some narrative information and some action in square brackets [ ]. When the play is staged, those lines in square brackets are spoken out loud. Sills does not tell you who says them. It might be an outside narrator, or speaker, who stands at the edge of the stage, although no narrator is included in Sills's cast of characters. One of the characters who is onstage during the action may speak those lines.

Reread the scene on page 242 in which the old man and the master thief talk about the birthmark that the old man's son has on his neck.

**Master Thief**   What did it look like?
**Old Man**  In the shape of a bean.
**Master Thief** and **Old Man**  A bean?

[The **Thief** then pulled his collar open and showed the **Old Man** his neck.]

**Old Man**   Yes, yes, that's it.

[Then the **Old Man** realized who the **Stranger** really was and, putting his arms around him, said:]

You are my son? Where have you been?

Because the playwright does not tell you who says the lines inside the brackets, you must decide for yourself. If the play is staged, a director must make that same decision.

*8. Who do you think should say the lines inside the brackets?*

# Humor and Irony

*The Master Thief* contains many kinds of humor. Much of that humor is developed through irony. For example, humor is created by the dramatic irony in the play. As you have learned, dramatic irony occurs when the audience knows something that a character in the play does not.

*9. What do the parson and the clerk think is happening in the cemetery? Why is the clerk willing to climb into the sack? When they meet the count in the pigeon coop, where does the parson think he and the count are? How is that scene an example of dramatic irony?*

Humor is also created by the situational irony in the play. <u>Situational irony</u> is a type of irony in which what happens is different from what you expect or what the characters expect. You have probably seen "situation comedies" on television. In those dramas the characters are faced with unusual, unexpected, or seemingly unsolvable problems. The situational irony develops from the improbable situations and from the unexpected problems that are created. Because neither you nor the characters expect those ridiculous problems, the situation is funny.

Like a situation comedy, *The Master Thief* uses situational irony in a humorous way. When the master thief tells his godfather, the count, his true identity, the count threatens the young man. Either the master thief must pass three tests or he will be hanged. The tests are ridiculous and nearly impossible.

*10. In your own words, describe the three tests. How does the master thief succeed at each test? Choose one test and explain the situational irony in the test.*

# Humor and Characterization

Sills also achieves humor through his characters. Playwrights can create many different kinds of humorous characters. In *The Master Thief* Sills uses two basic types of characters. One type is a witty, clever character who makes you laugh by making fools out of other characters. The second kind of humorous character is a fool. When you laugh at a foolish

*Staging a Skit*

character, you feel superior to him or her. You are happy that you are not as foolish as that person.

You will find humorous characters in both comedies and serious plays. In a tragedy, for example, a silly character often gives the audience a brief escape from grim or frightening events. Sometimes the foolish character reveals an important detail or helps to move the action along.

*11. Think about the characters in* The Master Thief. *Which character or characters are more skillful or clever than others? Give an example. Which characters are foolish? Give an example.*

*12. Which character in the play do you find the most humorous? Why?*

## Questions for Thought and Discussion

The questions and activities that follow will help you explore *The Master Thief* in more depth and at the same time develop your critical thinking skills.

1. **Analyzing Character.** In small groups discuss what kind of person the master thief is. Find evidence in the play to support your group's view. Each group should decide whether or not the master thief is likable, and why.

2. **Identifying a Theme.** In some plays the theme is stated directly. In others, the theme is implied. What do you think is the theme of *The Master Thief*? Is it stated or implied? Explain your answer.

3. **Evaluating.** Why do you think Sills mixes narration with dialogue in *The Master Thief*? Does it make the play easier or harder to read? Would it make the play more or less enjoyable to watch?

4. **Interpreting.** Do you think the ending of *The Master Thief* is a happy one? Why or why not?

5. **Comparing.** How is *The Master Thief* similar to an old-fashioned fairy tale? How is it different?

# Writing About Literature

Several suggestions for writing projects follow. You may be asked to complete one or more of these projects. If you have any questions about how to begin a writing assignment, review Using the Writing Process, beginning on page 385.

1. **Inventing Dialogue.** Imagine that the master thief is arrested and brought to trial before the count. Invent a page of dialogue in which the master thief tries to persuade the count not to hang him.

2. **Combining Narration and Dialogue.** Create a brief humorous skit in which you use both narration and dialogue as Paul Sills has done in *The Master Thief.* The skit can be based on a real incident or it can be wholly imaginary.

3. **Writing Stage Directions.** Imagine that you must stage a production of *The Master Thief.* According to your understanding of the play, prepare stage directions to answer the following questions: (1) What costumes should the actors wear? (2) What scenery, if any, should there be? (3) How should lighting be used to create certain effects? (4) Which characters, if any, should be played seriously? (5) Which character is likely to make the audience laugh? (6) How should the actor playing that part act in order to make the audience laugh?

## Chapter 7

**Selection**     *A Marriage Proposal*
ANTON CHEKHOV

**Lesson**     *Farce and Satire*

## About the Selection

When you think of a man proposing marriage to a woman, you probably imagine a romantic scene. A traditional image pictures a man kneeling as a humble suitor before a woman. That image is not accurate, of course, but most people do think of a proposal as a moment full of tender emotion.

Anton Chekhov's play *A Marriage Proposal* is a comedy. It creates a picture that contrasts sharply with the tender moments of a traditional proposal. The play begins with a landowner, Iván Vassílievich Lómov, calling on his neighbor. Lómov wants to ask his neighbor's daughter to marry him. But the solemn occasion quickly develops into an absurd and humorous quarrel.

You have already read two comedies and learned about the different elements of humor in each. Unlike *The Ugly Duckling* and *The Master Thief,* which are based on fairy tales, *A Marriage Proposal* has a real-life setting. It takes place in Russia in the late 1800s. Like all of Chekhov's plays, it deals with people of Chekhov's own time and place.

Anton Chekhov is one of the best-known Russian authors of the nineteenth century. He was born in 1860. Chekhov's grandfather had been a serf—a peasant who belonged to a landowner and was not free to leave the land. He eventually bought his freedom, and Chekhov's father worked hard to buy a grocery store.

As a boy, Chekhov worked in his father's store and went to school.

Young Anton had a difficult childhood. His father was a religious fanatic and frequently beat his son. The family had little money. While still a student, Chekhov began writing poems, essays, and sketches. His talent for comedy revealed itself when he created and produced humorous skits at home.

Through hard work, Chekhov managed to get into medical school. While studying to become a doctor, he supported himself by writing and selling more than three hundred humorous stories.

The years of struggle took their toll. At the age of twenty-four, Chekhov developed tuberculosis. Yet he continued to practice medicine and to write. He published two hundred more tales and became a skilled short-story writer. In addition, he wrote many plays. His illness progressed, however, and Chekhov died at the age of forty-four.

In his own time Chekhov's plays were not as popular as they are today. At the time he was writing, melodrama was in style. The melodramas of the 1800s centered on villains, dashing heroes, and helpless heroines. By contrast, Chekhov's plays were not romantic. They focused on people who were locked into their fates by forces such as heredity or environment. Because of the power of those forces, people could not escape their fates.

Among Chekhov's full-length plays are *The Cherry Orchard, The Three Sisters,* and *The Sea Gull.* Today, they are considered among the best plays ever written and are performed in theaters all over the world.

Chekhov wrote during the reign of Czar Alexander III. The powerful czar and his officials took harsh measures against anyone who criticized the government and especially against writers who called for reform. The government seized the works of many writers because the authors had suggested the need for change.

Chekhov was not a reformer, but he did see the weaknesses of Russian society at the time. In his stories and plays, he often wrote about Russian landowners. Like the czar, most landowners resisted change. Even though their way of life was threatened by the Industrial Revolution of the nineteenth century, they continued their traditional pastimes—hunting, gossiping, and socializing. By using humor, Chekhov was able to reveal their weaknesses without having his work seized by the government.

# Lesson Preview

The lesson that follows *A Marriage Proposal* examines the play as a farce. A <u>farce</u> is a type of comedy designed to provoke the audience to simple, hearty laughter. It contains ridiculous characters and improbable situations. A farce often relies on verbal and physical humor.

The questions that follow will help you to identify the elements of farce in this play. As you read, think about how you would answer these questions.

**1** Who are the main characters in the play? What is humorous about their behavior?

**2** What is absurd about the plot?

**3** How does the dialogue reflect the foolishness of the characters?

**4** What serious points do you think Chekhov is making in the play?

# Vocabulary

Here are some difficult words that appear in the selection that follows. Study the words and their definitions, as well as the sentences that show how the words are used. This will help you get the most from your reading.

**embezzlement** the theft of money or goods entrusted to one's care. *After being convicted of embezzlement, the bank employee returned all the money he had taken.*

**colossal** gigantic; enormous; extraordinary. *Although she knows that I'm allergic to dogs, my neighbor had the colossal nerve to bring her puppy into my house.*

**muzzle** the projecting jaws and nose of an animal. *The friendly dog pushed his muzzle into my hand and licked my fingers.*

**hypocrite** one who pretends to have qualities he or she does not have. *George disliked his job as a salesman, and he felt like a hypocrite every time he convinced someone to buy his product.*

# A Marriage Proposal

Anton Chekhov

*Translated by Joachim Neugroschel*

## Characters

Stepán Stepánovich Choobookóv,[1] *a landowner.*
Natália Stepánovna, *his twenty-five-year-old daughter.*
Iván Vassílievich Lómov, *Choobookóv's neighbor, a healthy
and well-fed, but terribly hypochondriac[2] landowner.*

*The action takes place in the drawing room of* **Choobookóv's** *country
house.*

## Scene 1

(**Choobookóv** *and* **Lómov.** *The latter enters, wearing tails and white
gloves.)*

**Choobookóv** *(going over to welcome his guest)* Why, of all people! My old
friend, Iván Vassílievich! How nice to see you! *(Shakes his hand.)* This
really is a surprise, old boy. . . . How *are* you?

**Lómov** Very well, thank you. And may I ask how *you* are?

**Choobookóv** Not bad at all, old friend, with the help of your prayers
and so on. . . . Please have a seat. . . . Now, really, it's not very nice
of you to neglect your neighbors, my dear boy. And what are you

---

**1.** The accent marks in the Russian names show on which syllable to place the emphasis.   **2. hypochondriac:** a person who is overly concerned with his or her health, often with imaginary illnesses.

all dressed up for? Morning coat,[3] gloves, and so on! Are you off on a visit, old boy?

**Lómov**   No, I'm just calling on you, my esteemed neighbor.

**Choobookóv**   But why the morning coat, old friend? This isn't New Year's Day!

**Lómov**   Well, you see, the fact of the matter is . . . *(Takes his arm.)* I've burst in on you like this, Stepán Stepánovich, my esteemed neighbor, in order to ask a favor of you. I've already had the honor more than once of turning to you for help and you've always, so to speak, uh! . . . But forgive me, my nerves . . . I must have a sip of water, dear Stepán Stepánovich.

*(Drinks some water.)*

**Choobookóv**   *(aside)* He's after money. Fat chance! *(To* **Lómov***)* What is it, my dear fellow?

**Lómov**   Well, you see, my Stepán dearovich, uh! I mean dear Stepánovich . . . uh! I mean, my nerves are in a terrible condition, which you yourself are so kind as to see. In short, you're the only one who can help me, although, of course, I've done nothing to deserve it and . . . and I don't even have the right to count on your help. . . .

**Choobookóv**   Now, now; don't beat about the bush, old friend. Out with it! . . . Well?

**Lómov**   All right, here you are. The fact of the matter is, I've come to ask for your daughter Natália's hand in marriage.

**Choobookóv**   *(overjoyed)* My *dearest* friend! Iván Vassílievich. Could you repeat that—I'm not sure I heard right!

**Lómov**   I have the honor of asking——

**Choobookóv**   *(breaking in)* My oldest and dearest friend . . . I'm *so* delighted and so on . . . Yes really, and all that sort of thing. *(Hugging and kissing him.)* I've been yearning for this for ages. It's been my constant desire. *(Sheds a tear.)* And I've always loved you like a son, you wonderful person, you. May God grant you love and

---

3. **morning coat:** a long, formal cutaway coat, worn at ceremonies such as weddings and funerals.

*Farce and Satire*

guidance and so on, it's been my most fervent wish. . . . But why am I standing here like a blockhead? I'm dumbstruck by the sheer joy of it, completely dumbstruck. Oh, with all my heart and soul . . . I'll go get Natasha, and so on.

**Lómov** *(deeply moved)* Stepán Stepánovich, my esteemed friend, do you think I may count on her accepting me?

**Choobookóv** A handsome devil like you? How could she possibly resist? She's *mad*ly in love with you, don't worry, *mad*ly, and so on . . . I'll call her right away.

*(Exit.)*

## Scene 2

**Lómov** *(alone)* It's so cold . . . I'm shaking all over, like before a final exam. The important thing is to make up your mind. If you think about it too long, or waver, talk about it too much, and wait for the ideal woman or for true love, you'll never marry. . . . Brr! It's cold! Natália Stepánovna is an excellent housekeeper, she's not bad-looking, and she's got some education. . . . What more could I ask for? Oh, I'm so nervous, I can hear a buzzing in my ears. *(Drinks some water.)* It would be best for me to get married . . . First of all, I'm thirty-five years old already—and that, as they say, is a critical age. And then, I have to start leading a steady and regular life. . . . I've got a heart condition, with palpitations[4] all the time. . . . I've got an awful temper and I'm always getting terribly wrought up. . . . Even now, my lips are trembling and my right eyelid is twitching. . . . But the worst thing is when I try to sleep. The instant I get to bed and start dropping off, something *stabs* me in my left side—ungh! And it cuts right through my shoulder straight into my head—ungh! I jump like a lunatic, walk about a little, and then I lie down again, but the moment I start to doze off, I feel it in my side again—ungh! And it keeps on and on for at least twenty times. . . .

---

4. **palpitations:** rapid flutterings, as of the heart.

## Scene 3

*(*Natália Stepánovna *and* Lómov.*)*

**Natália**    *(entering)* Ah, it's you. And Papa said a customer had come for the merchandise. How do you do Iván Vassílievich!

**Lómov**    How do you do, my esteemed Natália Stepánovna!

**Natália**    I'm sorry about my apron and not being dressed. . . . We're shelling peas for drying. Where've you been keeping yourself? Have a seat. . . . *(They sit down.)* Would you like a bite of lunch?

**Lómov**    Thank you so much, but I've already eaten.

**Natália**    Well, then have a cigarette. . . . The matches are over here. . . . The weather's magnificent today, but yesterday it rained so hard that the men couldn't do a thing all day long. How much hay did *you* get done? Can you imagine, I was so greedy that I had the whole meadow mown, and now I regret it, I'm scared that all my hay may rot. I should have waited. But what's this? I do believe you're wearing a morning coat! How original! Are you going to a ball or something? Incidentally, you're getting quite handsome. . . . But honestly, why are you all dolled up?

**Lómov**    *(nervously)* You see, my esteemed Natália Stepánovna . . . the fact is I've made up my mind to ask you to listen to me. . . . Naturally you'll be surprised and even angry, but I . . . *(Aside.)* God, it's cold!

**Natália**    What is it? *(Pause.)* Well?

**Lómov**    I'll try to be brief. You are well aware, my esteemed Natália Stepánovna, that for a long time now, in fact since my childhood, I have had the honor of knowing your family. My late aunt and her husband, whose estate as you know I inherited, always held your father and your late mother in utmost esteem. The Lómov family and the Choobookóv family have always maintained extremely friendly, one might even say, intimate relations. Furthermore, as you know, my property borders on yours. Perhaps you will be so kind as to recall that my Ox Meadows run along your birch forest.

**Natália**  Excuse me for interrupting you. You said *"my* Ox Meadows" . . . are they *yours?*

**Lómov**  Of course. . . .

**Natália**  Oh, come now! The Ox Meadows belong to us, not you!

**Lómov**  Oh no! They're mine, dear Natália Stepánovna.

**Natália**  That's news to me. How did they ever get to be yours?

**Lómov**  What do you mean? I'm talking about the Ox Meadows that are wedged in between your birch forest and the Burnt Marsh.

**Natália**  Exactly. . . . They're ours.

**Lómov**  No, you're mistaken, dear Natália Stepánovna—they're mine.

**Natália**  Do be reasonable, Iván Vassílievich! Since when have they been yours?

**Lómov**  Since when? They've always been ours, as far back as I can remember.

**Natália**  Excuse me, but this is too much!

**Lómov**  You can look at the documents, dear Natália Stepánovna. At one time, there *were* some quarrels about the Ox Meadows, you're quite right. But now, everyone knows they're mine. Why argue about it? If you will permit me to explain: my aunt's grandmother lent them to your paternal great-grandfather's peasants for an indefinite period and free of charge in return for their firing her bricks.[5] Your great-grandfather's peasants used the Meadows free of charge for some forty years and began thinking of them as their own . . . and then after the Emancipation,[6] when a statute was passed——

**Natália**  You've got it all wrong! Both my grandfather and great-grand-father regarded their property as reaching all the way to the Burnt Swamp—which means that the Ox Meadows were ours. What's there to argue about?—I don't understand. How annoying!

**Lómov**  I'll show you the documents, Natália Stepánovna.

**Natália**  No; you're joking or trying to tease me. . . . What a surprise!

---

**5. firing her bricks:** baking newly made bricks in an oven to harden them.   **6. Emancipation:** the Edict of Emancipation (1861) was a law freeing the Russian serfs, or peasants, from a kind of slavery to landlords.

We've owned the land for practically three hundred years and now suddenly we're told it's not ours! I'm sorry, Iván Vassílievich, but I just can't believe my ears. Those Meadows don't mean a thing to me. The whole area probably doesn't come to more than forty acres, it's worth about three hundred rubles;[7] but I'm terribly upset by the injustice of it all. You can say what you like, but I simply can't stand injustice.

**Lómov**   Please listen to me, I beseech you. Your paternal great-grandfather's peasants, as I have already had the honor of telling you, fired bricks for my aunt's grandmother. Now, my aunt's grandmother, wishing to do them a favor in return——

**Natália**   Grandfather, grandmother, aunt . . . I don't know *what* you're talking about! The Meadows are *ours,* and that's that.

**Lómov**   They're *mine!*

**Natália**   They're ours! You can keep arguing for two days, you can put on fifteen morning coats if you like, but they're ours, ours, ours! . . . I don't desire *your* property, but I don't care to lose mine. . . . Do as you like!

**Lómov**   I don't need the Meadows, Natália Stepánovna, but it's the principle of the thing. If you want, I'll *give* them to you.

**Natália**   It would be *my* privilege to give them to *you,* they're mine! . . . All this is rather odd—to put it mildly, Iván Vassílievich. Up till now we've always considered you a good neighbor and friend. Last year we let you borrow our threshing machine, and as a result we couldn't finish our own grain until November, and now you're treating us like Gypsies. You're *giving* me my own land. Excuse me, but that's not a neighborly thing to do! To *my* mind, it's impertinent,[8] if you care to——

**Lómov**   Are you trying to tell me that I'm a land-grabber? Madam, I've never seized anyone else's property, and I won't allow anyone to *say* I have. . . . *(Hurries over to the carafe and drinks some water.)* The Ox Meadows are mine!

---

**7. rubles:** Russian units of money.   **8. impertinent:** disrespectful.

*Farce and Satire*

**Natália**  That's not true, they're ours.

**Lómov**  They're mine.

**Natália**  That's not true. I'll prove it to you! I'll send my men over to mow them this afternoon.

**Lómov**  What?!

**Natália**  My men will be there this afternoon!

**Lómov**  I'll kick them out!

**Natália**  You wouldn't dare!

**Lómov**  *(clutching at his heart)* The Ox Meadows are mine! Do you hear! Mine!

**Natália**  Stop shouting! Please! You can shout your lungs out in your own place, but I must ask you to control yourself here.

**Lómov**  Madam, if it weren't for these awful, excruciating palpitations and the veins throbbing in my temples, I'd speak to you in a totally different way! *(Shouting.)* The Ox Meadows are mine.

**Natália**  Ours!

**Lómov**  Mine!

**Natália**  Ours!

**Lómov**  Mine!


## Scene 4

*(Enter **Choobookóv**.)*

**Choobookóv**  What's going on? What's all the shouting about?

**Natália**  Papa, please tell this gentleman whom the Ox Meadows belong to. Us or him.

**Choobookóv**  *(to **Lómov**)* Why, the Meadows belong to us, old friend.

**Lómov**  But for goodness' sake, Stepán Stepánovich, how can that be? Can't *you* be reasonable at least? My aunt's grandmother lent the Meadows to your grandfather's peasants for temporary use and free of charge. His peasants used the land for forty years and got in the habit of regarding it as their own, but after the Land Settlement——

**Choobookóv**   Excuse me, old boy . . . You're forgetting that our peasants didn't pay your grandmother and so on precisely *because* the Meadows were disputed and what not. . . . But now every child knows that they're ours. I guess you've never looked at the maps.

**Lómov**   I'll *prove* they're mine.

**Choobookóv**   You won't prove a thing, my boy.

**Lómov**   I will *so* prove it!

**Choobookóv**   My dear boy, why carry on like this? You won't prove a thing by shouting. I don't want anything of yours, but I don't intend to let go of what's mine. Why should I? If it comes to that, dear friend, if you mean to dispute my ownership of the Meadows, and so on, I'd sooner let my peasants have them than you. So there!

**Lómov**   I don't understand. What right do you have to give away other people's property?

**Choobookóv**   Allow me to decide whether or not I've got the right. Really, young man, I'm not accustomed to being spoken to in that tone of voice, and what not. I'm old enough to be your father, and I must ask you to calm down when you speak to me, and so forth.

**Lómov**   No! You're treating me like an idiot, and laughing at me. You tell me that *my* property is yours, and then you expect me to remain calm and talk to you in a normal fashion. That's not a very neighborly thing to do, Stepán Stepánovich. You're no neighbor, you're a robber baron.[9]

**Choobookóv**   What?! What did you say, my good man?

**Natália**   Papa, have the men mow the Ox Meadows right now!

**Choobookóv**   *(to* **Lómov***)* What did you say, sir?

**Natália**   The Ox Meadows are our property, and I won't let anyone else have them. I won't, I won't, I won't!

**Lómov**   We'll see about that! I'll prove to you in court that they're mine.

**Choobookóv**   In court? My good man, you can take it to court and what not. Go right ahead! I know you, you've just been waiting for

---

9. **robber baron:** a person who acquired wealth by taking advantage of others.

*Farce and Satire*

a chance to litigate, and so on. You're a quibbler from the word go. Your whole family's nothing but a bunch of pettifoggers.[10] All of them!

**Lómov**   I must ask you not to insult my family. The Lómovs have always been law-abiding folk. None of them was ever hauled into court for embezzlement the way your uncle was.

**Choobookóv**   Every last one of them was insane.

**Natália**   Every last one of them, every last one!

**Choobookóv**   Your grandfather drank like a fish, and the whole country knows that your youngest aunt, Nastasia, ran off with an architect, and what not——

**Lómov**   And your mother was a hunchback! *(Clutching at his heart.)* There's a twitching in my side. . . . My head's throbbing. . . . Oh, God . . . Water!

**Choobookóv**   And your father was a gambler and he ate like a pig!

**Natália**   And no one could beat your aunt at scandalmongering.[11]

**Lómov**   My left leg's paralyzed. . . . And you're a schemer. . . . Oooh! My heart! . . . And it's no secret to anyone that just before the elections you——There are stars bursting before my eyes. . . . Where's my hat?

**Natália**   Vermin! Liar! Brute!

**Choobookóv**   You're a spiteful, double-dealing schemer! So there!

**Lómov**   Ah, my hat . . . My heart. Where am I? Where's the door? Oooh! . . . I think I'm dying. . . . My foot's totally paralyzed.

*(Drags himself to the door.)*

**Choobookóv**   *(calling after him)* And don't ever set your foot in my home again!

**Natália**   Go to court! Sue us! Just wait and see!

*(**Lómov** staggers out.)*

---

10. **pettifoggers:** people who argue over insignificant matters.   11. **scandalmongering:** dealing or trading in scandals or gossip.

## Scene 5

*(***Choobookóv*** *and* **Natália Stepánovna.***)*

**Choobookóv**  He can go straight to hell, damn him!

*(Walks about, all wrought up.)*

**Natália**  Isn't he the worst crook? Catch me trusting a good neighbor after this!

**Choobookóv**  The chiseler! The scarecrow!

**Natália**  The monster! He not only grabs other people's property, he calls them names, to boot.

**Choobookóv**  And that clown, that . . . freak had the colossal nerve to ask me for your hand in marriage, and so on. Can you imagine? He wanted to propose.

**Natália**  Propose?

**Choobookóv**  Exactly? That's what he came for. To propose to you.

**Natália**  Propose? To me? Why didn't you *say* so?

**Choobookóv**  And he got all dolled up in a morning coat. That pipsqueak. That upstart.

**Natália**  Propose? To me? Ohhh! *(Collapses into an armchair and wails.)* Bring him back. Get him. Ohh! Get him!

**Choobookóv**  Get whom?

**Natália**  Hurry up, hurry! I feel sick. Bring him back. *(Hysterical.)*

**Choobookóv**  What is it? What's wrong? *(Grabbing his head.)* This is awful! I'll shoot myself. I'll hang myself. They've worn me out.

**Natália**  I'm dying! Bring him back!

**Choobookóv**  All right. Stop yelling!

*(Runs out.)*

**Natália**  *(alone, wailing)* What've we done? Bring him back! Bring him back!

**Choobookóv**  *(running in)* He's coming and all that, goddam him. Ughh! *You* talk to him, alone, I really don't feel like . . .

**Natália**  *(wailing)* Bring him back!

**Choobookóv**  *(shouting)* He's coming, I tell you. Oh God! What did I ever do to deserve a grown-up daughter? I'll cut my throat. I swear, I'll cut my throat. We insulted and abused him, and it's all your fault!

**Natália**  My fault? It was yours!

**Choobookóv**  Now *I'm* the culprit!

*(**Lómov** appears at the French doors. **Choobookóv** exits.)*


## Scene 6

*(**Natália** and **Lómov**.)*

**Lómov**  *(entering, exhausted)* What horrible palpitations . . . my foot's gone numb . . . there's a jabbing in my side . . .

**Natália**  My apologies, Iván Vassílievich, we got so worked up. . . . I do recall now that the Ox Meadows are actually *your* property.

**Lómov**  My heart's palpitating. . . . The Meadows *are* mine. . . . There are stars bursting in both my eyes.

*(They sit down.)*

**Natália**  We were wrong.

**Lómov**  It's the principle of the thing. . . . I don't care about the land, it's the principle of the thing——

**Natália**  Exactly, the principle . . . Let's talk about something else.

**Lómov**  Particularly since I have proof. My aunt's grandmother let your paternal great-grandfather's peasants——

**Natália**  All right, all right . . . *(Aside.)* I don't know how to go about it. . . . *(To **Lómov**)* Will you start hunting soon?

**Lómov**  Yes, for grouse,[12] Natália Stepánovna. I think I shall begin after the harvest. Oh, have you heard what bad luck I had? My hound Guess—you know the one—he's gone lame.

**Natália**  What a pity! How did it happen?

---

12. **grouse:** a kind of bird.

**Lómov**  I don't know. He must have twisted his leg, or else some other dog bit him. . . . *(Sighs.)* My very best hound, not to mention the money! Why, I paid Mirónov a hundred and twenty-five rubles for him.

**Natália**  You overpaid him, Iván Vassílievich.

**Lómov**  I don't think so. It was very little for a wonderful dog.

**Natália**  Papa bought his dog Leap for eighty-five rubles, and Leap is vastly superior to your Guess.

**Lómov**  Leap superior to Guess? Oh, come now. *(Laughs.)* Leap superior to Guess!

**Natália**  Of course he is! I know that Leap is still young, he's not a full-grown hound yet. But for points and action, not even Volchanietsky has a better dog.

**Lómov**  Excuse me, Natália Stepánovna, but you're forgetting that he's pug-jawed, which makes him a poor hunting dog.

**Natália**  Pug-jawed? That's news to me.

**Lómov**  I can assure you, his lower jaw is shorter than his upper jaw.

**Natália**  Have you measured it?

**Lómov**  Indeed, I have. He'll do for pointing, of course, but when it comes to retrieving, he can hardly hold a cand——

**Natália**  First of all, our Leap is a pedigreed grey-hound—he's the son of Harness and Chisel, whereas your Guess is so piebald[13] that not even Solomon could figure out his breed. . . . Furthermore, he's as old and ugly as a broken-down nag——

**Lómov**  He may be old, but I wouldn't trade him for five of your Leaps. . . . The very idea! Guess is a real hound, but Leap . . . Why argue? It's ridiculous. . . . Every huntsman's assistant has a dog like your Leap. At twenty-five rubles he'd be overpriced.

**Natália**  You seem to be possessed by some demon of contradiction, Iván Vassílievich. First you fancy that the Ox Meadows are yours, then you pretend that Guess is a better hound than Leap. If there's one thing I don't like it's a person who says the opposite of what

---

13. **piebald:** covered with patches or spots of two colors, usually white and black.

*Farce and Satire*

he thinks. You know perfectly well that Leap is a hundred times better than . . . than that stupid Guess of yours. Why do you insist on denying it?

**Lómov**   You obviously must think, Natália Stepánovna, that I'm either blind or mentally retarded. Can't you see that your Leap has a pug jaw?

**Natália**   That's not true.

**Lómov**   A pug jaw.

**Natália**   *(screaming)* That's not true.

**Lómov**   Why are you screaming, Madam?

**Natália**   Why are you talking such rubbish? It's exasperating! Your Guess is just about ready to be put out of his misery, and you compare him to Leap.

**Lómov**   Excuse me, but I can't keep on arguing like this. My heart's palpitating.

**Natália**   I've noticed that the sportsmen who argue most don't understand the first thing about hunting.

**Lómov**   Madam, pleeeease, keep quiet . . . My heart's bursting. . . . *(Shouts.)* Keep quiet!

**Natália**   I won't keep quiet until you admit that Leap is a hundred times superior to your Guess.

**Lómov**   He's a hundred times *in*ferior. Someone ought to shoot him. My temples . . . my eyes . . . my shoulder . . .

**Natália**   No one has to wish that idiotic mutt of yours dead, because he's just skin and bones anyway.

**Lómov**   Keep quiet! I'm having heart failure!

**Natália**   I will *not* keep quiet!

## Scene 7

**Choobookóv**   *(entering)* What's going on now?

**Natália**   Papa, tell me, honestly and sincerely: which is the better dog— our Leap, or his Guess?

**Lómov**  Stepán Stepánovich, I beseech you, just tell me one thing: is your Leap pug-jawed or isn't he? Yes or no?

**Choobookóv**  So what! Who cares? He's still the best hound in the country, and what not.

**Lómov**  And my Guess isn't better? Tell the truth.

**Choobookóv**  Don't get all worked up, old boy. . . . Let me explain. . . . Your Guess *does* have a few good qualities. . . . He's pure-bred, he's got solid legs, he's well put together, and what not. But if you must know, my good man, your dog's got two basic faults: he's old, and his muzzle's too short.

**Lómov**  Excuse me, my heart's racing madly. . . . Let's examine the facts. . . . Please don't forget that when we were hunting in the Mapooskin Fields, my Guess ran neck and neck with the count's dog Waggy, while your Leap lagged behind by half a mile.

**Choobookóv**  That was because the count's assistant struck him with his riding crop.

**Lómov**  Naturally. All the other dogs were chasing the fox, but yours started running after sheep.

**Choobookóv**  That's a lie! My dear boy, I fly off the handle easily, so please let's stop arguing. The man whipped him because people are always envious of everyone else's dogs. Yes, they're all filled with spite! And you, sir, are no exception. Why, the minute you notice that anyone else's dog is better than your Guess, you instantly start up something or other . . . and what not. I've got the memory of an elephant!

**Lómov**  And so do I.

**Choobookóv**  *(mimicking him)* "And so do I." . . . And what does your memory tell you?

**Lómov**  My heart's palpitating. . . . My foot's paralyzed. . . . I can't anymore . . .

**Natália**  *(mimicking)* "My heart's palpitating . . . " What kind of hunter are you anyway? You ought to be home in bed catching cockroaches instead of out hunting foxes. Palpitations! . . .

*Farce and Satire*

**Choobookóv**  That's right, what kind of hunter are you? If you've got palpitations, stay home; don't go wobbling around the countryside on horseback. It wouldn't be so bad if you really hunted, but you only tag along in order to start arguments or meddle with other people's dogs, and what not. We'd better stop, I fly off the handle easily. You, sir, are not a hunter, and that's that.

**Lómov**  And you *are*, I suppose. The only reason *you* go hunting is to flatter the count and carry on your backstabbing little intrigues. . . . Oh, my heart! . . . You schemer!

**Choobookóv**  Me, a schemer. *(Shouting.)* Shut up!

**Lómov**  Schemer!

**Choobookóv**  Upstart! Pipsqueak!

**Lómov**  You old fogy! You hypocrite!

**Choobookóv**  Shut up, or I'll blast you with a shot gun like a partridge.

**Lómov**  The whole county knows that—Oh, my heart!—your late wife used to beat you. . . . My leg . . . my temples . . . I see stars . . . I'm falling, falling . . .

**Choobookóv**  And your housekeeper henpecks you all over the place!

**Lómov**  There, you see . . . my heart's burst! My shoulder's torn off. . . . Where's my shoulder? . . . I'm dying! *(Collapses into armchair.)* Get a doctor! *(Faints.)*

**Choobookóv**  Pipsqueak. Weakling. Windbag. I feel sick. *(Drinks some water.)* I feel sick.

**Natália**  What kind of hunter are you anyway? You don't even know how to sit in a saddle! *(To her father)* Papa! What's the matter with him? Papa! Look, Papa! *(Screams.)* Iván Vassílievich! He's dead!

**Choobookóv**  I feel sick! . . . I can't breathe! . . . Air!

**Natália**  He's dead! *(Tugs at Lómov's sleeve.)* Iván Vassílievich! Iván Vassílievich! What've we done? He's dead. *(Collapses into easy chair.)* Get a doctor. *(She becomes hysterical.)*

**Choobookóv**  Oh! . . . What is it? What's wrong?

**Natália**  *(moaning)* He's dead . . . he's dead!

**Choobookóv**  Who's dead? *(Glancing at Lómov.)* He really is dead! Oh, my God! Get some water! Get a doctor! (*Holds a glass to* **Lómov's** *mouth.*) Go ahead and drink! . . . He won't drink. . . . I guess he's dead and so on. . . . Why does everything have to happen to me? Why didn't I put a bullet through my head long ago? Why didn't I cut my throat? What am I waiting for? Give me a knife! Give me a gun! (**Lómov** *stirs.*) He's reviving, I think. . . . Drink some water! . . . That's right.

**Lómov**   Stars . . . fog . . . where am I?

**Choobookóv**   You two'd better hurry up and get married . . . Dammit! She accepts. . . . (*Joins* **Lómov's** *hand with* **Natália's.**) She accepts. . . . My blessings and so forth. . . . Just do me a favor and leave me in peace.

**Lómov**   What? (*Getting up.*) Who?

**Choobookóv**   She accepts. Well? Kiss her and . . . the two of you can go straight to hell.

**Natália**   (*moaning*) He's alive. . . . I accept, I accept. . . .

**Choobookóv**   Kiss and make up.

**Lómov**   What? Who? (*Kisses* **Natália.**) *Enchanté*[14] . . . Excuse me, but what's going on? Oh yes, I remember. . . . My heart . . . stars . . . I'm very happy, Natália Stepánovna. (*Kisses her hands.*) My leg's paralyzed. . . .

**Natália**   I . . . I'm very happy, too. . . .

**Choobookóv**   That's a load off my back. . . . Whew!

**Natália**   But . . . all the same, why don't you finally admit that Guess isn't as good as Leap.

**Lómov**   He's much better.

**Natália**   He's worse.

**Choobookóv**   The launching of marital bliss! Champagne!

**Lómov**   He's better.

**Natália**   Worse! Worse! Worse!

**Choobookóv**   (*trying to outshout them*) Champagne! Champagne!

---

14. *Enchanté*: a French word meaning "I'm enchanted" or "I'm delighted."

# Reviewing the Selection

Answer each of the following questions without looking back at the play.

*Recalling Facts*

1. Lómov goes to visit Choobookóv in order to
   - ☐ a. borrow money from him.
   - ☐ b. discuss who owns the Ox Meadows.
   - ☐ c. propose marriage to Natália.
   - ☐ d. sell his dog, Guess.

*Understanding Main Ideas*

2. In this play Chekhov seems to be saying that
   - ☐ a. men are more selfish than women.
   - ☐ b. love will make everyone happy.
   - ☐ c. neighbors are never good friends.
   - ☐ d. adults sometimes behave like children.

*Placing Events in Order*

3. After Lómov and Natália argue about who owns the Ox Meadows, they disagree about
   - ☐ a. who has more money.
   - ☐ b. whose house is larger.
   - ☐ c. who is the better neighbor.
   - ☐ d. whose dog is better.

*Finding Supporting Details*

4. Natália is desperate to get married. You know this because of the way she behaves when
   - ☐ a. she greets Lómov for the first time.
   - ☐ b. Lómov brings up the subject of the Ox Meadows.
   - ☐ c. her father tells her why Lómov came to visit.
   - ☐ d. Lómov brings up the subject of their dogs.

5. "May God grant you love and guidance and so on, it's been my most <u>fervent</u> wish." In this context *fervent* means
   ☐ a. fevered.
   ☐ b. dreaded.
   ☐ c. sincere.
   ☐ d. happy.

## Interpreting the Selection

Answer each of the following questions. You may look back at the play if necessary.

6. Lómov has decided to marry Natália because he
   ☐ a. is deeply in love with her.
   ☐ b. thinks it is time to settle down.
   ☐ c. likes Choobookóv as a father-in-law.
   ☐ d. wants to own the Ox Meadows.

7. All three characters in this play could be described as
   ☐ a. highly intelligent, well-educated people.
   ☐ b. hypochondriacs.
   ☐ c. anxious to please.
   ☐ d. easily roused to anger.

8. In this play Chekhov was probably trying to
   show the
   ☐ a. backwardness of Russian marriage
   customs.
   ☐ b. ridiculous behavior of people who think
   only of themselves.
   ☐ c. harsh life of Russian peasants.
   ☐ d. importance of hunting to Russian
   landowners.

9. Lómov suffers from various ailments that get
   worse whenever he
   ☐ a. goes hunting.
   ☐ b. drinks water.
   ☐ c. thinks of doing any work.
   ☐ d. argues.

10. Which of the following conclusions can you
    draw about Choobookóv?
    ☐ a. He is a man with superficial feelings.
    ☐ b. He is an excellent judge of character.
    ☐ c. He thinks his daughter will make a
    loving wife for Lómov.
    ☐ d. He is a hardworking landowner.

# Farce and Satire

People enjoy comedies because comedies are amusing and entertaining. Writers of comedies often use their plays to ridicule certain attitudes, behaviors, or human weaknesses. Most comedies, however, have a serious message below the surface humor.

Comedy can take different forms. Some comedies, such as *The Ugly Duckling,* humorously imitate particular kinds of literature. Others, such as *The Master Thief,* develop their humor from the situations and characters. *A Marriage Proposal* is a particular kind of comedy known as a farce. A farce is a play that arouses laughter through ridiculous characters and an improbable plot. A farce may include slapstick—the kind of humor that depends on fast, foolish action to make people laugh. Slapstick often involves comic physical action.

In this lesson you will study some of the elements of humor in a farce. You will also examine the satire in *A Marriage Proposal.* Satire is the kind of writing in which certain aspects of human behavior are ridiculed by the writer. As you will learn, Chekhov uses satire to convey a serious message about human weakness.

## Exaggeration

Humor in a farce is often based on exaggeration. Exaggeration refers to an intentional overstatement of facts or events so that their meanings are intensified. Exaggeration is not meant to deceive you but to create humorous results.

In a farce a comic actor might speak with an exaggerated accent or move in an exaggerated way. The exaggeration is absurd and usually points out some kind of human foolishness. Much of the humor of *A Marriage Proposal* comes from the exaggerated behavior and language of the characters.

**Behavior.** The play opens with Lómov dressed in tails and white gloves. Why is he dressed so formally when he is merely visiting a neighbor? This costume, we learn, is meant to suit the occasion. He plans to propose to Choobookóv's daughter, Natália. Still, his dressing in formal clothes is ridiculous.

In the opening scene Lómov and Choobookóv treat each other with exaggerated politeness. When Choobookóv learns why Lómov has called, his behavior becomes even more exaggerated. He hugs and kisses Lómov and even *"sheds a tear."* His language mirrors his extreme emotion. Such strong emotion, under the circumstances, is silly.

*1. Read Choobookóv's speech in response to Lómov's request for Natália's hand. List the phrases he uses to express his emotions.*

The characters also respond in exaggerated ways to other incidents. In Scene 3 you expect Lómov to make his proposal to Natália. Instead, the couple quickly gets sidetracked into a long and violent argument about who owns the Ox Meadows. As soon as Lómov mentions that piece of land, Natália reacts strongly.

**Natália**   Excuse me for interrupting you. You said *"my* Ox
            Meadows" . . . are they *yours?*
**Lómov**   Of course. . . .
**Natália**   Oh, come now! The Ox Meadows belong to us, not you!

After that exchange, the argument continues to grow. Each character claims the land. At the same time, each denies that the land has worth. Their exaggerated squabble becomes overblown and senseless:

**Lómov**   . . . The Ox Meadows are mine!
**Natália**   That's not true, they're ours.
**Lómov**   They're mine.
**Natália**   That's not true. I'll prove it to you! I'll send my men
            over to mow them this afternoon!

**Lómov**   What?!

**Natália**   My men will be there this afternoon!

**Lómov**   I'll kick them out!

**Natália**   You wouldn't dare!

The argument continues into Scene 4. In response to the noisy argument, Choobookóv reappears. Soon both father and daughter are furious at their neighbor. All three characters fling claims, counterclaims, and insults at one another. Finally, Choobookóv turns Lómov out of the house.

The scene is humorous because of the extreme contrast of emotions. A short time earlier, Choobookóv was embracing Lómov as his future son-in-law. Now he is telling him never to set foot in the house again.

 *2. Review the last three scenes of the play. Choose at least two examples of exaggerated behavior. Explain why each example is humorous.*

**Language.** Exaggerated language also contributes to the humor of the farce. Study the insults that Choobookóv showers on Lómov and his family. "Your whole family's nothing but a bunch of pettifoggers. All of them!" "Every last one of them was insane." "You're a spiteful, double-dealing schemer! So there!" Choobookóv's word choice is exaggerated and ridiculous. You cannot help laughing at the extremes to which Choobookóv's anger has carried him.

 *3. Find three other examples of exaggerated language that are humorous.*

## Farce and Character

The characters in a farce are often stereotypes. As you learned in Chapter 5, a stereotype is a stock character who matches a fixed idea held by a number of people. In *A Marriage Proposal* Choobookóv creates characters who are stereotypes. Each character is meant to stand for a type of person in nineteenth-century Russian society.

Lómov, for example, is a typical hypochondriac. In the description of characters at the beginning of the play, you learn that Lómov is *"healthy and well-fed."* Yet in the play, he is constantly complaining about his aches and pains. In Scene 1 he keeps telling Choobookóv how bad his nerves are. In Scene 2 he gives a long speech in which he describes his health problems. When the arguments rage over who owns the Ox Meadows and whose dog is superior, Lómov continues to complain about his health.

*4. What do you think Lómov's married life will be like? Why?*

Choobookóv is another stereotype. He reflects Chekhov's view of nineteenth-century Russian landowners. Outwardly, Choobookóv is polite and friendly. Yet he is really stubborn, superficial, and lazy—especially in his speech. Instead of completing a thought, he often ends by saying "and so on" or "and what not." Those phrases make him sound as foolish as Lómov, who is always exclaiming about his health.

*5. Skim the scenes in which Choobookóv appears. Find two examples of his foolishness in behavior or in language. What do you learn about his character from those examples?*

Natália is much like her father. She is stubborn and willful. She is also a stereotypical spinster desperate for a husband. In nineteenth-century society Natália would have been considered an "old maid." By twenty-five, she should have been married for several years.

*6. How do you know that Natália is anxious to be married? Does she treat Lómov as a romantic figure? Explain your answer. What is humorous about the way she treats Lómov?*

## The Improbable Plot

Another element of farce is contained in the ridiculous situation in which the characters find themselves. The plot of *A Marriage Proposal* is highly improbable. It moves from one absurdity to the next.

At first, the plot seems reasonable. A landowner, Lómov, calls on his neighbor, Choobookóv, to ask for the hand of the neighbor's daughter in marriage. Although Lómov is overdressed and Choobookóv overreacts to the proposal, the story seems almost believable. When Natália appears in Scene 3, Lómov tries to make his proposal. He seems to be a typical, shy suitor. Then suddenly the couple is in the midst of an argument. The conflict becomes ridiculously exaggerated. Choobookóv joins the argument. The climax occurs when Lómov leaves the house.

*7. What is absurd about the situation that develops in Scenes 3 and 4?*

In Scene 5 Choobookóv and Natália are alone. They agree that Lómov is a "crook" and a "chiseler." Then Choobookóv reveals that Lómov had come to propose to Natália.

*8. What is Natália's response to that news? What does she make her father do? Why is that scene humorous?*

Lómov returns, but once again the meeting between the couple involves an argument. Instead of discussing Lómov's marriage proposal, the two end up fighting about their hunting dogs. They insult each other's dogs, and the argument develops just as their earlier conflict did. When Choobookóv returns, he again joins the battle.

*9. What crisis develops in Scene 7?*

*10. Examine Choobookóv's response to Natália's statement on page 281 that Lómov is dead. What is absurd about his reaction? What is improbable about the last part of Scene 7?*

## Satire and Irony

Although *A Marriage Proposal* is a farce, Chekhov uses the play to make some serious points. He does so by combining farce and satire. Satire, you will recall, is the kind of writing in which certain aspects of human behavior are ridiculed by the writer. Writers often use satire to improve society or to change social standards.

In *A Marriage Proposal* Chekhov exposes the childish behavior of adults. You cannot help but laugh at the way Lómov, Natália, and Choobookóv shout and argue. Yet think about how often adults get involved in silly quarrels. Chekhov's satire shows that adults can react in foolish ways, especially in stressful situations. As the stress increases in *A Marriage Proposal,* so does the foolish behavior of the characters.

11. *What other human weaknesses are satirized in the play?*

Satire can be light and friendly; a writer may use satire to gently smile at human foolishness. Some satire, however, is harsh and cruel. For example, the well-known writer Mark Twain wrote such bitter satire against religion that some people refused to read his works.

12. *Would you call Chekhov's satire good-natured and gentle or cruel and angry? Why?*

Like many satirists, Chekhov uses irony to create humor. Irony, you will recall, is a contrast between what is expected and what happens, or between what is said and what is meant. The situation in *A Marriage Proposal* is ironic. You expect Lómov to propose to Natália. Instead, the two battle violently.

Chekhov uses verbal irony effectively. Verbal irony is the type of irony in which a writer or a character says one thing but means something entirely different.

13. *Read the two passages that follow. The first passage comes from the beginning of Scene 3. The second comes almost at the end of the play. Find each passage in the play. Then explain how each is an example of verbal irony.*

a. **Natália** (entering) *Ah, it's you. And Papa said a customer had come for the merchandise. How do you do, Iván Vassílievich!*

b. **Choobookóv** *The launching of marital bliss! Champagne!*

## Questions for Thought and Discussion

The questions and activities that follow will help you explore *A Marriage Proposal* in more depth and at the same time develop your critical thinking skills.

1. **Drawing a Conclusion.** Reread Scene 2. On the basis of Lómov's monologue, what kind of person do you think he is? Why do you think he has finally decided to get married? Why do you think he has chosen Natália Stepánovna?

2. **Preparing a Scene for Performance.** Divide the class into six groups. Each group should choose a scene (but do not use Scene 2) from *A Marriage Proposal.* Then divide your group's scene so that each person gets a turn to speak. Practice saying the lines, and decide what gestures and expressions you will use. Each group should then perform its scene.

3. **Comparing.** Compare Natália in *A Marriage Proposal* to Princess Camilla in *The Ugly Duckling.* How are they similar? How are they different?

4. **Inferring.** What comments do you think Chekhov is making about the Russian landowning class in *A Marriage Proposal?* Why do you think he chose to present his ideas in a farce rather than in a serious play?

## Writing About Literature

Several suggestions for writing projects follow. You may be asked to complete one or more of these projects. If you have any questions about how to begin a writing assignment, review Using the Writing Process, beginning on page 385.

1. **Creating Dialogue.** Think about a conversation that might take place between Lómov and Natália after they have been married for several months. The dialogue could be about one of the issues discussed before their marriage, or about some other issue. Then write the conversation in dialogue form, trying to make the characters sound the way Chekhov made them sound. Try to give the characters the same personalities that they had in the play.

2. **Writing an Eyewitness Account.** Imagine that you were in the room on the day that Lómov called on his neighbor. In the form of a letter to a friend, write an eyewitness account of the events that took place. Include your opinion of the characters and their behavior.

3. **Describing a Personal Experience.** Have you ever found yourself caught up in an argument that you knew was pointless? Describe a personal experience that was similar to the quarrels between Lómov and his neighbors. Try to use both description and dialogue.

# Plays for Radio, Television, and Movies

*Excerpt from*
## War of the Worlds
RADIO PLAY BY HOWARD KOCH
BASED ON THE NOVEL BY H. G. WELLS

### The Radio Drama

*Excerpt from*
## The Death of Billy the Kid
GORE VIDAL

### The Television Play

*Excerpt from*
## The Treasure of the Sierra Madre
SCREENPLAY BY JOHN HUSTON
BASED ON THE NOVEL BY B. TRAVEN

### The Screenplay

$T$he plays you studied in earlier units were written to be performed on a stage in front of an audience. For thousands of years, that was the only way in which plays were performed. In the twentieth century, however, new technologies led to the development of radio, television, and movies. Each of those media opened up new worlds for playwrights.

In Unit Three you will study plays that were developed for radio, television, and movies. Radio plays were especially popular from the 1920s through the early 1950s. Television plays were popular in the 1950s and 1960s, and screenplays for movies have been popular since the early 1900s.

Twentieth-century technology has allowed plays to be broadcast to huge audiences separated by distance from the performers. The technology involves new ways of communicating by sound and sight. Audiences that listen to radio plays can only *hear* what the play is about. They cannot *see* a performance. Images suggested by the playwright and the sound effects used by the actors stimulate the imaginations of the listening audience.

Unlike plays written for radio, television plays and screenplays use cameras. The plays written for both media are shown on screens, although a television screen is usually smaller than a movie screen. Cameras give the playwright the ability to show varied kinds of events and actions and to focus closely on the actors.

Despite the changes brought about by technology, many elements of radio plays, television plays, and screenplays are similar to the basic elements of a stage play. Like playwrights for the stage, playwrights for the new media build plots, develop characters, and create conflicts. In this unit you will read examples of famous scripts developed for radio, television, and movies. Each play contains both traditional elements of a stage play as well as elements unique to its medium.

## Chapter 8

**Selection**

*Excerpt from*
# War of the Worlds
RADIO PLAY BY HOWARD KOCH
BASED ON THE NOVEL BY H. G. WELLS

**Lesson**

## The Radio Drama

## About the Selection

Try to imagine evenings at home without television. Until the 1950s few families had television sets. Families gathered around their radios. Just as watching football on Monday night has become a ritual in many homes, listening to a favorite radio program was a common pastime in the days when radio first became popular.

The first radio show went on the air in 1922. Within ten years, millions of Americans owned radios. During the Great Depression in 1929, people turned to the radio to escape their troubles. The entertainment helped to ease the minds of the millions of people who were suffering from unemployment or were worrying about how to make ends meet.

Every night people listened to comedy and drama programs. These programs were not prerecorded; they were all live performances. One popular drama program was the "Mercury Theatre on the Air." It starred Orson Welles, John Houseman, and several other young actors and actresses. Welles acted in and directed many of the weekly programs.

During the 1938 season, Welles had an idea for a special Halloween-night production. He planned to broadcast a radio play based on a popular science fiction novel called *War of the Worlds*. The novel had been written in 1898 by H. G. Wells. It was a frightening story about the invasion of Earth by terrible but intelligent creatures from Mars. Orson

Welles asked playwright Howard Koch to adapt the novel for a radio drama. In this chapter you will read an excerpt from Koch's radio drama.

Koch wrote the radio script in the form of a series of news bulletins. When the program was broadcast on October 30, 1938, its effect was amazing. Some listeners tuned in after the broadcast had begun. They heard reporters and experts explaining the extraordinary events of the evening. Listeners thought they were hearing real news reports. People became so involved in the program that they did not think about the impossibility of reporters reaching the various scenes in a matter of seconds.

Rumors and fears spread quickly as the story of the Martian invasion came across the airwaves. Thousands of people on the East Coast of the United States panicked. Some packed their belongings and fled their homes. Others ran screaming through the streets. Police stations in New Jersey—the site of the supposed invasion—were flooded with phone calls.

The panic lasted only a few hours. People soon learned that no Martians had landed and that the broadcast was about an imaginary event. The program, however, showed the power of radio. Young Orson Welles, only twenty-five years old at the time, became world famous. Today he is still remembered as the creator of one of the most famous incidents in broadcasting history.

Orson Welles went on to a successful career in the movies. In 1940 he directed and starred in *Citizen Kane.* He later acted in or directed more than fifty other movies.

H. G. Wells and Howard Koch were also important contributors to the radio drama you will read. Herbert George Wells was an English writer and philosopher. In addition to *War of the Worlds,* he wrote several science fiction novels, including *The Time Machine.* Playwright Howard Koch was born and raised in New York. In 1942 Koch received an Academy Award for his screenplay *Casablanca.* In the 1950s he moved to England, where he continued to write. Later he returned to the United States and taught screenwriting classes to college students.

## Lesson Preview

The lesson that follows the excerpt from *War of the Worlds* focuses on the elements of a radio drama. Like any other play, a radio play has a plot, characters, and a theme. What makes a radio play different from other plays is that it depends entirely on sound. The writer's words, the actors' voices, and the sound effects are the only means by which the audience learns what is happening.

The questions that follow will help you notice ways in which a radio play differs from a stage play. As you read, think about how you would answer these questions.

**1** How do you learn about the setting of the play? How do you know when the scenes change?

**2** What sound effects are used? What purposes do you think the various sound effects have?

**3** How does the suspense build in the play? How do you think the actors' voices sound as the suspense increases?

## Vocabulary

Here are some difficult words that appear in the selection that follows. Study the words and their definitions, as well as the sentences that show how the words are used. This will help you get the most from your reading.

**scrutinized** examined closely. *The surgeon scrutinized the patient's health records before prescribing a pain medication.*

**transient** passing quickly; temporary. *Highway motels cater to transient visitors who generally only stay there overnight.*

**complacence** self-satisfaction. *Sue's complacence about her scholarship award was annoying to all the other students who had applied for it.*

**ethereal** relating to the regions beyond the Earth. *Tom bought a telescope because he was interested in learning more about the ethereal regions beyond our atmosphere.*

**disillusionment** disenchantment; disappointment. *Her disillusionment with the organization stemmed from the petty jealousies of her coworkers.*

*Excerpt from*

# War of the Worlds

RADIO PLAY BY HOWARD KOCH
BASED ON THE NOVEL BY H. G. WELLS

## Characters

Announcer
Orson Welles
Announcer Three
Announcer Two
Carl Phillips
Professor Richard Pierson
Policeman
Mr. Wilmuth
Voices of the Crowd
Brigadier General Montgomery Smith
Mr. Harry McDonald
Captain Lansing

**Columbia Broadcasting System
Orson Welles and Mercury Theatre
On the Air
Sunday, October 30, 1938
8:00 to 9:00 P.M.**

*Cue: (Columbia Broadcasting System)*
*( . . . 30 seconds . . . . )*

**Announcer**  The Columbia Broadcasting System and its affiliated stations present Orson Welles and the Mercury Theatre on the Air in *War of the Worlds* by H. G. Wells.

*(Theme)*

**Announcer**  Ladies and gentlemen: the director of the Mercury Theatre and star of these broadcasts, Orson Welles. . . .

**Orson Welles**  We know now that in the early years of the twentieth century this world was being watched closely by intelligences greater than man's and yet as mortal as his own. We know now that as human beings busied themselves about their various concerns they were scrutinized and studied, perhaps almost as narrowly as a man with a microscope might scrutinize the transient creatures that swarm and multiply in a drop of water. With infinite complacence people went to and fro over the earth about their little affairs, serene in the assurance of their dominion over this small spinning fragment of solar driftwood which by chance or design man has inherited out of the dark mystery of Time and Space. Yet across an immense ethereal gulf, minds that are to our minds as ours are to the beasts in the jungle, intellects vast, cool and unsympathetic regarded this earth with envious eyes and slowly and surely drew their plans against us. In the thirty-ninth year of the twentieth century came the great disillusionment.

It was near the end of October. Business was better. The war scare was over. More men were back at work. Sales were picking up. On this particular evening, October 30, the Crossley service[1] estimated that thirty-two million people were listening in on radios.

**Announcer Cue**  . . . for the next twenty-four hours not much change in temperature. A slight atmospheric disturbance of undetermined origin is reported over Nova Scotia, causing a low pressure area to move down rather rapidly over the northeastern states, bringing a

---

1. **Crossley service:** a ratings company that regularly surveyed people to find out what programs they listened to.

forecast of rain, accompanied by winds of light gale force. Maximum temperature 66; minimum 48. This weather report comes to you from the Government Weather Bureau.

. . . We now take you to the Meridian Room in the Hotel Park Plaza in downtown New York, where you will be entertained by the music of Ramon Raquello and his orchestra.

*(Spanish theme song . . . fades)*

**Announcer Three**   Good evening, ladies and gentlemen. From the Meridian Room in the Park Plaza in New York City, we bring you the music of Ramon Raquello and his orchestra. With a touch of the Spanish, Ramon Raquello leads off with "La Cumparsita."

*(Piece starts playing)*

**Announcer Two**   Ladies and gentlemen, we interrupt our program of dance music to bring you a special bulletin from the Intercontinental Radio News. At twenty minutes before eight, central time, Professor Farrell of the Mount Jennings Observatory, Chicago, Illinois, reports observing several explosions of incandescent gas, occurring at regular intervals on the planet Mars.

The spectroscope indicates the gas to be hydrogen and moving towards the earth with enormous velocity. Professor Pierson of the observatory at Princeton confirms Farrell's observation, and describes the phenomenon as *(quote)* like a jet of blue flame shot from a gun *(unquote)*. We now return you to the music of Ramon Raquello, playing for you in the Meridian Room of the Park Plaza Hotel, situated in downtown New York.

*(Music plays for a few moments until piece ends. . . . sound of applause)*

Now a tune that never loses favor, the ever-popular "Star Dust." Ramon Raquello and his orchestra. . . .

*(Music)*

**Announcer Two**   Ladies and gentlemen, following on the news given in our bulletin a moment ago, the Government Meteorological Bureau has requested the large observatories of the country to keep an astronomical watch on any further disturbances occurring on the planet Mars. Due to the unusual nature of this occurrence, we have arranged an interview with the noted astronomer, Professor Pierson, who will give us his views on this event. In a few moments we will take you to the Princeton Observatory at Princeton, New Jersey. We return you until then to the music of Ramon Raquello and his orchestra.

*(Music)*

**Announcer Two**   We are ready now to take you to the Princeton Observatory at Princeton where Carl Phillips, our commentator, will interview Professor Richard Pierson, famous astronomer. We take you now to Princeton, New Jersey.

*(Echo chamber)*

**Phillips**   Good evening, ladies and gentlemen. This is Carl Phillips, speaking to you from the observatory at Princeton. I am standing in a large semicircular room, pitch black except for an oblong split in the ceiling. Through this opening I can see a sprinkling of stars that cast a kind of frosty glow over the intricate mechanism of the huge telescope. The ticking sound you hear is the vibration of the clockwork. Professor Pierson stands directly above me on a small platform, peering through the giant lens. I ask you to be patient, ladies and gentlemen, during any delay that may arise during our interview. Beside his ceaseless watch of the heavens, Professor Pierson may be interrupted by telephone or other communications. During this period he is in constant touch with the astronomical centers of the world. . . . Professor, may I begin our questions?

**Pierson**   At any time, Mr. Phillips.

**Phillips**   Professor, would you please tell our radio audience exactly what you see as you observe the planet Mars through your telescope?

**Pierson**   Nothing unusual at the moment, Mr. Phillips. A red disk swimming in a blue sea. Transverse[2] stripes across the disk. Quite distinct now because Mars happens to be at the point nearest the earth . . . in opposition, as we call it.

**Phillips**   In your opinion, what do these transverse stripes signify, Professor Pierson?

**Pierson**   Not canals, I can assure you, Mr. Phillips, although that's the popular conjecture of those who imagine Mars to be inhabited. From a scientific viewpoint the stripes are merely the result of atmospheric conditions peculiar to the planet.

**Phillips**   Then you're convinced as a scientist that living intelligence as we know it does not exist on Mars?

**Pierson**   I should say the chances against it are a thousand to one.

**Phillips**   And yet how do you account for these gas eruptions occurring on the surface of the planet at regular intervals?

**Pierson**   Mr. Phillips, I cannot account for it.

**Phillips**   By the way, Professor, for the benefit of our listeners, how far is Mars from the earth?

**Pierson**   Approximately forty million miles.

**Phillips**   Well, that seems a safe enough distance.

**Phillips**   Just a moment, ladies and gentlemen, someone has just handed Professor Pierson a message. While he reads it, let me remind you that we are speaking to you from the observatory in Princeton, New Jersey, where we are interviewing the world-famous astronomer, Professor Pierson. . . . One moment, please. Professor Pierson has passed me a message which he has just received. . . . Professor, may I read the message to the listening audience?

**Pierson**   Certainly, Mr. Phillips.

**Phillips**   Ladies and gentlemen, I shall read you a wire addressed to Professor Pierson from Dr. Gray of the National History Museum, New York. "9:15 P.M. eastern standard time. Seismograph[3] registered

---

**2. transverse:** crossing from side to side.   **3. seismograph:** an instrument that measures the strength of earthquakes.

shock of almost earthquake intensity occurring within a radius of twenty miles of Princeton. Please investigate. Signed, Lloyd Gray, Chief of Astronomical Division." . . . Professor Pierson, could this occurrence possibly have something to do with the disturbances observed on the planet Mars?

**Pierson**  Hardly, Mr. Phillips. This is probably a meteorite of unusual size and its arrival at this particular time is merely a coincidence. However, we shall conduct a search, as soon as daylight permits.

**Phillips**  Thank you, Professor. Ladies and gentlemen, for the past ten minutes we've been speaking to you from the observatory at Princeton, bringing you a special interview with Professor Pierson, noted astronomer. This is Carl Phillips speaking. We now return you to our New York studio.

*(Fade in piano playing)*

**Announcer Two**  Ladies and gentlemen, here is the latest bulletin from the Intercontinental Radio News. Toronto, Canada: Professor Morse of Macmillan University reports observing a total of three explosions on the planet Mars, between the hours 7:45 P.M. and 9:20 P.M., eastern standard time. This confirms earlier reports received from American observatories. Now, nearer home, comes a special announcement from Trenton, New Jersey. It is reported that at 8:50 P.M. a huge, flaming object, believed to be a meteorite, fell on a farm in the neighborhood of Grovers Mill, New Jersey, twenty-two miles from Trenton. The flash in the sky was visible within a radius of several hundred miles and the noise of the impact was heard as far north as Elizabeth.

We have dispatched a special mobile unit to the scene, and will have our commentator, Mr. Phillips, give you a word description as soon as he can reach there from Princeton. In the meantime, we take you to the Hotel Martinet in Brooklyn, where Bobby Millette and his orchestra are offering a program of dance music.

*(Swing band for 20 seconds . . . then cut)*

*The Radio Drama*

**Announcer Two**   We take you now to Grovers Mill, New Jersey.

*(Crowd noises . . . police sirens)*

**Phillips**   Ladies and gentlemen, this is Carl Phillips again, at the Wilmuth farm, Grovers Mill, New Jersey. Professor Pierson and myself made the eleven miles from Princeton in ten minutes. Well, I . . . I hardly know where to begin, to paint for you a word picture of the strange scene before my eyes, like something out of a modern Arabian Nights.[4] Well, I just got here. I haven't had a chance to look around yet. I guess that's *it*. Yes, I guess that's the . . . *thing*, directly in front of me, half buried in a vast pit. Must have struck with terrific force. The ground is covered with splinters of a tree it must have struck on its way down. What I can see of the . . . object itself doesn't look very much like a meteor, at least not the meteors I've seen. It looks more like a huge cylinder. It has a diameter of . . . what would you say, Professor Pierson?

**Pierson**   *(off)* About thirty yards.

**Phillips**   About thirty yards. . . . The metal on the sheath is . . . well, I've never seen anything like it. The color is sort of yellowish-white. Curious spectators now are pressing close to the object in spite of the efforts of the police to keep them back. They're getting in front of my line of vision. Would you mind standing on one side, please?

**Policeman**   One side, there, one side.

**Phillips**   While the policemen are pushing the crowd back, here's Mr. Wilmuth, owner of the farm here. He may have some interesting facts to add. . . . Mr. Wilmuth, would you please tell the radio audience as much as you remember of this rather unusual visitor that dropped in your backyard? Step closer, please. Ladies and gentlemen, this is Mr. Wilmuth.

**Wilmuth**   I was listenin' to the radio.

**Phillips**   Closer and louder, please.

**Wilmuth**   Pardon me!

---

4. **Arabian Nights:** a collection of fantastic adventure stories.

**Phillips** Louder, please, and closer.

**Wilmuth** Yes, sir—while I was listening to the radio and kinda drowsin,' that Professor fellow was talkin' about Mars, so I was half dozin' and half . . .

**Phillips** Yes, Mr. Wilmuth. Then what happened?

**Wilmuth** As I was sayin', I was listenin' to the radio kinda halfways . . .

**Phillips** Yes, Mr. Wilmuth, and then you saw something?

**Wilmuth** Not first off. I heard something.

**Phillips** And what did you hear?

**Wilmuth** A hissing sound. Like this: sssssssss . . . kinda like a fourt' of July rocket.

**Phillips** Then what?

**Wilmuth** Turned my head out the window and would have swore I was to sleep and dreamin.'

**Phillips** Yes?

**Wilmuth** I seen a kinda greenish streak and then zingo! Somethin' smacked the ground. Knocked me clear out of my chair!

**Phillips** Well, were you frightened, Mr. Wilmuth?

**Wilmuth** Well, I—I ain't quite sure. I reckon I—I was kinda riled.[5]

**Phillips** Thank you, Mr. Wilmuth. Thank you.

**Wilmuth** Want me to tell you some more?

**Phillips** No. . . . That's quite all right, that's plenty.

**Phillips** Ladies and gentlemen, you've just heard Mr. Wilmuth, owner of the farm where this thing has fallen. I wish I could convey the atmosphere . . . the background of this . . . fantastic scene. Hundreds of cars are parked in a field in back of us. Police are trying to rope off the roadway leading into the farm. But it's no use. They're breaking right through. Their headlights throw an enormous spot on the pit where the object's half-buried. Some of the more daring souls are venturing near the edge. Their silhouettes stand out against the metal sheen.

*(Faint humming sound)*

---

5. **riled:** irritated.

One man wants to touch the thing . . . he's having an argument with a policeman. The policeman wins. . . . Now, ladies and gentlemen, there's something I haven't mentioned in all this excitement, but it's becoming more distinct. Perhaps you've caught it already on your radio. Listen: *(Long pause)* . . . Do you hear it? It's a curious humming sound that seems to come from inside the object. I'll move the microphone nearer. Here. *(Pause)* Now we're not more than twenty-five feet away. Can you hear it now? Oh, Professor Pierson!

**Pierson**   Yes, Mr. Phillips?

**Phillips**   Can you tell us the meaning of that scraping noise inside the thing?

**Pierson**   Possibly the unequal cooling of its surface.

**Phillips**   Do you still think it's a meteor, Professor?

**Pierson**   I don't know what to think. The metal casing is definitely extra-terrestrial . . . not found on this earth. Friction with the earth's atmosphere usually tears holes in a meteorite. This thing is smooth and, as you can see, of cylindrical shape.

**Phillips**   Just a minute! Something's happening! Ladies and gentlemen, this is terrific! This end of the thing is beginning to flake off! The top is beginning to rotate like a screw! The thing must be hollow!

**Voices**   She's a movin'!
Look, the darn thing's unscrewing!
Keep back, there! Keep back, I tell you.
Maybe there's men in it trying to escape!
It's red hot, they'll burn to a cinder!
Keep back there! Keep those idiots back!

*(Suddenly the clanking sound of a huge piece of falling metal)*

**Voices**   She's off! The top's loose!
Look out there! Stand back!

**Phillips**   Ladies and gentlemen, this is the most terrifying thing I have ever witnessed. . . . Wait a minute! Someone's *crawling out of the hollow* *top.* Some one or . . . something. I can see peering out of that black hole two luminous disks . . . are they eyes? It might be a face. It might be. . . .

*(Shout of awe from the crowd)*

Good heavens, something's wriggling out of the shadow like a grey snake. Now it's another one, and another. They look like tentacles to me. There, I can see the thing's body. It's large as a bear and it glistens like wet leather. But that face. It . . . it's indescribable. I can hardly force myself to keep looking at it. The eyes are black and gleam like a serpent. The mouth is V-shaped with saliva dripping from its rimless lips that seem to quiver and pulsate. The monster or what-ever it is can hardly move. It seems weighed down by . . . possibly gravity or something. The thing's raising up. The crowd falls back. They've seen enough. This is the most extraordinary experience. I can't find words. . . . I'm pulling this microphone with me as I talk. I'll have to stop the description until I've taken a new position. Hold on, will you please, I'll be back in a minute.

*(Fade into piano)*

**Announcer Two**   We are bringing you an eyewitness account of what's happening on the Wilmuth farm, Grovers Mill, New Jersey.

*(More piano)*

We now return you to Carl Phillips at Grovers Mill.

**Phillips**   Ladies and gentlemen (Am I on?). Ladies and gentlemen, here I am, back of a stone wall that adjoins Mr. Wilmuth's garden. From here I get a sweep of the whole scene. I'll give you every detail as long as I can talk. As long as I can see. More state police have arrived. They're drawing up a cordon[6] in front of the pit, about thirty of them. No need to push the crowd back now. They're willing to keep their distance. The captain is conferring with

---

6. **cordon:** line of people or objects stationed around an area to guard it.

someone. We can't quite see who. Oh yes, I believe it's Professor Pierson. Yes, it is. Now they've parted. The professor moves around one side, studying the object, while the captain and two policemen advance with something in their hands. I can see it now. It's a white handkerchief tied to a pole . . . a flag of truce. If those creatures know what that means . . . what anything means! . . . *Wait!* Something's happening!

*(Hissing sound followed by a humming that increases in intensity)*

A humped shape is rising out of the pit. I can make out a small beam of light against a mirror. What's that? There's a jet of flame springing from that mirror, and it leaps right at the advancing men. It strikes them head on! Good Lord, they're turning into flame!

*(Screams and unearthly shrieks)*

Now the whole field's caught fire. *(Explosion.)* The woods . . . the barns . . . the gas tanks of automobiles . . . it's spreading everywhere. It's coming this way. About twenty yards to my right. . . .

*(Crash of microphone . . . then dead silence . . . )*

**Announcer Two**   Ladies and gentlemen, due to circumstances beyond our control, we are unable to continue the broadcast from Grovers Mill. Evidently there's some difficulty with our field transmission. However, we will return to that point at the earliest opportunity. In the meantime, we have a late bulletin from San Diego, California. Professor Indellkoffer, speaking at a dinner of the California Astronomical Society, expressed the opinion that the explosions on Mars are undoubtedly nothing more than severe volcanic disturbances on the surface of the planet. We continue now with our piano interlude.

*(Piano . . . then cut)*

Ladies and gentlemen, I have just been handed a message that came in from Grovers Mill by telephone. Just a moment. At least forty people, including six State Troopers lie dead in a field east of the village of Grovers Mill, their bodies burned and distorted beyond all possible recognition. The next voice you hear will be that of Brigadier General Montgomery Smith, commander of the State Militia at Trenton, New Jersey.

**Smith**  I have been requested by the governor of New Jersey to place the counties of Mercer and Middlesex as far west as Princeton, and east to Jamesburg, under martial law.[7] No one will be permitted to enter this area except by special pass issued by state or military authorities. Four companies of State Militia are proceeding from Trenton to Grovers Mill, and will aid in the evacuation of homes within the range of military operations. Thank you.

**Announcer**  You have just been listening to General Montgomery Smith commanding the State Militia at Trenton. In the meantime, further details of the catastrophe at Grovers Mill are coming in. The strange creatures after unleashing their deadly assault, crawled back in their pit and made no attempt to prevent the efforts of the firemen to recover the bodies and extinguish the fire. Combined fire departments of Mercer County are fighting the flames which menace the entire countryside.

We have been unable to establish any contact with our mobile unit at Grovers Mill, but we hope to be able to return you there at the earliest possible moment. In the meantime we take you—uh, just one moment please.

*(Long pause)*     *(Whisper)*

Ladies and gentlemen, I have just been informed that we have finally established communication with an eyewitness of the tragedy. Professor Pierson has been located at a farmhouse near Grovers Mill where he has established an emergency observation post. As a scientist,

---

**7. martial law:** temporary rule by the military, usually in time of war.

he will give you his explanation of the calamity. The next voice you hear will be that of Professor Pierson, brought to you by direct wire. Professor Pierson.

**Pierson**   Of the creatures in the rocket cylinder at Grovers Mill, I can give you no authoritative information—either as to their nature, their origin, or their purposes here on earth. Of their destructive instrument I might venture some conjectural[8] explanation. For want of a better term, I shall refer to the mysterious weapon as a heat-ray. It's all too evident that these creatures have scientific knowledge far in advance of our own. It is my guess that in some way they are able to generate an intense heat in a chamber of practically absolute nonconductivity. This intense heat they project in a parallel beam against any object they choose, by means of a polished parabolic[9] mirror of unknown composition, much as the mirror of a lighthouse projects a beam of light. That is my conjecture of the origin of the heat-ray. . . .

**Announcer Two**   Thank you, Professor Pierson. Ladies and gentlemen, here is a bulletin from Trenton. It is a brief statement informing us that the charred body of Carl Phillips has been identified in a Trenton Hospital. Now here's another bulletin from Washington, D.C.

Office of the director of the National Red Cross reports ten units of Red Cross emergency workers have been assigned to the headquarters of the State Militia stationed outside of Grovers Mill, New Jersey. Here's a bulletin from State Police, Princeton Junction: The fires at Grovers Mill and vicinity now under control. Scouts report all quiet in the pit, and no sign of life appearing from the mouth of the cylinder. . . . And now, ladies and gentlemen, we have a special statement from Mr. Harry McDonald, vice-president in charge of operations.

**McDonald**   We have received a request from the militia at Trenton to place at their disposal our entire broadcasting facilities. In view of

---

8. **conjectural:** based on guesses.   9. **parabolic:** curved.

the gravity of the situation, and believing that radio has a definite responsibility to serve in the public interest at all times, we are turning over our facilities to the State Militia at Trenton.

**Announcer**   We take you now to the field headquarters of the State Militia near Grovers Mill, New Jersey.

**Captain**   This is Captain Lansing of the Signal Corps, attached to the State Militia now engaged in military operations in the vicinity of Grovers Mill. Situation arising from the reported presence of certain individuals of unidentified nature, is now under complete control.

The cylindrical object which lies in a pit directly below our position is surrounded on all sides by eight battalions of infantry, without heavy fieldpieces,[10] but adequately armed with rifles and machine guns. All cause for alarm, if such cause ever existed, is now entirely unjustified. The things, whatever they are, do not even venture to poke their heads above the pit. I can see their hiding place plainly in the glare of the searchlights here. With all their reported resources, these creatures can scarcely stand up against heavy machine-gun fire. Anyway, it's an interesting outing for the troops. I can make out their khaki uniforms, crossing back and forth in front of the lights. It looks almost like a real war. There appears to be some slight smoke in the woods bordering the Millstone River. Probably fire started by campers. Well, we ought to see some action soon. One of the companies is deploying on the left flank. A quick thrust and it will all be over. Now wait a minute! I see something on top of the cylinder. No, it's nothing but a shadow. Now the troops are on the edge of the Wilmuth farm. Seven thousand armed men closing in on an old metal tube. Wait, that wasn't a shadow! It's something moving . . . solid metal . . . kind of a shield-like affair rising up out of the cylinder. . . . It's going higher and higher. Why, it's standing on legs . . . actually rearing up on a sort of metal framework. Now it's reaching above the trees and the searchlights are on it! Hold on!

---

10. **fieldpieces:** heavy artillery, such as cannon.

*The Radio Drama*

**Announcer Two**   Ladies and gentlemen, I have a grave announcement to make. Incredible as it may seem, both the observations of science and the evidence of our eyes lead to the inescapable assumption that those strange beings who landed in the Jersey farmlands tonight are the vanguard[11] of an invading army from the planet Mars. The battle which took place tonight at Grovers Mill has ended in one of the most startling defeats ever suffered by an army in modern times; seven thousand men armed with rifles and machine guns pitted against a single fighting machine of the invaders from Mars. One hundred and twenty known survivors. The rest strewn over the battle area from Grovers Mill to Plainsboro crushed and trampled to death under the metal feet of the monster, or burned to cinders by its heat-ray. The monster is now in control of the middle section of New Jersey and has effectively cut the state through its center. Communication lines are down from Pennsylvania to the Atlantic Ocean. Railroad tracks are torn and service from New York to Philadelphia discontinued except routing some of the trains through Allentown and Phoenixville. Highways to the north, south, and west are clogged with frantic human traffic. Police and army reserves are unable to control the mad flight. By morning the fugitives will have swelled Philadelphia, Camden and Trenton, it is estimated, to twice their normal population.

At this time martial law prevails throughout New Jersey and eastern Pennsylvania. We take you now to Washington for a special broadcast on the National Emergency . . . the Secretary of the Interior. . . .

> *Summary of the Remainder of the Play. After the speech by the Secretary of the Interior, various military announcements describe the disorderly retreat of the United States armed forces, chased by the invaders. An announcer, speaking from the roof of the broadcasting building, describes the approach of the Martians.*

---

11. **vanguard:** the part of an army that moves ahead of the main army.

*The population of New York flees. Many people dive into the East River to escape the invaders. Then the radio transmission suddenly stops.*

*After a pause, the broadcast begins again. Professor Pierson, who has been hiding in an abandoned house, narrates. He ventures into the open but finds the countryside deserted. He learns that the invaders have conquered the human race and plan to breed people as livestock.*

*Pierson makes his way to New York City, which is also deserted. In Central Park, however, he discovers the first dead Martians. He learns that the invaders are dying from a virus to which human beings are immune.*

# Reviewing the Selection

Answer each of the following questions without looking back at the play.

*Recalling Facts*

1. In this excerpt from the *War of the Worlds* radio broadcast, the audience hears all of the following *except*
   - ☐ a. a weather report.
   - ☐ b. the music of Ramon Raquello and his orchestra.
   - ☐ c. an interview with a well-known scientist.
   - ☐ d. the voices of the creatures from Mars.

*Understanding Main Ideas*

2. Orson Welles begins his broadcast with an introduction. In it he makes the point that
   - ☐ a. humans might someday travel in space.
   - ☐ b. scientists know about extraterrestrial life but most people do not.
   - ☐ c. outside the Earth exist creatures that are more intelligent than humans.
   - ☐ d. space travel will not be possible for at least another hundred years.

*Placing Events in Order*

3. The first news bulletin that suggests that something odd is happening is the
   - ☐ a. weather report.
   - ☐ b. information about explosions on Mars.
   - ☐ c. report of a strange flying ship.
   - ☐ d. firsthand report on the meteorite in New Jersey.

4. Which of these events lets the listeners know
   that *War of the Worlds* is not a real newscast?
   ☐ a. the report of explosions on Mars
   ☐ b. the interview with the professor
      at Princeton
   ☐ c. the introduction by Orson Welles
   ☐ d. the interview with Mr. Wilmuth

5. "The spectroscope indicates the gas to be
   hydrogen and moving towards the earth with
   enormous <u>velocity</u>." In this context *velocity*
   means
   ☐ a. speed.
   ☐ b. power.
   ☐ c. brilliance.
   ☐ d. winds.

## Interpreting the Selection

Answer each of the following questions. You may look back at the play
if necessary.

6. Many people listening to this broadcast
   believed that the Earth was being invaded
   by Martians. People probably felt that way
   because they
   ☐ a. were uneducated.
   ☐ b. believed whatever they heard on
      the radio.
   ☐ c. never read the newspapers.
   ☐ d. wanted to meet Martians.

*Generalizing*

7. The *War of the Worlds* broadcast takes advantage of the following feelings *except*
   ☐ a. fear of invasion.
   ☐ b. fear of the unknown.
   ☐ c. respect for religion.
   ☐ d. trust in scientific experts.

*Finding the Author's Purpose*

8. By writing this broadcast, Howard Koch probably wanted to
   ☐ a. entertain the audience.
   ☐ b. prove that Martians did exist.
   ☐ c. show the dangers faced by radio reporters.
   ☐ d. teach the audience about extraterrestrial life.

*Analyzing the Evidence*

9. The Martians seem to have landed in order to
   ☐ a. conquer the planet.
   ☐ b. negotiate with humans.
   ☐ c. refuel their ship.
   ☐ d. explore the planet.

*Drawing Conclusions*

10. The radio broadcast is narrated by a number of people in order to
    ☐ a. give work to more actors.
    ☐ b. confuse listeners about what is happening.
    ☐ c. make it sound more believable.
    ☐ d. show that everyone saw the Martians.

# The Radio Drama

The radio broadcast of *War of the Worlds* had a great impact on its audience. Although you have only read a part of the broadcast, perhaps you can understand why it sounded so real to listeners. Millions of people listened closely to the voices that carried into their own homes the news of the strange events. The voices sounded convincing, and people found themselves thinking that their own worst fears had come true. Of course, most radio broadcasts do not have such an unsettling effect. They do, however, force the listener to use his or her imagination to picture the events described in the broadcast.

Today, tapes of some old radio dramas are being replayed, and some new radio dramas are being aired. Such programs—both old and new—include family comedies, serious plays, and science fiction works such as Koch's adaptation of H. G. Wells's novel.

Radio plays are different from the plays that you have already read in this book. Unlike stage plays, which an audience watches *and* hears, a radio play can only be heard. A commentator once said that radio has "an audience of the blind." People listening to the radio are affected only by the words and sounds they hear. Listeners must rely on their imaginations to make those words and sounds come alive. In this lesson you will learn how an effective drama can be created for and presented on the radio.

# The Setting of a Radio Play

As you know, the setting of any play is the time and place of the action of a story. In a play setting also refers to the scenery onstage. The setting gives the audience a hint about what the play will be like.

The setting is usually established as soon as the curtain rises. If a play takes place in the 1990s, the setting will prepare you for how the characters might dress, how they will speak, and even what kinds of events may affect their lives. A setting in the 1890s or in ancient Rome will create different expectations. If you were seeing a performance of *Julius Caesar*, for example, the setting might include certain props, scenery, and costumes to suggest the time and place of the action.

Radio plays are different, of course. You see nothing. All the information comes to you through your ears. The setting must be suggested to you so that you can imagine the time and place of the action. A playwright creating a radio script could include a detailed description of the setting. But most radio dramas are quite short—only thirty or sixty minutes long. Therefore the writer would probably not want to spend a lot of time describing the setting.

In a radio play, as in other kinds of plays, the setting changes as the scenes change. The radio writer can only spend a few seconds letting you know the new time and place of the action.

In the radio broadcast of *War of the Worlds,* the setting changes frequently. A change in setting is signaled by dialogue, by narration, and by background sounds. The broadcast begins with the announcer giving information about the play. The station plays its theme, and the announcer introduces Orson Welles.

*1. When and where is this radio drama taking place? Review Orson Welles's long introduction. What details about the setting does he reveal?*

*2. What new setting does the announcer introduce after Welles's speech? What sounds suggest that setting?*

Early in this radio drama, you realize that Howard Koch has adapted *War of the Worlds* for radio in an unusual way. He has made it into a series of news broadcasts and announcements.

Several speakers are reporters or announcers. You have probably noticed that reporters and announcers on radio and television usually begin by telling the place from which they are speaking. So that Koch can easily establish each scene change, he has the speaker introduce the scene with an opening line that sounds natural. Read the first sentences of three opening scenes:

"From the Meridian Room in the Park Plaza . . ."

"This is Carl Phillips, speaking to you from the observatory at Princeton."

"Ladies and gentlemen, this is Carl Phillips again, at the Wilmuth farm, Grovers Mill, New Jersey."

Those bulletins give you only the barest idea of the setting. In many other places, however, you get a much more complete picture of the setting.

*3. Skim the play to find a detailed description of a scene. Who is giving the description? Why is he giving it? What effect do you think the description would have on an audience?*

## Sound Effects

Sound effects are the sounds called for in the script of a play, radio or television program, or motion picture. Sound effects can be used to give you a sense of place or to make a scene more realistic.

*4. Imagine a radio scene that takes place inside a railroad car on a moving train. What sound effects could be used to let the audience know where the scene is taking place?*

**Setting.** In a radio play sound effects remind the audience of the setting. A car horn lets you know that a scene is taking place on a street. In a restaurant scene you might hear the occasional clinking of glasses or plates. The sound of footsteps would tell you that the characters are walking as they talk.

Sound effects are important in a radio script. Koch's *War of the Worlds* has several examples.

*5. What sound effects are used to suggest the Meridian Room in the Park Plaza? Why do you think an echo chamber is used during the interview at Princeton University? What sound effects are used when Carl Phillips begins reporting from Grovers Mill?*

**Suspense.** In addition to letting you picture the setting, sound effects serve another purpose in this drama: They contribute to the mood and the suspense. The feeling of uncertainty and tension builds gradually in the play. At the beginning, the broadcast seems unthreatening. Orson Welles's introduction hints of disillusionment but he ends his introduction on a calm note. He explains that life is improving for most people.

The broadcast shifts to a weather report and then to dance music. The dance music program is interrupted for a special bulletin about explosions on Mars. That announcement is followed by Carl Phillips's interview with Professor Pierson. The scientist speaks with the calm, authoritative voice of an expert.

When the scene switches to Grovers Mill, however, the tension begins to build. Phillips describes an unusual sight:

> Well, I . . . I hardly know where to begin, to paint for you a word picture of the strange scene before my eyes, like something out of a modern Arabian Nights.

Even though Phillips tries to remain calm and professional, he is clearly unsettled.

*6. Make a list of the various sound effects behind Phillips's report from Grovers Mill. How do they make the scene more realistic? How do they contribute to the suspense?*

## Radio Acting

A radio drama is made believable by the way the actors deliver their lines. The actors must play their parts as realistically as possible. In most stage productions, actors use more than just their voices to create characters. They use costumes, body movements, gestures, and facial expressions to bring their characters to life onstage. In radio plays, however, the actors face the same limitations that radio scriptwriters do. They can only use sound. How, then, do they create effective characters?

The first task of any actor is to develop a character's personality from the written dialogue. The actor's second task is to convey the character's personality to the audience. For a radio actor, that can be done only by speaking the lines.

To help the actors, a good writer will create dialogue that hints at a character's personality. For example, read the dialogue of Professor Pierson. He is a scientist who is speaking about his special field.

*7. How do you think the actor portraying Pierson would sound? How do Pierson's answers to the reporter's questions give you a clue to the way the professor might speak on the air?*

The actor playing Pierson would study the scientist's lines to get an idea of the kind of man Pierson is, at least in public. Then the actor would have to decide how to let the audience "see" Pierson. He would have to decide how loud Pierson's voice should be. How fast should he speak? Should his voice be high-pitched or low-pitched? A talented actor would make listeners believe that they were actually hearing the voice of Professor Pierson, a world-famous astronomer.

Radio actors have only one tool for conveying a character's personality to an audience. Through their voices, actors let the audience know if the characters are strong or weak, happy or sad, certain or unsure. The actors must use pauses, loudness, and pitch to emphasize the feeling behind their character's lines.

*8. Read aloud Phillips's report from the moment the top of the capsule opens to his last words before the microphone crashes (pages 308 to 310). Imagine what his voice would sound like. Make a list of the emotions Phillips probably felt. How do you think the actor playing Phillips would convey the reporter's emotions to radio listeners?*

During the days when radio dramas were very popular, some actors played several characters in the same play. Some even played both characters in conversation.

9. *Suppose the actor who played Phillips was also the second announcer. Describe how the actor would have to change his voice to go from one character to the other.*

## Audience Involvement

Radio drama demands more of the audience than other plays do. It requires an audience to use its imagination. In a radio play the writer develops a plot and gives the audience a sense of the characters through the dialogue. The actors add to the image of the characters by the way they speak their lines. Each listener, however, must fill in all the visual details. On the basis of what they hear, listeners must imagine the setting, clothing, physical appearance, facial expressions, and actions of the characters.

10. *Reread Captain Lansing's report at the end of the excerpt. In your own words, describe the scene you imagine as you read the report.*

## Questions for Thought and Discussion

The questions and activities that follow will help you explore the excerpt from *War of the Worlds* in more depth and at the same time develop your critical thinking skills.

1. **Evaluating.** Would this broadcast of *War of the Worlds* be as effective today as it was in 1938? Would some people believe that it was a real newscast? Give reasons for your answers.

2. **Analyzing the Uses of Radio.** What makes this broadcast of *War of the Worlds* a convincing newscast? Which parts did you think were most effective? Why? Do you think it would make a good television play? Why or why not?

3. **Interpreting.** In small groups write a description of the creatures that came out of the spacecraft. Do not look back at the play. Compare your description with those of the other groups. Then reread Phillips's

description of the creatures. Finally, make a list of the features that appeared in your description but not in the play. Discuss why you included those features.

4. **Recognizing Humor.** Although this radio drama is organized like a serious news broadcast, it has elements of humor. What parts of the play did you find amusing? Why?

## Writing About Literature

Several suggestions for writing projects are given below. You may be asked to complete one or more of these projects. If you have any questions about how to begin a writing assignment, review Using the Writing Process, beginning on page 385.

1. **Describing a Place or an Object.** An announcer in *War of the Worlds* says he will try to paint a "word picture" for his listeners. Choose a place or an object that you know well. Paint a word picture of it for someone who has never seen the place or object.

2. **Creating a News Report.** You have probably heard hundreds, maybe even thousands, of newscasts in your life. The *War of the Worlds* broadcast is effective in part because it makes use of your familiarity with the language of newscasts. Create a fake news report about any topic. You may invent an incident or use some actual event. Your report may be serious or funny, realistic or fantastic.

3. **Reporting on Research.** People are fascinated with the idea of intelligent life in space. Use library sources, including books, newspapers, and magazines, to prepare a short report on *one* of the following topics: (a) Can Mars support life? (b) Have UFOs (unidentified flying objects) ever actually landed on Earth?

## Chapter 9

**Selection**

*Excerpt from*
## The Death of Billy the Kid
GORE VIDAL

**Lesson**

*The Television Play*

❖

## About the Selection

In the days of William Shakespeare, English audiences were fascinated by the great figures of Roman history, such as Julius Caesar and Mark Antony. Since the late 1800s, audiences in the United States have been just as fascinated by the famous outlaws and lawmen of the Old West.

Billy the Kid was one of those legendary figures. Like Jesse James, Wyatt Earp, and Butch Cassidy, Billy the Kid became the subject of many fantastic stories. Although he was wanted for murder, he was often thought of as a hero.

Even the true story of Billy the Kid is surrounded by legend. His real name was Henry McCarty, although he later called himself William Bonney. He was born in New York City in 1859. He and his mother moved to New Mexico when Billy was very young. Billy's mother died in 1874, leaving the boy a homeless orphan. Young Billy survived, living mostly in alleys and barrooms. During those years he acquired his nickname, Billy the Kid. Despite his youth, Billy soon earned his reputation as a killer after he shot a man in a barroom fight. In the excerpt from the play that you will read, Billy is said to have killed his first man at the age of twelve. Researchers, however, are not sure whether or not that story is really true.

According to legend, Billy stole cattle, robbed banks and trains, and murdered twenty-one men. Although the legend has been exaggerated, he did kill seven or eight men, and he was charged with three murders. Most of the killings occurred during the range wars in New Mexico. During that period, wealthy ranchers fought one another over cattle rights and property lines. These ranchers often hired gunmen, such as Billy and his friend Pat Garrett, to do the fighting for them.

When the range wars ended, Pat Garrett was elected sheriff of Lincoln County, New Mexico. He then had the job of hunting down his old friend. In 1880 Garrett captured Billy the Kid, but the young outlaw killed two prison guards and escaped. In 1881 Garrett caught up with Billy in Fort Sumner, New Mexico, and killed him. Billy was only twenty-two years old.

The violent, colorful stories of the western frontier have long provided material for writers. When Gore Vidal wrote *The Death of Billy the Kid*, he was not trying to add to the legend of the young outlaw. Rather, he was interested in the character of Billy. He wanted his play to explore what the real Billy the Kid was like. Although you will only read Act 1 of Vidal's play, you can begin to understand what the playwright thought of Billy.

Gore Vidal was born in West Point, New York, in 1925. At the age of nineteen he published his first novel, *Williwaw*. In the late 1940s Vidal wrote and sold several plays to television producers.

At the time, many theater people looked down on television productions. Because television plays were performed before a camera, they were considered to be more like movies than like stage plays. Many young writers, directors, and actors, however, saw television as a medium in which they could make a name for themselves. Vidal was among the most successful of these young artists.

*The Death of Billy the Kid* is a play written for television in the days before videotape existed. As a result, the play was broadcast live. The audience saw the performance as it was being acted on the studio stage.

Since the 1940s, television has become more sophisticated. This play, however, is an excellent example of a character study written in the early days of television.

## Lesson Preview

The lesson that follows *The Death of Billy the Kid* focuses on the elements of a television play. A television play is a drama written expressly for television. It is not a stage play adapted for television or a movie shown on television. As you have learned, early television plays were broadcast live. Today, fewer plays are written for TV. What was once a television play is now a made-for-television movie. Such movies are videotaped to include scenes such as car chases and airplane travel. The action in *The Death of Billy the Kid*, however, was limited to what could be broadcast from a studio.

Like any other play, a television play has a plot, characters, dialogue, and themes. A television play also has elements unique to the medium. Those unique elements affect both the production of the play and the performances of the actors.

A television script contains <u>technical directions</u>—instructions telling the camera crew, sound crew, and actors how the scenes and sounds should be presented to the viewers. Learn the meaning of the following terms so that you can understand how they affect the play.

**fade in**   cause an image to gradually appear and fill a previously blank screen. This technique is often used to begin a scene.

**fade out**   cause an image to gradually disappear from the screen, leaving the screen blank for a few seconds. This technique is often used to end a scene.

**dissolve to**   cause an image to gradually disappear while having another image slowly replace it. This technique is often used to accomplish a change of scene or to indicate the passage of time.

**cut to**   switch abruptly from one scene to another. The first image disappears suddenly from the screen and is immediately replaced by a new image. This technique is often used to show different parts of the same setting during a scene, or to show the scene from different angles.

**superimpose**   place one image over another so that both images appear on the screen at the same time. This technique is often used to show titles or other printed information against the background action of a scene.

**montage**   a series of rapidly changing images appearing one after another. This technique is often used to show a series of events that happen between one scene of a movie and the next.

The questions that follow will help you notice some ways in which a television play differs from a stage play or a radio play. As you read, think about how you would answer these questions.

**1** What different settings do you see in Act 1 of *The Death of Billy the Kid?*

**2** When the setting or location changes, what does the audience see on the screen?

**3** What kinds of instructions does the playwright give for televising this play?

**4** What kind of person is Billy? Who are the other major characters? How are they similar to or different from Billy?

**Note:**  The selection in this chapter does not have difficult vocabulary.

*Excerpt from*

# The Death of Billy the Kid

## ACT 1

Gore Vidal

### Characters

Billy the Kid
Pat Garrett
John Poe
Charlie Bowdre
Saval Guiterrez
Celsa Guiterrez
Pete Maxwell
General Lew Wallace
Joe Grant
A Drunk

*Fade in on a saloon in Ft. Sumner, New Mexico; the year is 1878. In the room—a bar, tables, a pool table—are* **Charlie Bowdre**, *a young outlaw;* **Saval Guiterrez**, *an older resident of the town;* **Joe Grant**, *a heavy-drinking, boastful man; and* **A Drunk** *whose name no one knows. The* **Drunk** *stands nearest the door; he has cadged[1] all the drinks he can from the three men. Sadly, he waits for a newcomer.*

---

**1. cadged:** begged.

**Grant**   I tell you one thing: the governor'll have Billy teaching Sunday School when he gets through with him, and that's the truth.

**Charlie**   Not Billy. He's got a long memory.

**Saval**   But the fighting's over now. McSween is dead. Nothing will bring him back, or any of the others gone. *(Proposing toast)* Well, Charlie . . . Joe, here's to peace in Lincoln County.

**Charlie**   No more Murphys fighting McSweens.

**Grant**   In fact there ain't no more Murphys and McSweens to speak of.

**Saval**   No, nor a lot of others just as fine.

(**Pat Garrett**, *a tall, slow man, a former gunfighter and rancher, enters.*)

**Charlie**   Hey, Pat Garrett. Come on over . . . have a drink.

**Garrett**   Thank you. Hello, Charlie, Saval . . . Joe. Billy showed up yet?

**Charlie**   He's on his way. You heard the news?

**Garrett**   *(nods)* I heard.

**Saval**   Our Billy's a big man now with Governor Wallace himself begging to talk to him. Pete Maxwell just brought Billy the message. The governor's at Lincoln now, waiting on him.

**Garrett**   Bill going to see him?

**Charlie**   He ain't said.

**Saval**   Just think! The governor's at Lincoln, waiting on him.

**Grant**   Well, it's luck, that's all . . . him so famous when there's a hundred men in the Territory shoot better than him. Men too . . . not green boys.

**Charlie**   Don't let Billy hear you talk that way.

**Grant**   I talked that way before he was born, and that's the truth. I got no fear of boys.

**Charlie**   Joe Grant's drinking a lot.

**Saval**   What you doing next, Pat?

**Garrett**   Don't know. Maybe start ranching again.

**Charlie**   Going to be dull with no fighting in Lincoln County.

**Garrett**   I don't mind one bit. Just as long as I find me a way to live.

**Grant**   *(bitterly)* The best shot in the Territory! And all them stories back East about Billy the Kid: made-up stories, that's what they are! Just because he got luck, because he's shot with it[2] like gold in a hill.

**Charlie**   Keep dreaming, Joe Grant, keep drinking and dreaming . . .

**Grant**   I ain't drunk.

*(Cut to door as* **Billy***, a blond youth wearing a Mexican sombrero, enters. The* **Drunk** *approaches him.)*

**Drunk**   Good evening, Mr. Bonney. I am a senior citizen of this Territory and an admirer of yours, Mr. Bonney, a great admirer. Will you pause for one instant in eternity . . . *(***Billy** *hands him a coin.)* Thank you, Mr. Bonney.

**Billy**   Hello, Pat.

**Garrett**   Hi, Billy.

**Saval**   You been with ladies?

**Grant**   *(sneering)* Drinking tea with ladies . . .

**Garrett**   That's just what he was doing, drinking tea with my cousin Maria.

**Billy**   That's right, Pat. I was with Maria, rocking on the porch.

**Grant**   Rocking on the porch, playing house . . .

**Charlie**   *(to* **Billy***)* The boys are collecting,[3] like you wanted.

**Billy**   You joining us, Pat?

**Garrett**   Stealing cattle?

**Billy**   Stealing? No, we just pick up these stray heifers[4] and we take them down to Old Mexico to sell. Come on with us. You're the best gun in the Territory.

**Garrett**   Second best.

**Billy**   *(smiles)* I won't dispute your word.

*(***Billy** *crosses to the pool table, starts to play.)*

---

**2. shot with it:** filled with it.   **3. collecting:** getting together.   **4. heifers:** young cows.

**Garrett**   What are you gonna do when you see the governor?

**Billy**   I just want to look at him. You know, he's a real general from the war.[5] I never saw a general.

**Garrett**   Never saw a governor either.

**Billy**   I don't care about them, but a general, now that's something, fighting them Johnny Rebs[6] down there.

**Garrett**   You were born the wrong time, Kid.

**Billy**   Well, I was born. That's the most a man can ask. You join us, Pat?

**Garrett**   No, Billy. I'm sick of trouble.

**Billy**   We going to miss you.

(**Joe Grant** *suddenly approaches from the bar.*)

**Grant**   Billy! I make you a bet.

**Billy**   What's that?

**Grant**   I bet I kill a man tonight before you do.

**Billy**   Who's talking about killing tonight? We're all friends, ain't we?

**Grant**   *(producing money)* Twenty-five dollars. Here it is. Now you put up, Billy, unless you're afraid of losing. Saval, you're the nearest one to an honest man. You hold the stakes.

**Saval**   Now, no trouble, please. Joe, forget this bet, eh?

**Grant**   Forget this bet? Not with these odds. Why, look at me: betting with the Kid himself, the famous Kid, so famous there's a price on his head.

**Charlie**   You drinking too much, Joe Grant. You starting to dream again.

**Billy**   *(softly)* I'll bet, if it makes you happy. Let me see what kind of gun you got.

**Grant**   *(hands over pistol)* This old gun's the last thing many a man saw, and that's the truth.

**Billy**   It's real fancy. Real fancy. Covered with pearl, too. I like things covered with pearl.

---

**5. war:** the Civil War, 1861–65.   **6. Johnny Rebs:** soldiers of the Confederate Army in the Civil War.

*(While **Billy** examines it, he opens the chamber and, unobserved, slips out two cartridges.)*

**Charlie**   Watch out for him, Billy. He's in a mean mood. He's all likkered up.[7]

**Billy**   I'll watch out, Charlie. *(**Billy** returns the gun.)* I'll bet you already got somebody picked out, Joe.

*(**Billy** crosses to pool table. When **Billy's** back is to him, **Grant**, with a sudden shout, takes aim and fires, but there is only an empty click. **Billy** turns and slowly, with one easy gesture, shoots him. **Grant** falls. There is silence in the saloon. No one moves.)*

**Charlie**   He was wanting the reward on your head.

*(**Saval**, without a word, puts the money, the stakes, on the pool table.)*

**Garrett**   Good thing his gun jammed.

**Billy**   Thank you, Pat. *(He opens his right hand and shows the cartridges. He grins.)*

**Garrett**   That's a good trick! You couldn't lend me a bit of that betting money, could you? I'm broke again.

**Billy**   Sure. Take it all.

**Garrett**   *(collecting money)* That Joe Grant was one precious fool.

**Billy**   *(smiles)* And that's the truth.

*Dissolve to the courthouse room at Lincoln: a table, two chairs, a portait of Lincoln, two windows and a door. **General Lew Wallace**, U.S. **Marshall Poe** and **Pete Maxwell**, a middle-aged friend of **Billy's**, are there. It is noon the next day. **Poe** is at the window. There is a sound of horse's hoofs.*

**Wallace**   Is that he, Mr. Poe?

*(**Poe** looks out window.)*

---

7. **all likkered up:** drunk.

**Poe**   Yes, General, that's him, riding down the street of Lincoln with his gun on his knee.

*(**Wallace** and **Maxwell** join **Poe** at the window.)*

**Wallace**   He' so young . . .

**Poe**   That trigger finger ain't young.

**Maxwell**   You notice, General, there's no one in the street when Billy rides through town. . . . I'd better go bring him up.

**Wallace**   All right, Mr. Maxwell.

*(**Poe** starts to follow him.)*

**Maxwell**   *(stops him)* I think it would be wise for Billy to see a friendly face first. Don't you agree, Mr. Poe?

*(**Poe** nods and turns back into room, but **Billy** is already at the door.)*

**Maxwell**   Hello, Billy.

**Billy**   Hello, Pete. *(To **Poe**)* You the general?

**Maxwell**   No, Billy, that's John Poe, the U.S. Marshal. *(Leads him to* **Wallace***)* This is the governor, General Lew Wallace. William Bonney, General.

**Billy**   Hello, General.

**Wallace**   Mr. Bonney, you . . . you're not what I thought.

**Billy**   Well, I left my horns and my tail up in Ft. Sumner.

**Wallace**   Will you excuse us, gentlemen? *(**Maxwell** and **Poe** leave.)* Sit down. I've heard a lot about you, Billy. The whole country has. The President and I had a long talk about you before I came West.

**Billy**   Were you a general of cavalry or foot?

**Wallace**   Both. I commanded a division at Shiloh.[8]

**Billy**   *(nods)* And you saved Cincinnati from the Rebels. I heard tell about you, and about the war.

**Wallace**   Sit down, Billy. *(Both sit.)* Where were you born?

**Billy**   New York City.

---

8. **Shiloh:** the scene of a famous Civil War battle.

**Wallace**   You came West with your mother when you were a boy. You killed your first man on her account when you were twelve years old.

**Billy**   *(smiles)* I guess we both heard about each other.

**Wallace**   Yes, most everyone's heard of Billy the Kid.

**Billy**   Not all of it's true.

**Wallace**   How many men have you killed?

**Billy**   Maybe twenty. How many men you killed, General?

**Wallace**   That was war.

**Billy**   This is war, too.

**Wallace**   It was, but it's over now and we're offering amnesty for everyone involved in the McSween-Murphy dispute. I want this to be a peaceful territory.

**Billy**   I'm sure it will be, General.

**Wallace**   Then you'll help us? You'll settle down?

**Billy**   No, sir, I will not. Why, you know what'd happen to me if I put this gun down? I'd be killed in a day. You watched me riding down that street—I saw you in the window—well, there were guns in windows and doors all up and down that street, just waiting for me to look away.

**Wallace**   But if you were to change?

**Billy**   They'd kill me just as dead.

**Wallace**   You could go West, to California. Start over: a new life, where no one knows you.

**Billy**   Would *you* start a new life where no one knows you? No, this is where I'll live as long as I live.

**Wallace**   You know you can't stand up to all of us. You have no chance. One man's too small, even Billy the Kid.

**Billy**   I never planned on a long life. One day I'll be too slow or there'll be too many . . . but between now and that day I'll live the way I like.

**Wallace**   You were fond of McSween, weren't you, Billy? Well, he was an honest man, a brave one.

**Billy**   McSween's dead. So are the men who killed him.

**Wallace**   I am told he regarded you as his son.

**Billy**   Well, I'm an orphan now, General. Sad, ain't it?

**Wallace**   (*officially*) William Bonney, do you accept the amnesty offered all who were involved in the Lincoln County cattle war with the understanding you cease violence and obey the law of the United States?

**Billy**   No, sir.

**Wallace**   Are we to be enemies?

**Billy**   I don't see why. I leave you alone in Santa Fe. You leave me be in Lincoln County. (**Wallace** *doesn't answer.*) Well, I guess I better be going now.

**Wallace**   I wish you would help me.

**Billy**   (*pauses at door*) You know . . . it ain't such a long way, General, from here to Shiloh.

**Wallace**   The distance is no greater than a man's honor.

(**Billy** *looks at him with disgust; then he goes.* **Maxwell** *and* **Poe** *return.*)

**Maxwell**   Well, Governor?

**Wallace**   He refuses.

**Maxwell**   I told you he would.

**Wallace**   We'll need a new sheriff down here. Whom do you propose?

**Maxwell**   Pat Garrett.

**Poe**   Isn't he a friend of Billy's?

**Maxwell**   We're all friends, but Pat wants a job, and Pat's a great fighter: he's cold, he's hard . . . he's a rock.

**Wallace**   Would he shoot his friend if the law required it?

**Maxwell**   Yes, Pat would.

**Wallace**   Send him to me in Santa Fe.

(*He crosses to window. During this we hear horse's hoofs retreating.*)

**Wallace**   (*softly*) What a man that boy could be.

*Montage:* **Billy** *firing.* **Pat Garrett** *in pursuit. The dates 1878, 1879, 1880 are superimposed in quick succession.*

*Dissolve to the kitchen of* **Saval Guiterrez's** *house in Ft. Sumner.* **Saval** *and his young wife* **Celsa** *sit at dinner as* **Pete Maxwell** *enters excitedly.*

**Maxwell**   Saval! Saval! Saval, they've got him trapped!
**Saval**   Got who?
**Celsa**   Billy.
**Maxwell**   The Kid. Pat Garrett and his men got Billy holed up in an old cabin at Stinking Spring.
**Saval**   As long as he's *in* the cabin they haven't caught him yet.
**Maxwell**   He'll never escape. Not now. And they'll hang him for sure.
**Saval**   Are you glad, Pete?
**Maxwell**   *(startled)* Glad? No, no, I guess I'm not. Relieved, but not glad. It's like killing a fine hawk who's been raiding your chickens. . . .
**Celsa**   *(nods)* He *is* like a bird, like a hawk.

*Dissolve to* **Garrett** *and* **Poe** *and two men outdoors; it is a moonlit night. All are armed.*

**Poe**   How many do you think there are, Pat?
**Garrett**   Four, maybe five.
**Poe**   *(nervously)* We ought to send for more men. We ain't got enough.
**Garrett**   We got as many as they got, Poe.
**Poe**   I know, but *he's* in there.
**Garrett**   I can handle Billy.
**Poe**   *(nervously)* I'm sure you can, Sheriff. I'm sure you can.
**Garrett**   You been reading those storybooks about him? The ones they print back East?
**Poe**   No, but I just hope you know what you're doing, Pat.
**Garrett**   I make you a promise. We'll go back to Lincoln with Billy tomorrow—maybe alive, maybe dead—but we'll have that boy slung over a saddle.

*Dissolve to interior of the cabin.* **Charlie Bowdre** *is at one window,* **Billy** *at another. Two other men keep watch.*

**Charlie**   Wish we had a fire going in here. Billy, I'm half froze.

**Billy**   *(grimly)* If I know Pat, we'll be plenty warm soon.

**Charlie**   You think he'll set us afire?

**Billy**   If we let him get near enough he will.

**Charlie**   My hands are turning blue. *(Beat[9])* Billy.

**Billy**   Yes, Charlie.

**Charlie**   What chance we got?

**Billy**   No chance at all I can see.

**Charlie**   Think we ought to give up?

**Billy**   And go back to Lincoln and get hung?

**Charlie**   *(shudders)* It's going to be a long, cold night. Wonder how many of 'em there are?

**Billy**   Enough. *(To one of the men)* You see anything?

**Man**   No.

**Charlie**   Billy.

**Billy**   Yes?

**Charlie**   You know what day this is?

**Billy**   I don't keep no track of days, Charlie.

**Charlie**   Well, it's Christmas.

**Billy**   Yes, Charlie.

**Charlie**   Well, don't you know about Christmas?

**Billy**   Yes, I heard tell, Charlie. Keep your eye on what you're doing.

**Charlie**   When I was a kid we always had a big dinner come Christmas Day. That was on a farm where we lived, nine of us kids, in the South before the war, before we moved West. . . .

**Billy**   Charlie, watch what you're doing. There's men moving around out there. They can see you.

**Charlie**   So every Christmas—this is before we came West from Carolina—well, we would all get together just about this time . . .

---

9. *Beat:* pause.

*(A pistol shot. **Charlie** gasps and falls. **Billy** crosses to him.)*

**Billy**   Charlie, I told you . . . now look! You gone and got yourself killed!

**Charlie**   Help me up, Billy. Help me up.

**Billy**   What for, Charlie?

**Charlie**   Help me, Billy.

**Billy**   There's no point.

**Charlie**   For the love of God, Billy, help me! Let me stand up. I'll be all right standing up. Nobody dies standing up. Billy, Billy, please.

**Billy**   All right.

*(He helps **Bowdre** to his feet. He puts a gun in his hand and leads him to the door.)*

**Billy**   *(carefully)* You're going to help me, Charlie. You're going out there, firing, and you're going to run and you're going to keep running . . .

**Charlie**   Keep ahold of me, Billy. I'm going to fall.

**Billy**   You hear me now? You keep running. You keep firing. *(He opens door.)*

**Charlie**   Billy, don't let go of me. Please!

**Billy**   Good-by, Charlie.

*(He shoves **Bowdre** out into the night and slams the door. Two gun shots.)*

**Billy**   *(disgustedly)* He just stood there.

Cut to **Garrett** and **Poe.**

**Poe**   Which one was it?

**Garrett**   Charlie Bowdre, old friend of mine . . . a good boy.

**Poe**   It must be hard for you, hunting down old friends.

**Garrett**   They'd do the same to me in my place.

**Poe**   It's a cold night. Think we could have a fire?

**Garrett**   No fire till we set the cabin going. *(Shouts)* Billy, you ready to come out?

**Poe**   He'll never budge.

**Garrett**   We'll give him a little while longer. We'll pick off a few more of the gang. None of them's going to slip away in all this moon.

*Cut to cabin.* **Billy** *is at the window. Beside him is one of his men.*

**Man**   What do we do now, Billy?

**Billy**   Wait.

**Man**   They got us holed up proper.

**Billy**   *(softly)* How I'd love to get me a bead on[10] Pat Garrett. He knows me too well. Oh, Pat, you hold out a little longer, keep the fire off us and when that moon sets . . .

**Garrett**   *(offstage)* We're setting fire to you, Billy! Come on out!

*(***Billy*** *looks at the others.)*

*Cut to* **Pat** *and his men as the cabin door opens and* **Billy's** *two men step out. They are led away. Then* **Garrett** *goes cautiously to the door as* **Billy** *appears, smiling.*

**Billy**   Hi, Pat.

**Garrett**   Hi, Billy.

**Billy**   How you been, Pat?

**Garrett**   Pretty good. Except when *you* worried me.

**Billy**   Like the new job?

**Garrett**   I like being sheriff.

**Billy**   The pay pretty good?

**Garrett**   Good enough.

**Billy**   Then maybe you can pay me back that fifty dollars you borrowed in Ft. Sumner.

**Garrett**   *(nods)* I owe you money. I aim to pay you back.

**Billy**   Well, we'll be seeing a lot of each other, I guess.

**Garrett**   For a while.

**Billy**   Then what?

---

10. **get me a bead on:** line up in my gun sights.

**Garrett**   They'll put you on trial in Lincoln.

**Billy**   Then what?

**Garrett**   Then they'll hang you, Billy.

**Billy**   *(softly)* No, no, Pat. You ain't going to *hang* me.

*Fade out on **Billy's** face, still smiling.*

> ***Summary of the Remainder of the Play.*** *Act 2 opens with Billy in prison in Lincoln. He is scheduled to be hanged in a week. Suddenly he disarms and kills his guards. Billy then escapes and makes his way to Saval's house in Fort Sumner. He wants to stay there until Maria Gonzalez, the woman he loves, returns from Santa Fe. However, Pat Garrett is on Billy's trail, and he soon arrives in Fort Sumner. Billy visits the local bar, where he is recognized by the drunk, who betrays his presence in town to Pat Garrett.*
>
> *In Act 3, Garrett questions Saval and his wife, Celsa, but they do not reveal Billy's whereabouts. Pete Maxwell urges Billy to leave the country, but Billy refuses. That night, as Billy approaches Maxwell's house, Pat Garrett shoots and kills him.*

# Reviewing the Selection

Answer each of the following questions without looking back at the play.

*Recalling Facts*

1. When the governor meets with Billy the Kid, he
   - ☐ a. threatens to hang Billy.
   - ☐ b. asks Billy to become sheriff.
   - ☐ c. tells Billy how many men were killed in the war.
   - ☐ d. offers Billy the chance to start a new life.

*Understanding Main Ideas*

2. Gore Vidal would most likely describe Billy the Kid as
   - ☐ a. fearless.
   - ☐ b. amusing.
   - ☐ c. kind.
   - ☐ d. loyal.

*Placing Events in Order*

3. Which of the following events happens first?
   - ☐ a. Pat Garrett is elected sheriff.
   - ☐ b. Billy meets General Lew Wallace.
   - ☐ c. Billy sends Charlie Bowdre out to face the lawmen.
   - ☐ d. Billy shoots Joe Grant.

*Finding Supporting Details*

4. Billy is called the Kid because he
   - ☐ a. is young.
   - ☐ b. likes to make jokes.
   - ☐ c. is shorter than most men.
   - ☐ d. treats adults like children.

5. "It was, but it's over now and we're offering <u>amnesty</u> for everyone involved in the McSween-Murphy dispute." In this context *amnesty* means
   - ☐ a. a reward.
   - ☐ b. a pardon.
   - ☐ c. freedom.
   - ☐ d. land.

## Interpreting the Selection

Answer each of the following questions. You may look back at the play if necessary.

6. Billy probably avoids discussing McSween with General Wallace because
   - ☐ a. he hated McSween.
   - ☐ b. McSween had betrayed him.
   - ☐ c. he regarded McSween's death as something long past.
   - ☐ d. McSween had opposed his friendship with Maria.

7. Which of the following statements best describes Billy's attitude toward death?
   - ☐ a. He is afraid of dying.
   - ☐ b. He knows he will live to be an old man.
   - ☐ c. He believes most people deserve to die young.
   - ☐ d. He looks on death as a necessary evil.

8. Vidal has Billy kill Joe Grant to show that Billy
   - ☐ a. is a good shot.
   - ☐ b. is a troublemaker.
   - ☐ c. kills without reason.
   - ☐ d. picks on weak men.

9. After Charlie is shot, Billy pushes him out of the cabin. Billy does this to
   - ☐ a. punish Charlie for complaining about the cold.
   - ☐ b. silence Charlie's pleas for help as he is dying.
   - ☐ c. show how cruel he can be.
   - ☐ d. force Garrett to stop firing.

10. When Billy rides into Lincoln to meet the governor, the streets are empty because
    - ☐ a. the governor has ordered everyone to stay inside.
    - ☐ b. Billy has threatened the town.
    - ☐ c. no one is interested in Billy's arrival.
    - ☐ d. everyone is afraid of Billy.

# *The Television Play*

Think of the television programs you watch regularly. How many of them take place as you see them? Except for news and sports events, very little of what you see on television is live. Most programs are recorded in advance on videotape.

That was not always true. When television was first developed in the late 1940s, videotape did not exist. For the first fifteen years of television history, all television performances were live.

Live television plays had elements of both movies and stage plays. Like movies, they were performed before cameras. As with stage plays, scenes could not be redone if something went wrong. In addition, the camera could broadcast scenes only in a television studio. The audience saw the play complete with any mistakes. Because today's television plays are taped, directors can redo scenes in which mistakes are made. The use of color and other new technologies have changed some aspects of television. Today's television plays, however, still have many of the same features they had in the past.

Gore Vidal wrote *The Death of Billy the Kid* for television. In this lesson you will examine some concerns of the writer, director, and actors in a television play. Television plays do have some things in common with weekly TV shows. Both kinds of television programs are written for limited time slots, are interrupted by commercials, and use cameras. But there are differences between a television play and a weekly show. For example, unlike ongoing programs in which the same characters reappear in a new plot each week, a television play introduces its characters and tells its story only once.

## Writing for Television

When Gore Vidal wrote *The Death of Billy the Kid,* he knew that the medium of television had both advantages and disadvantages when compared with the stage. The major advantage of television is the camera. It can zoom in from a distance to show a face or even a tiny gesture. It can direct the audience's attention to one particular character or to the whole set. The television viewer, sitting in front of a screen at home, sees exactly what the camera shows. In addition, television's sound system allows audiences to hear even small sighs and low-voiced conversations.

By contrast, the audience in a theater is usually at a distance from the actors. Actors use large, expansive gestures in order to be seen and to fill the stage with their presence. Although the actor who is speaking may be the focus of attention, members of the theater audience see the whole stage all the time. Because of that difference, television often seems more personal than the theater.

Writers of television plays are aware of the camera's potential, and they know that the camera can be used to develop the characters and to advance the plot.

*1. Read the opening scene of* The Death of Billy the Kid. *Give one example of how the camera might be used to develop the characters you see in that scene.*

Despite the advantages of the camera, writing for television involves certain restrictions that writing for the stage does not. A major restriction has to do with time. A television play is written to fill a certain time period, usually 30, 60, 90, or 120 minutes. Most television programs also have commercial breaks at regular intervals. Scenes are usually structured to fit into specific time frames. Because of the enforced time restrictions, television plays have a structure that is not necessary in stage plays.

*2. Suppose that in Act 1 of* The Death of Billy the Kid *you had to plan for two commercial breaks. Where would you choose to interrupt the action? Why?*

## Directing for Television

Like writers of television plays, the directors of television plays are also aware of the advantages and disadvantages of the medium. One important consideration for any television director is space.

Television plays are usually performed in very small spaces, especially if the play is being performed live. The studio is usually filled with cameras and other equipment. Actors, technicians, and other workers are also in the studio.

The director must avoid giving an audience the impression that the set is cramped or crowded. By carefully positioning the cameras and the actors, the director can make a setting look more spacious than it really is. For example, you may see actors in a corner of a room. In the studio the whole room does not exist. Yet you get the feeling that the room is complete. Watching the scene, you feel as though you are standing in the room with the characters.

By using cameras, a television director can do things that a stage director cannot. The director can use cameras to make scenes more personal or intense than they might be on a stage. One way to create that kind of intimacy is by using close-up shots.

A close-up shot is a picture taken with the camera very close to the subject. A close-up might fill the television screen with an actor's face. When you see the actor's face and expression so clearly, the dialogue can seem much more immediate—almost as if the character is speaking to you.

The imaginative use of cameras can give a scene greater impact. Think about Act 1 of *The Death of Billy the Kid*. It includes several conversations that reveal Billy's character. One conversation involves Billy and General Wallace. Imagine the scene played before one camera. You would see the room with Billy and the general facing each other as they speak.

Now imagine the same scene played before three cameras. One camera focuses on the room. The second shows a close-up of Billy's face, and the third shows a close-up of Wallace's face. As the characters speak, the director switches the focus back and forth from one face to another. When the two men are about to part, the camera shows the whole room.

*3. Imagine that you are directing this play. In what scene would you use close-ups? How would you use the close-ups?*

*4. Find a scene that would not work well with close-ups. Why do you think close-ups are not desirable in that scene?*

## Acting for Television

In Chapter 8 you read about the special skills that radio actors need. Because radio conveys all its information through sound, the actors have to communicate the moods and personalities of their characters through their voices. Radio acting calls for different skills than stage acting. Television actors, too, perform differently from stage actors.

*5. What is one major difference between radio and television that affects the work of television actors?*

Stage actors know that their audiences are in the room when the play is being performed. Some people in the audience are only a few feet away from the stage. Others are quite far away, often in balconies high above the stage. As you have read, that distance means that the actors onstage often have to exaggerate their movements, gestures, and speaking voices in order to be seen and heard. They use a lot of makeup so that their features and expressions will be visible to the entire audience.

Television actors have different concerns. They generally do not perform before a live audience, but in front of cameras. The audience watches the actors' performances on the small screen of a television set. The cameras can give the audience the feeling of looking at something from several yards away or from just a few inches away.

Because the camera is so revealing and so close, television actors need to move and speak as naturally as possible. They need to keep their gestures small and their voices quiet. Unlike stage actors, who must project their voices to be heard, television actors need to speak only loud enough for sensitive microphones to pick up their voices. Makeup has to look natural in the close-up camera shots.

Every television actor learns to be aware of the camera at all times. At the same time, the actor learns to ignore the camera. While they are performing, experienced actors know exactly what the audience will see on the screen. Yet they know that they must never show that they are concerned about the camera. To become involved in a television program, the audience needs to forget that there *is* a camera.

As you have read, *The Death of Billy the Kid* was written for television actors. Vidal's characters, especially Billy, seem very realistic. In many stories western outlaws are shown as arrogant and proud. In Vidal's play Billy is quiet, low-key, and almost humble. Yet Billy is still dangerous.

Early in the play, Billy shoots Joe Grant without regret. Of course, Grant tried to kill him first. Billy knows that he faces a threat from every ambitious or envious gunfighter. He accepts the challenge just as he seems to accept his way of life.

Billy is a young man. Yet he seems old and hardened in many ways. He has a chance to live in peace, but he rejects the governor's offer. "What a man that boy could be," says General Wallace after his interview with Billy.

*6. What do you think the actor playing Billy the Kid should look like?*

*7. Choose one scene in which Billy reveals something about his character through his words or actions. Explain how you think an actor should play this scene. What should he try to show about Billy?*

# Television Productions of Stage Plays

Some plays, such as *The Death of Billy the Kid,* are written especially for television. Other plays that appear on television were originally written as stage plays. You might, for example, see *Julius Caesar* on television. When you watch such a production, are you seeing a stage play or a television play?

You are actually seeing both at the same time. The television script will usually be the same script used for the stage production. But the director and the actors work differently. The director, for example, has to think about camera placement and plan each actor's movements with the cameras in mind. The actors have to adjust their movements and voices for the cameras rather than for the audience in the balcony.

*8. Review Act 5, Scene 5, of* Julius Caesar, *in which Brutus dies. Describe how the scene might be played on the stage. How might the same scene be staged for a television production?*

# Questions for Thought and Discussion

The questions and activities that follow will help you explore the excerpt from *The Death of Billy the Kid* in more depth and at the same time develop your critical thinking skills.

1. **Evaluating.** Think about the scene in which Billy meets the governor. How do you think each views the other? Why?

2. **Analyzing a Character.** How does Billy see himself? Do you think he feels any conflict about his way of life? Give reasons for your answer.

3. **Comparing.** In *The Death of Billy the Kid,* what television technique is used to show the passing of time? How might Shakespeare have shown what happened over a period of years in one of his plays?

4. **Inferring.** How do you think the ordinary people of Fort Sumner feel about Billy the Kid? Find evidence from the play to support your answer.

# Writing About Literature

Several suggestions for writing projects are given below. You may be asked to complete one or more of these projects. If you have any questions about how to begin a writing assignment, review Using the Writing Process, beginning on page 385.

1. **Writing a Soliloquy.** Write a soliloquy for Billy to give during the play. Remember that a soliloquy expresses a character's thoughts. It is not intended to be heard by other characters. Be sure to indicate at what point in Act 1 Billy's soliloquy would appear.

2. **Reporting on Research.** Use books, magazines, and encyclopedias to find out about the real Billy the Kid. Then prepare a report in which you compare Billy the Kid in real life to the character in the play. How are the two similar? How are they different? What were the actual circumstances under which Billy was captured?

3. **Writing a Newspaper Article.** Write a newspaper article about the capture of Billy the Kid. Use information from the play and details based on what you think might have happened. Include a physical description of Billy when he is captured.

680-66

## Chapter 10

*Excerpt from*

**Selection**
# The Treasure of the Sierra Madre
SCREENPLAY BY JOHN HUSTON
BASED ON THE NOVEL BY B. TRAVEN

**Lesson**
## The Screenplay

## About the Selection

In the 1920s and 1930s new technology led to the popularity of radio and movies. With this new technology came new forms of drama: radio plays and screenplays. You have already read an excerpt from one of the best-known radio plays, Orson Welles's presentation of *War of the Worlds*.

In this chapter you will read an excerpt from the film classic, *The Treasure of the Sierra Madre*. The film was made in 1948. Humphrey Bogart starred as Dobbs, a desperate and bitter man who has fallen on hard times. John Huston wrote the screenplay and directed the movie. He won Academy Awards for both writing the screenplay and directing the film. His father, Walter Huston, also won an Academy Award for his portrayal of Howard, the oldest of the three prospectors hunting for gold in the Sierra Madre.

The Sierra Madre is a mountain range in Mexico. The story takes place in northwestern Mexico, near the town of Durango. Durango lies halfway between Mexico City and the Texas border.

The three main characters are Dobbs, Curtin, and Howard. Dobbs and Curtin are unemployed, having lost their jobs when the Mexican oil boom ended. Dobbs is so short of money that he is reduced to begging. Compared to the hardened Dobbs, Curtin, the youngest of the three, seems very young and innocent.

From Howard, the old prospector, the other two men learn about

*The Screenplay*

the gold of the Sierra Madre. As he tells his gold-hunting stories, however, Howard warns that the sight of gold changes people.

Dobbs and Curtin collect some money that is owed to them by their former employer. They then ask Howard to take them hunting for gold. He readily agrees, but warns them of the dangers and hardships they will face. In the excerpt that you will read, the men have discovered gold, not in nuggets, but in fine flakes, mixed with sand.

Like many screenplays, *The Treasure of the Sierra Madre* was adapted from a novel. The author of the novel was B. Traven, a mysterious man about whom little is known. He became a best-selling writer in the 1930s and 1940s, but he lived in isolation in Mexico. He refused to give interviews or to meet reporters. Traven claimed to be a citizen of the United States, but some evidence suggests he may have been born in Germany. Because so little is known about Traven, many legends and stories have been told about him.

John Huston, who wrote the screenplay, asked to meet Traven when Huston was in Mexico making the movie. One day a man calling himself Hal Croves called on Huston. Croves said he was a friend of Traven's. Huston always thought Croves was Traven, but he could not be sure.

John Huston was one of the most famous directors and screenwriters in Hollywood. In his youth he traveled across the country and worked as a boxer, a painter, a writer, an actor, and an officer in the Mexican cavalry. In 1937 he went to Hollywood, where he wrote screenplays for Warner Brothers. He directed his first movie in 1941. That movie was *The Maltese Falcon*, one of the most popular detective movies ever made.

Huston continued to direct many successful movies, including *The Asphalt Jungle, The Red Badge of Courage, The African Queen, Annie,* and *Prizzi's Honor*. In *Prizzi's Honor* his daughter, Anjelica, won an Academy Award for best supporting actress. Her success made the Hustons the only family in which three generations have won Oscars. Walter, John, and Anjelica all won their Oscars in movies directed by John Huston.

## Lesson Preview

The lesson that follows the excerpt from *The Treasure of the Sierra Madre* focuses on the elements of a screenplay. A <u>screenplay</u> is the script prepared for a movie production. It provides the director with the information necessary to film the movie. A screenplay contains the basic elements of plot, characters, and theme as well as additional information for the film crew and the actors.

Writers of screenplays treat a subject differently for the screen than they would for the stage. They give almost as much thought to how scenes will look on film as they do to what the characters will say and do.

Like the television script for *The Death of Billy the Kid,* the screenplay for *The Treasure of the Sierra Madre* includes technical directions. Here are some technical directions that appear in the selection that follows.

**pan shot**    a camera shot in which a camera set on a tripod turns to the left or to the right in a smooth, sweeping motion. A pan shot slowly takes in a large scene or a landscape.

**pull back to**    the camera retreats from a close-up shot to show more of a scene than was shown before.

**full shot**    a wide-angle shot that provides a complete view of a person, an object, or a scene.

**cut back to**    switch abruptly from one scene of a movie to an earlier scene.

The questions that follow will help you understand how a screenplay is put together. As you read, think about how you would answer these questions.

**1** How does this excerpt from a screenplay differ from the scripts of the other plays you have read?

**2** Who are the main characters in this screenplay? How do you learn about each of them?

**3** Notice that there are shots in which no characters appear. What do those shots add to the play?

**4** What kinds of details does the screenplay direct the camera to give?

**Note:** The selection in this chapter does not have difficult vocabulary.

*The Screenplay*

*Excerpt from*

# The Treasure of the Sierra Madre

SCREENPLAY BY JOHN HUSTON
BASED ON THE NOVEL BY B. TRAVEN

## Characters

Dobbs
Howard
Curtin

*In the scenes leading up to this excerpt, the three prospectors, Howard, Curtin, and Dobbs, have struggled up into the rugged Sierra Madre. They have found gold, in the form of tiny flakes mixed with sand. Howard, the "old-timer," has shown Curtin and Dobbs how to use a water wheel to wash the sand for gold—to separate the gold from the sand.*

**36**  **Camp  Close-up  Of Dobbs**                          **Night**
*His eyes, reflecting the light of the campfire, glitter in their sockets. He leans forward and we see a Mexican calendar tacked to the wall. Lines have been drawn across all the dates up to October 21.*

**37    Close-up    Of a Scale**
*as the proceeds of the day's work are weighed.* **Camera pulls back** *to a* **close shot** *of the three men.* **Howard** *measures dust onto the scale.*

**Curtin**    How much do you figure it is now?
**Howard**    Close on to five thousand dollars worth.
**Dobbs**    When're we going to start dividing it?

**Howard** *looks at him keenly.*

**Howard**    Any time you say.
**Curtin**    Why divide it at all? I don't see any point. We're all going back together, when the time comes. Why not wait until we get paid for the stuff, then just divide the money?
**Howard**    Either way suits me. You fellers decide.
**Dobbs**    I'm for dividing it up as we go along and leaving it up to each man to be responsible for his own goods.
**Howard**    I reckon I'd rather have it that way, too. I haven't liked the responsibility of guarding your treasure any too well.
**Dobbs**    Nobody asked you.
**Howard**    *(smilingly)* That's right—you never asked me. I only thought I was the most trustworthy among us three.
**Dobbs**    You? How come?
**Howard**    I said the most trustworthy. As for being the most honest, no one can say.
**Dobbs**    I don't get you.
**Howard**    Well, let's look the thing straight in the face. Suppose you were charged with taking care of the goods. All right, I'm somewhere deep in the brush one day getting timber and Curtin here is on his way to the village for provisions. That'd be your big chance to pack up and leave us in the cold.
**Dobbs**    Only a guy that's a thief at heart would think me likely to do a thing like that!

**Howard**  Right now it wouldn't be worthwhile. But when our pile has grown to let's say three hundred ounces, think of such things, you will . . .

**Curtin**  How's about yourself?

**Howard**  I'm not quick on my feet any longer. You fellers are a lot tougher than when we started out. And by the time the pile is big enough to be really tempting I won't be able to run half as fast as either one of you. You'd get me by the collar and string me up in no time. And that's why I think I'm the most trustworthy in this outfit.

**Curtin** *grins.*

**Curtin**  Looking at it that way I guess you're right. But perhaps it would be better to cut the proceeds three ways every night. It'd relieve you of a responsibility you don't like.

**Howard**  Swell by me. After we've gotten more than a couple hundred ounces it'll be a nuisance to carry it around in little bags hanging from our necks, so each of us will have to hide his share of the treasure from the other two. And having done so he'll have to be forever on the watch in case his hiding place is discovered.

**Dobbs**  What a dirty filthy mind you have.

**Howard**  Not dirty, baby. No, not dirty. Only I know what sort of ideas even supposedly decent people can get in their heads when gold's at stake.

**Dissolve to:**

38    **Full Shot   Of the Mine**
*There are two tunnels now into the rocky shoulder.* **Over Scene** *the* **sound** *of picks.* **Camera moves** *into the interior of one of the tunnels.* **Howard** *puts down his pick, starts shoveling the rocky debris out of the cave into the open.* **Camera moves** *to the opening of the other tunnel.* **Dobbs**, *some twenty feet in, is swinging away with his pick.*

**39**    **A Crack in the Ceiling**
*of the tunnel over* **Dobbs's** *head.*

**40**     **Dobbs's Pick Biting into the Rock**
**Over Scene** *we hear* **Dobbs's** *voice.*

**Dobbs's Voice**     *(he grunts)* Whew! Hot! Geez . . . hot.

**Cut Back to:**

**41**    **Crack in Ceiling**
*It lengthens by half an inch.*

**42**    **Ext. Tunnel**
*as* **Curtin** *drives his burro up the trail. He is hauling water for the tank. He unloads the burro, pours the water into the tank, then starts back down the trail.*

**43**    **Int. Tunnel**
 **Dobbs** *swinging his pick.*

**44**    **Crack in Ceiling**
*It is twice as long now as before, and with each blow from the pick it gets wider.*

**45**    **Curtin**
*starting his burro down the trail. He takes a few strides, hesitates, turns back up toward the tunnels. At the mouth of the first tunnel he calls to the old man.*

**Curtin**    Hey, Howard, want me to spell you?
**Howard**    Thanks, not right yet, baby. I'm just getting my second wind. *(He turns around; with a movement of his arm he wipes the sweat and grime out of his eyes.)*

**Curtin** *moves on to the next tunnel. There has been a cave-in. The ceiling is hanging so low at the opening that there is not enough room for a body to pass through. Curtin doesn't take time to yell for Howard* *but starts clawing rubble aside. When he has made a big enough opening he wriggles into the tunnel.*

**46     Int. Tunnel**

**Dobbs** *is lying unconscious, half covered with rock.* **Curtin** *works* **Dobbs's** *body free, then starts pulling him out. It is an inch-by-inch proposition getting the unconscious man through the narrow opening, but at last he succeeds.*

**Curtin**     *(shouting)* Howard! Howard!

> **Howard's** *voice answers hollowly from inside the tunnel.*

**Howard's Voice**     Yes?

> *The ring of* **Howard's** *pick against the stones stops.*

**Curtin**     Come quick. Howard!

*The old man comes on the run. One look at* **Dobbs's** *tunnel tells him what has happened. He immediately goes to work on* **Dobbs.**

**Howard**     *(presently)* He's coming around.

> **Dobbs** *groans. His eyelids flicker, then open.*

**Howard**     Lie still for a minute till you get your senses back.
**Dobbs**     What happened?
**Howard**     Tunnel caved in on you.
**Dobbs**     *(remembers)* Yeah . . . I tell you I heard the harps playing sure enough. *(He sits up now, tests his arms and legs.)*
**Howard**     Nothing broken.
**Dobbs**     Guess I'm almost good as new. Who pulled me out?
**Howard**     Curtin did.

*There is a sound of falling rubble and the three men turn in time to see the tunnel sealed off for good. Dobbs shivers, then he stretches out his hand to Curtin.*

**Dobbs**   I owe you my life, partner.
**Curtin**   Forget it.

**Dissolve to:**

47   **Night**

*Howard is measuring out the yellow sand into three equal parts.* **Curtin** *and* **Dobbs** *follow his every move. Presently it is divided.*

*Dobbs takes up his share and leaves the circle of light the campfire makes to go off into the dark. The old man takes out his harmonica, begins to play softly.*

**Curtin**   What are you going to do with your hard-earned money, old-timer, when you get back and cash in?

**Howard**   I'm getting along in years. Oh, I can still hold up my end when it comes to a hard day's work, but I ain't the man I was once, and next year, next month, next week, by thunder, I won't be the man I am today. Reckon I'll find me some quiet place to settle down. Buy a business maybe . . . a grocery or a hardware store, and spend the better part of my time reading the comic strips and adventure stories. One thing's for sure . . . I ain't going to go prospecting again and waste my time and money trying to find another gold mine . . . How's about yourself? What are your plans, if any?

**Curtin**   I figure on buying some land and growing fruit—peaches maybe.

**Howard**   How'd you happen to settle on peaches?

**Curtin**   One summer when I was a kid I worked as a picker in a peach harvest in the San Joaquin Valley.[1] It sure was something. Hundreds of people—old and young—whole families working together. After the day's work we used to build big bonfires and sit around 'em and sing to guitar music, till morning sometimes. You'd go to sleep, wake up and sing, and go to sleep again. Everybody had a wonderful time . . .

---

1. **San Joaquin Valley:** a rich farming area in California.

**Dobbs** *comes back into the light of the campfire.*

**Curtin**   *(continuing)* . . . Ever since, I've had a hankering to be a fruit grower. Must be grand watching your own trees put on leaves, come into blossom and bear . . . watching the fruit get big and ripe on the bough, ready for picking . . .

**Dobbs**   What's all that about?

**Howard**   We've been telling each other what we aim to do when we get back.

**Dobbs**   Me now, I got it all figured out what I'm going to do.

**Curtin**   Tell us, Dobbsie.

**Dobbs**   First off I'm going to the Turkish bath and sweat and soak till I get all the grime out of my pores. Then I'm going to a barber shop and after I've had my hair cut and've been shaved and so on, I'm going to have 'em douse me out of every bottle on the shelf. Then I'm going to a haberdasher's and buy brand new duds . . . a dozen of everything. And then I'm going to a swell cafe—and if anything ain't just right, and maybe if it is, I'm going to raise hell, bawl the waiter out, and have him take it back . . . *(He smiles, thoroughly enjoying this imaginary scene at table.)*

**Curtin**   What's next on the program?

**Dobbs**   What would be . . . a dame!

**Curtin**   Only one?

**Dobbs**   That'll all depend on how good she is. Maybe one—maybe half a dozen.

**Howard**   If I were you boys I wouldn't talk or even think women. It ain't too good for your health.

**Dobbs**   Guess you're right, seeing the prospect is so far off.

**Howard**   You know what. We ought to put some kind of limit on our take. Agree between ourselves that when we get exactly so much we pull up stakes and beat it.

**Curtin**   What do you think the limit ought to be?

**Howard**   Oh, say twenty-five thousand dollars worth apiece.

**Dobbs**   Twenty-five thousand? That's small potatoes.

**Curtin**   How much do you say?

**Dobbs**   Fifty thousand anyway. Seventy-five's more like it.

**Howard**   That'd take another year at least . . . if the vein held out, which wouldn't be likely.

**Dobbs**   What's a year more or less when that kind of dough's to be made?

**Howard**   Twenty-five's plenty far as I'm concerned. More'n enough to last me out my lifetime.

**Dobbs**   Sure, you're old. But I'm still young. I need dough and plenty of it.

**Curtin**   Twenty-five thousand in one piece is more'n I ever expected to get my hands on.

**Dobbs**   *(snorts)* Small potatoes!

**Curtin**   No use making hogs of ourselves.

**Dobbs**   Hog am I! Why, I'd be within my rights if I demanded half again what you get.

**Curtin**   How come?

**Dobbs**   There's no denying, is there, I put up the lion's share of the cash?

**Curtin**   So you did, Dobbsie—and I always meant to pay you back.

**Dobbs**   *(pointedly)* In civilized places the biggest investor always gets the biggest return.

**Howard**   That's one thing in favor of the wilds.

**Dobbs**   Not that I intend to make any such demand, you understand, but I'd be within my rights if I did. Next time you go calling me a hog, remember what I could'a done if I'd'a wanted . . .

**Howard**   I think you're wise not to put things on a strictly money basis, partner. Curtin might take it into his head he was a capitalist instead of a guy with a shovel and just sit back and take things easy and let you and me do all the work.

*While the old man talks,* **Curtin** *uses the scales to weigh out a portion of his dust.*

*The Screenplay*

**Howard** *(continuing)* He'd stand to realize a tidy sum on his investment without so much as turning his hand over. If anybody's to get more, I reckon it ought to be the one who does the most work.

**Curtin** *(giving the dust to **Dobbs**)* There you are, Dobbsie. What I owe you with interest.

**Dobbs** *(he takes the dust, weighs it in his hand, then, with a sudden gesture, flings it away so that it falls, a little shower, into the fire)* I just don't like being told I'm a hog, that's all.

**Howard** *(addressing **Dobbs**)* Other things aside, there's a lot of truth in what you were saying about being younger than me and needing more dough therefore. I'm willing to make it forty thousand apiece. *(To **Curtin**.)* What do you say, partner?

**Curtin** How long will it take?

**Howard** Oh, another six months, I reckon.

**Curtin** *(after a moment's debate)* Make it forty thousand or six months.

**Howard** Suits me. Okay, Dobbs?

**Dobbs** *(sourly)* Okay.

**Howard** Let's shake on it then.

*The three men shake hands solemnly. Then **Curtin** gets up, starts away from the fire to hide his goods.*

**Dissolve to:**

48    **Int. Tent    Close Shot    On Dobbs**                    **Night**
*sleeping, a bar of moonlight across his face.* **Over Scene** *the* **scream** *of a tiger. He stirs, turns over. The* **scream** *is repeated.* **Dobbs** *opens his eyes. Then he sits up, leaning on an elbow.*

49    **Howard's blankets**
*They're empty.* **Camera pulls back to full shot interior tent**.

**Curtin** *is in his blankets sound asleep.* **Dobbs** *frowns. After a moment* **Dobbs** *sits all the way up, throws back his blankets, reaches for his shoes, and puts them on. Then, picking up his revolver, he moves silently out of the tent and heads across the campsite. He's gone perhaps a dozen steps when he hears* **Howard** *coming. He draws back into the shadows. When* **Howard** *is scarcely three feet away,* **Dobbs** *steps out, suddenly confronting him.*

**Dobbs**    That you, Howard?

**Howard**    *(startled)* You oughtn't to go jumping out at me like that. I might've let you have it.

**Dobbs**    Out for a midnight stroll?

**Howard**    There's a tiger[2] around. I went to see if the burros were all right.

**Dobbs**    *(grunts skeptically, then)* So!

**Howard**    What's the matter, Dobbsie?

**Dobbs**    Think I'll make *sure* the burros are all right.

**Howard**    Help yourself.

*He walks away in the direction of the tent.*

**50**    **Int. Tent**

*as* **Howard** *enters.* **Curtin** *stirs.*

**Curtin**    *(to* **Howard** *sleepily)* What's up?

**Howard**    Nothing's up.

*   **Curtin** *sees that* **Dobbs's** *blankets are empty.*

**Curtin**    Where's Dobbs?

**Howard**    Poking around in the dark out there.

**51**    **Dobbs**

*taking sacks of the precious dust out of his hiding place—a hole underneath a rock. He is counting the sacks aloud.*

---

**2. tiger:** probably a jaguar, an animal that is native to Mexico.

*The Screenplay*

**Dobbs**   Three—four—five—six.
> *He gives a satisfied grunt, then starts putting them back.*

**52**   **Int. Tent**
**Howard** *has got back in his blankets.*

**Curtin**   He's sure taking a long time . . .

> **Curtin** *throws his blankets off, puts on his shoes.*

**Curtin**   *(continuing)* I'm going to have a look-see.

**53**   **Ext. Tent**
**Camera pans** *with* **Curtin** *to his hiding place—a hollow tree. He begins to pick out his sacks of gold.*

**54**   **Int. Tent**
*as* **Dobbs** *enters. He starts to take his shoes off, then notices* **Curtin's** *absence.*

**Dobbs**   *(sharply)* Where's Curtin?
**Howard**   Out there some place. He said something about having a look-see.

*Again* **Dobbs's** *brow becomes furrowed with suspicion. He puts his shoe back on, gets up, and is about to leave the tent when* **Curtin** *enters. He and* **Dobbs** *survey each other wordlessly.*

**Howard**   It's come around to me again, but I won't take my turn if you guys'll quit worrying about your goods and go to bed. We got work to do tomorrow.

**Dobbs** *grunts, turns back into the tent.* **Curtin** *drops down on his blankets.*

**55**     **Ext. the Mine    Close Shot    Dobbs**
*at the sluice,*[3] *washing sand and talking to himself.*

**Dobbs**    You can't catch me sleeping . . . Don't you ever believe that. I'm not so dumb. The day you try to put anything over on me will be a costly one for both of you.

*At the **Over Scene sound** of hoofs on rock, **Dobbs** stops talking. **Camera pulls back** to show **Curtin** driving two of the burros. **Dobbs** keeps his face averted and **Curtin** passes without any words being exchanged. As the **sound** of the hoofs fades, Dobbs resumes his monologue.*

**Dobbs**    Any more lip out of you and I'll pull off and let you have it. If you know what's good for you, you won't monkey around with Fred C. Dobbs.

**56**     **Curtin**
*at a turn of the trail. He comes upon the old man repairing a tool.*

**Curtin**    You ought to get a load of Dobbsie. He's talking away to himself a mile a minute.

**Howard**    *(shaking his head)* Something's eating him. I don't know what. He's spoiling for trouble.

*        **Curtin** grunts, proceeds on down the trail.*

**57**     **Dobbs**

**Dobbs**    *(mimicking **Howard's** voice)* We're low on provisions, Dobbsie. How about you going to the village. *(Then as **Dobbs** again.)* Who does Howard think he is, ordering me around?

**Howard's Voice**    **(Over Scene)** What's that, Dobbsie?

---

3. **sluice:** a long, narrow channel through which water is run. The water is used to wash gravel for gold.

**Dobbs** *looks up in surprise.* **Camera pulls back** *to a* **close shot** *of* **Howard** *and* **Dobbs**.

**Dobbs**  Nothing.

**Howard**  Better look out. It's a bad sign when a guy starts talking to himself.

**Dobbs**  *(angrily)* Who else have I got to talk to? Certainly not you or Curtin. Fine partners, I must say.

**Howard**  Got something up your nose?

**Dobbs** *doesn't answer*

**Howard**  Blow it out. It'll do you good.

**Dobbs**  *(shouts suddenly)* Don't get the idea you two are putting anything over on me.

**Howard**  Take it easy, Dobbsie.

**Dobbs**  *(still louder)* I know what your game is.

**Howard**  Then you know more than I do.

**Dobbs**  *(railing)* Why am I elected to go to the village for provisions— why me instead of you or Curtin? Don't think I don't see through that. I know you've thrown together against me. The two days I'd be gone would give you plenty of time to discover where my dust is, wouldn't it?

**Howard**  If you have fears along those lines, why don't you take your dust along with you?

**Dobbs**  And run the risk of having it taken from me by bandits.

**Howard**  If you were to run into bandits, you'd be out of luck anyway. They'd kill you for the shoes on your feet.

**Dobbs**  So that's it. Everything is clear now. You're hoping bandits'll get me. That would save you a lot of trouble, wouldn't it? And your consciences wouldn't bother you either!

**Howard**  Okay, Dobbs, you just forget about going. Curtin or I'll go.

**Dobbs** *turns on his heel, stalks off.*

**58    Pan Shot of Curtin**

*Something he sees out of scene causes him to stop.*

**59    A Gila Monster** [4]

**Curtin** *picks up a rock, but before he can heave it the big yellow and black lizard has disappeared under a boulder.* **Curtin** *drops the rock, picks up a piece of timber, runs one end underneath the rock making a lever. He leans his weight on the end of the timber.*

**Dobbs's Voice    (Over Scene)** Just like I thought.

**Curtin** *turns.* **Camera pulls back** *to show* **Dobbs** *covering* **Curtin** *with his gun.*

**Curtin**    What's the idea?

**Dobbs**    Put your hands up.

> (**Curtin** *obeys.* **Dobbs** *takes* **Curtin's** *gun away from him.*)

**Dobbs**    I got a good mind to pull off and pump you up, chest and belly alike.

**Curtin**    Go ahead and pull, but would you mind telling me first what it's all about?

**Dobbs**    It won't get you anywhere playin' dumb.

**Curtin**    *(comprehension dawning on his face)* Well, I'll be—so that's where your dust is hidden, Dobbsie?

> **Howard** *comes up.*

**Howard**    What's all the hollerin' for?

**Curtin**    Seems like I stumbled accidentally on Dobbs's treasure.

**Dobbs**    *(snorts)* Accidentally! What were you trying to pry up that rock for? Tell me that!

**Curtin**    I saw a gila monster crawl under it.

**Dobbs**    Brother, I got to hand it to you. You can sure think up a good story when you need one.

---

**4. gila monster:** a poisonous lizard.

**Curtin**   Okay. I'm a liar. There isn't any gila monster under there. Let's see you stick your hand in and get your goods out. Go ahead.

**Dobbs**   Sure I will. But don't you make a move or I'll . . .

**Curtin**   Don't worry. I'll stand right where I am. I want to see this.

**Dobbs** *goes down on one knee beside the boulder. He starts to put his hand in, hesitates, then bends forward to look into the hole.)*

**Curtin**   Reach right in and get your goods. If you don't we'll think you're plain yellow, won't we, Howard?

**Dobbs** *sneaks his hand forward toward the opening beneath the rock.*

**Curtin**   They never let go, do they, Howard, once they grab onto you—gila monsters. You can cut 'em in half at the neck and their heads'll still hang on till sundown, I hear, but by that time the victim don't usually care anymore because he's dead. Isn't that right, Howard?

**Howard**   I reckon.

**Curtin**   What's the matter, Dobbs, why don't you reach your hand right in and get your treasure? It couldn't be you're scared to, could it, after the way you shot off your mouth. Show us you aren't yellow, Dobbsie. I'd hate to think my partner had a yellow streak up his back.

**Dobbs**   *(sweat showing on his face—the sweat of fear; he springs to his feet, aims wildly at **Curtin**, shouting)* I'll kill you, you dirty, thieving . . .

*But before he can pull the trigger **Howard** has knocked up his arm. Then both men close in on him. **Curtin** gets the gun away from him.*

**Curtin**   Okay, Howard, I got him covered. Dobbs, another bad move out of you, and I'll blow you to kingdom come. Hey, Howard, turn that rock over, will you.

**Howard** *obeys, leaning his weight on one end of the timber until the rock rolls over. **Camera moves into a close-up** of a gila monster, its*

body arched, hissing, atop **Dobbs's** treasure. **Over Scene** the **sound** of a shot. The slug bores through the lizard's head, its body rises, its tail threshes.)

60      **Close-up    Dobbs**
his face is white, his eyes are staring.

**Cut Back To:**

61      **Close-up    The Gila Monster**
lying belly up on **Dobbs's** treasure, his arms clawing at the air.

> *Summary of the Remainder of the Screenplay.* Dobbs becomes increasingly suspicious of his partners, but it is an attack by bandits that forces the three to quit their claim earlier than they planned.
>
> On their return to Durango, Howard helps save the life of a boy. The boy's grateful family and friends force him to stay in their village. Howard promises to catch up with his partners soon. Left alone with Curtin, Dobbs's suspicions take over completely. He shoots Curtin, leaving him for dead. Curtin manages to find Howard, and they ride to catch Dobbs at Durango.
>
> Before they find him, Dobbs is taken and killed by the same bandits who had attacked their camp. They steal his burros but are arrested in Durango just before Curtin and Howard arrive. On the outskirts of the town, the two prospectors find the empty bags that had been filled with their gold dust. The bandits had slit open the bags, thinking they contained nothing but sand.
>
> Howard laughs almost hysterically. The gold, he says, has been blown back to where they found it. When Curtin recovers from the shock, he, too, laughs. Howard plans to stay with the villagers who are grateful to him for saving the boy's life. Curtin decides to go to Texas.

# Reviewing the Selection

Answer each of the following questions without looking back at the play.

*Recalling Facts*

1. Unlike the other two men, Howard is
   - ☐ a. a thief.
   - ☐ b. an experienced prospector.
   - ☐ c. very young.
   - ☐ d. not interested in gold.

*Understanding Main Ideas*

2. What is the main cause of the conflict that separates the three men from one another?
   - ☐ a. lack of food
   - ☐ b. suspicion
   - ☐ c. unwillingness to share the work
   - ☐ d. cowardice

*Placing Events in Order*

3. After Dobbs accuses Curtin of trying to steal his gold, Curtin
   - ☐ a. saves Dobbs's life.
   - ☐ b. pays Dobbs back for an earlier loan.
   - ☐ c. dares Dobbs to reach under the rock where the gold is hidden.
   - ☐ d. talks about growing peaches in the San Joaquin Valley.

*Finding Supporting Details*

4. To show that he is not "a hog," Dobbs
   - ☐ a. suggests that they stop looking for gold.
   - ☐ b. hides his gold under a boulder.
   - ☐ c. checks on the burros during the night.
   - ☐ d. flings a packet of gold dust into the fire.

5. "Howard looks at him <u>keenly</u>." In this context *keenly* means
   - ☐ a. sharply.
   - ☐ b. sadly.
   - ☐ c. with amusement.
   - ☐ d. without interest.

## Interpreting the Selection

Answer each of the following questions. You may look back at the play if necessary.

6. One night when Dobbs notices that Howard's blankets are empty he goes outside to investigate. When he meets Howard and says, "Out for a midnight stroll?" he is probably being
   - ☐ a. friendly.
   - ☐ b. sarcastic.
   - ☐ c. helpful.
   - ☐ d. concerned.

7. Dobbs's major concern seems to be
   - ☐ a. finding more gold than the other two.
   - ☐ b. protecting his treasure.
   - ☐ c. getting food.
   - ☐ d. returning to civilization as soon as possible.

8. In the scenes in which Dobbs is talking to himself, John Huston is trying to show that Dobbs
   - ☐ a. is lonely.
   - ☐ b. is a thinking man.
   - ☐ c. feels angry and persecuted.
   - ☐ d. feels he can control the other two men.

9. After he is rescued from the cave-in, Dobbs says that he "heard the harps playing." What does he mean by that statement?
   - ☐ a. He thought he was dying.
   - ☐ b. He thought he was back in civilization.
   - ☐ c. He dreamed of music.
   - ☐ d. He thought visitors had come to the mine.

10. What conclusion can you draw about the characters in this excerpt?
    - ☐ a. They are not likely to steal from one another.
    - ☐ b. Curtin is the most violent of the three.
    - ☐ c. Dobbs is more levelheaded than Curtin.
    - ☐ d. Howard is the most practical of the three.

# *The Screenplay*

In the two previous chapters, you studied a radio script and a script for a live television play. As you learned, radio plays rely on dialogue and sound effects as the only means of communicating with listeners. The television script adds a visual element. You learned, for example, how the television scriptwriter must include details about the use of the camera. The movie script, or screenplay, for *The Treasure of the Sierra Madre* gives even more detailed instructions about the use of the camera.

Making a movie involves many steps. First, someone has to write a screenplay. Like the script for a stage play, a screenplay has a plot, characters, and dialogue, but it also includes other important elements.

The second step is filming. Filming can be done in a studio or on location. Filming on location means filming in the actual setting in which the action is supposed to take place. Parts of *The Treasure of the Sierra Madre* were filmed on location in Mexico.

The screenplay is an important tool during the filming because it details not only the words and motions of the actors but also the pictures that should appear on the screen. The director uses the screenplay as a guide to the shots to be filmed, the placement of the cameras, and the staging of the action.

The final step in filmmaking is often called the postproduction stage. After the scenes have been shot, the director and the editors must decide what to include in the final version of the movie. The movie is shaped at this stage. Often many scenes are dropped. The movie that you see usually contains only a fraction of the film that was actually shot.

In this lesson you will examine various elements of the screenplay. Many of those elements, such as the technical directions, are also found in television scripts, because both movies and television rely on the effective use of the camera.

## Elements of the Screenplay

When you begin reading a screenplay such as John Huston's, you notice right away that it looks different from the other plays in this book. The first thing you notice is the series of numbers in the left margin.

*1. What numbers do you find in the excerpt you read? What do you think the numbers mean?*

If you said the numbers indicate the different camera shots, you were right. Unlike stage plays, which are divided into just a few acts and scenes, a screenplay has numerous shots. The complete screenplay of *The Treasure of the Sierra Madre* has 138 shots. Sometimes several shots make up a scene. In a screenplay a new scene begins when you see words such as "dissolve to" or "slow dissolve." Those directions indicate a change to a new setting.

**Visual and Spoken Elements.** In addition to descriptions of the many shots, another special feature you notice is the relatively small amount of dialogue. Think about the plays you read in Chapters 1 through 8. One feature they all have in common is their dependence on dialogue. When you look at the screenplay of *The Treasure of the Sierra Madre,* you notice that it relies much less on dialogue. A great deal of information is communicated visually. You may have heard the expression "A picture is worth a thousand words." Movies rely on that idea. They tell a story with less dialogue than other forms of drama do. Some movies tell their stories with no spoken dialogue at all.

Remember that early movies had no soundtracks. In those "silent movies," live music and an occasional filmed poster containing a few lines of dialogue helped to tell the story. But the silent movie relied mainly on the visual image—what people saw on the screen—to tell the story. That is still true today. Like other writers, screenwriters are concerned with plot, character development, and theme. They use an additional communication tool, the camera, to tell their stories.

**Kinds of Instructions.** If you examine the screenplay, you will notice that it includes various kinds of instructions or directions. Some may be meant solely for the director, the actors, the set designer, or the camera people. Others may be meant for all the people involved in the movie. Notice that some instructions are printed in different types. Read, for example, the information in shot 36 at the beginning of the excerpt. Notice that the type in the first line is all in **boldface**. The type for the rest of the shot is set in *italics*.

*2. To whom do you think the instructions printed in boldface are addressed?*

*3. Study all of shot 36 carefully. Make a list of the kinds of instructions that are given and state to whom the various instructions are directed. (They might be meant for more than one person.) In your own words, describe what takes place in that shot.*

**Purposes of a Shot.** Huston had at least two purposes in including shot 36. First, he wanted to help the audience see or sense something about Dobbs. In the scenes right before this one, Howard showed Dobbs how to wash the sand to separate out the gold. Dobbs felt the joy of holding tiny flakes of gold in his hand. Dobbs's character is easily excited, probably dangerous, and certainly suspicious of his companions.

In shot 36 the campfire light makes Dobbs's eyes glitter in their sockets. When the camera shows Dobbs's face and eyes close up, you get a strong feeling about his character. The scene also suggests that gold sparks greed.

Huston's second purpose was to let the audience know that time has passed. In the opening scene of the movie, the camera shows a lottery list dated August 5, 1924. In shot 36 you learn that it is now

October 21. The days crossed out on the calendar show that the men have been working in the mine for several months.

In shot 36 Huston has achieved two important goals. He has developed the character of Dobbs, and he has advanced the plot. He has also increased the suspense. By suggesting Dobbs's greed, he leaves the audience wondering what Dobbs will do next. Huston has given all that information without a word of dialogue.

*4. Review the script from shots 38 through 44. Explain three pieces of visual or sound information that Huston conveys in those shots. What is the most important plot development shown by the camera?*

*5. If Huston had used dialogue to convey that information, how might he have done it? Do you think it would have been more or less effective than the method he chose? Explain.*

## Filming a Screenplay

As you know, a movie is recorded on film scene by scene and is eventually shown to an audience as a complete work. Because movies are recorded on film, they are seldom shot as a continuous story. Usually, all the scenes that take place in a particular studio setting or location are shot together, even though they may occur at different points in the story. Filmmakers shoot in that way in order to keep from having to move people and complicated equipment back and forth. The scenes are put in the right order in the editing room.

**Setting Up the Shots.** The director and the crew take as much time as necessary to set up a scene to get it exactly right. A shot that may last less than a minute on the screen might take hours to set up. It might also be filmed over and over until the director is satisfied that it has been acted and filmed in the best way possible.

You may have watched a shot being filmed over and over. Each filming is called a take. When you think about all the elements that go into some scenes, you can see why many takes may be needed to get a scene right.

Think about the scene with the gila monster. That scene goes from shots 59 through 61. Before that scene could be filmed, Huston had to make many decisions. He had to decide where the actors would be placed and discuss how they would deliver their lines. He had to decide where to place the cameras, which camera lenses to use, and what level of sound would be best. He even had to think about how much sweat was needed on Dobbs's face.

*6. Reread the scene involving the gila monster. What are two other things that the director had to coordinate in that scene?*

A scene like that would have to be staged very differently if it were part of a stage play. On the stage, a director could only use the actors and the lighting to focus the attention of the audience on the gila monster. In a film, however, the camera can zoom in on the lizard, which is at the center of the crisis in this scene.

*7. Review shots 38 and 49. Which of those shots could be done as effectively onstage as on-screen? Why?*

**Changes in Filming.** Because the scenes are not filmed in order, the director is often the only person who has an overview of the whole movie. Each actor appears on the set only when he or she is needed for a particular scene. Even the screenwriter does not necessarily know which scenes have been filmed and kept and which have been discarded.

In making the movie, the director is far more important than the writer of the screenplay. In *The Treasure of the Sierra Madre,* however, John Huston was both director and screenwriter. As a result, the relationship between the screenplay and the finished film is unusually close. Still, Huston made changes while filming, adding elements that were not in the screenplay.

In shot 45, for example, a cave-in traps Dobbs. In the screenplay Curtin sees the cave-in and rushes to save Dobbs. In the filming, however, Huston has Curtin hesitate before rescuing Dobbs. The hesitation in the filming increases the tension and adds an element of complexity to Curtin's character.

*8. In the movie why do you think Huston makes Curtin hesitate before rescuing his partner?*

*The Screenplay*

# Characterization in the Screenplay

In the excerpt that you read from *The Treasure of the Sierra Madre,* you need to decide what each character is like on the basis of his words and actions.

*9. Who are the main characters in this excerpt? Skim shots 36 through 46. What do you learn about each character?*

In shot 47 the three men discuss what they will do with their newfound wealth.

*10. What does each character say he will do? What do their choices tell you about their characters?*

In the excerpt that you read, you see the three main characters at a turning point in their relationship. In earlier scenes the three joined forces to prospect for gold. After various struggles, they reached their goal and began to reap the reward—gold. In the scenes in this excerpt, you see how the finding of gold affects the three partners.

Once the men realize they can become rich, they must decide how much gold they will take. In shot 47 they discuss how much is enough. Howard, the old man, would be satisfied with twenty-five thousand dollars. Dobbs rejects this amount as "small potatoes." He wants twice or three times as much. In the end the men agree on forty thousand dollars or six months.

In the middle of their discussion, an odd event takes place. Curtin weighs out some gold dust to repay Dobbs for a loan. Dobbs, who was penniless at the beginning of the movie, takes the gold dust and "flings it away."

*11. Why do you think Dobbs throws away the gold? What does that action tell you about his character?*

Dividing up the gold leads to new problems. Each man hides his share in a different place. After the gold is hidden, Dobbs becomes even more suspicious of the others. Curtin, too, takes precautions and checks on his hidden treasure.

*12. In the excerpt you read, describe how the relationship among the three men changes. What do you think is the theme, or underlying message, of the screenplay?*

## Questions for Thought and Discussion

The questions and activities that follow will help you explore the excerpt from *The Treasure of the Sierra Madre* in more depth and at the same time develop your critical thinking skills.

1. **Analyzing Character.** In the middle of shot 37, find Howard's speech that begins, "I'm not quick on my feet. . . ." What reason does Howard give for being the most trustworthy of the three men? Do you agree that he is the most trustworthy? Why or why not?

2. **Understanding Suspense.** What do you think is the most suspenseful moment in the excerpt you read? Explain what makes the scene you chose suspenseful.

3. **Comparing Soliloquies.** Compare Dobbs's soliloquy in shot 55 with Antony's soliloquy in *Julius Caesar*, Act 3, Scene 1, lines 254 to 275. What is the purpose of each soliloquy? What are the major differences in the two speeches?

4. **Expressing an Opinion.** B. Traven, who wrote the novel *The Treasure of the Sierra Madre,* believed that gold makes a man "the slave of his property." Do you agree with Traven's view? Give reasons for your opinion.

## Writing About Literature

Several suggestions for writing projects follow. You may be asked to complete one or more of these projects. If you have any questions about how to begin a writing assignment, review Using the Writing Process, beginning on page 385.

1. **Creating a Scene.** Imagine that you are writing the screenplay for *The Treasure of the Sierra Madre.* Think about a scene that you would write

to follow the incident of the gila monster. Then write that follow-up scene—with or without dialogue—and include the three main characters.

2. **Writing an Evaluation.** Decide which scene in the excerpt you thought was most effective. Then write a paragraph or two describing the scene to someone who has not read the screenplay or seen the movie. Give your reasons for liking the scene.

3. **Writing a Character Sketch.** Imagine that you are going to prospect for gold. In several paragraphs describe what kind of person you would want your partner to be.

4. **Reporting on Research.** Find out all you can about B. Traven, using at least three sources. Then write a brief report explaining why he remains a "mystery man."

# *Using the Writing Process*

*The lesson that follows is designed to help you with the writing assignments you will meet in this book. It explains the major steps in the writing process. Read the lesson carefully so that you understand the writing process thoroughly. On pages 395–396, following the lesson, is a checklist. Whenever you are asked to complete a writing assignment, you can just refer to the checklist as a reminder of the things you should consider as you're working on the assignment. The lesson can then serve as a reference—an information source. Turn to it whenever you feel that it would be helpful to review part or all of the process.*

When presented with a writing assignment, many people's instant response is panic. What will I write about? Do I have anything to say? To ease the panic, remind yourself that writing is something that *no one* simply sits down and does with the words flowing freely and perfectly from first sentence to last. Rather, writing is a *process*; that is, it involves a number of steps. The writing process is not a straightforward, mechanical one, such as that involved in solving a mathematical problem. These pages give you a plan that you can follow to sensibly work through the complex task of presenting your ideas on paper.

Keep in mind that writing is not simply the act of filling a piece of paper with words. It is a sophisticated act of communication. The purpose of writing is to put *ideas* across to other people. Since ideas come from your mind, not your pen, the writing process begins with the work that takes place in your mind: the creation and organization of ideas. The process then proceeds to the expression of ideas—the actual setting down of words on paper. The final stage is the polishing of both the ideas and the words that express them.

As they work, writers engage in a variety of activities—thinking, planning, organizing, writing, revising, rethinking. For clarity, we label the various stages in the process prewriting, writing, and revising. However, the stages are not so straightforward and separate. One blends into the next, and sometimes a writer returns to a previous activity, moving back and forth through the process. When you write, your goal should be to produce a clear and lively work that expresses interesting ideas. The writing process can help you in that effort.

# Stage 1: Prewriting
## Define Your Task

The first stage in the writing process is prewriting. At this stage, your goal is to choose a topic, to figure out what you are going to say about it, and to decide what style and tone you are going to use. Making these decisions is essential if you are going to write something interesting and to express your ideas clearly and vividly. At this stage you jot down thoughts and ideas—the material that you will eventually organize and write about in detail. During the prewriting stage, you should search for answers to the following questions:

**What Will I Write About?** This question must be answered before you do anything else. You need to choose a topic. Then you need to *focus* the topic. A focused topic directs your thinking as you write. This is important whether you are writing a brief description, a short story, an essay, or a research paper. Deciding just what issues you want to address, what kind of character you want to develop, or what theme and events you want a story to revolve around will focus your thinking and help you create a bright, strong piece of writing.

A careful decision is called for here. A good topic is neither too broad nor too narrow. The length of what you are writing and your purpose for writing often dictate how broad your focus should be. In an essay or a research paper, for instance, you need to choose a topic that's defined enough to explore in depth. You don't want to choose a topic that's so broad that you can only touch on the main ideas. If your assignment is to write a short story, you'll want to focus on perhaps one main relationship between characters, one important conflict, just a few related events.

You can then write in detail to create full, interesting characters and a well-developed story. When you need to focus a topic, think about what would be practical for the given task.

**What Do I Want to Say?** You need to think about what information you want or need to include, and what ideas you want to communicate.

**What Is My Purpose for Writing?** Will you try to persuade, to inform, to explain, or to entertain your readers?

**What Style Will I Use?** Do you want to write formally or in a casual, conversational style? Will you use the first person, I, or the third-person, he, she, or they? Will you write seriously or use jokes and humor? If you are writing a story, will you use dialogue?

**How Will I Organize My Ideas?** What will you start with? In what order will you present and develop your ideas?

**Who Is My Audience?** Who will be reading your work? Are you writing for other students? For people who already have some background in the subject? For people who know nothing about the subject? For children or for adults? Your audience will dictate the approach you take—whether you will write in a formal or an informal tone, whether you will provide a lot of background information or very little, what kind of words you will use.

## Generate and Organize Ideas

Although most of the writing assignments in this book provide fairly specific directions about the type of writing to be done, they leave lots of room for imagination. By using your imagination, you can discover fresh and exciting ideas that are distinctly yours. How can you come up with those bright ideas? Below are some techniques that can help you tap your creative powers. They can help you at the prewriting stage and any time you need to generate new ideas. You might use them to come up with a topic for a research paper, an essay, or a short story. You might use them to focus a topic or to generate ideas about a topic you've already chosen. Techniques such as outlining and clustering are also useful for organizing ideas. Try each of the techniques, and eventually you'll find the ones that work best for you for a particular purpose.

**Free Writing.** Have you ever been given a writing assignment and found that you had no idea what to write? Free writing is an activity for getting started—for coming up with ideas to write about. To free write, write anything that comes to mind, no matter how far off the topic it seems. At first it may seem silly, but eventually your mind will start associating ideas. Soon you will be writing complete thoughts about the topic.

Suppose you were asked to write about winter. How to begin? Start writing. Put down the first thought that comes to mind and let ideas begin to flow. You might come up with something like this:

> I don't know what to write. Winter. What can I say that hasn't already been said about winter? It's cold, there's lots of snow . . . well, not in all places I guess. Actually when it's cold here, it's warm on the other side of the world. Do they call that winter then, or summer . . . ?

Can you see how you might go from thoughts that are totally off the track to thoughts that are intriguing? When you have finished, look at all the ideas you've written down. Perhaps there are whole sentences or paragraphs that can go into your story or essay. This exercise will have gotten you started.

**Brainstorming.** This also is an activity to generate ideas. It can be done alone or in a group. When brainstorming, you want to come up with as many ideas as possible. Each idea will spur a new idea. As you or others in a brainstorming group think of ideas, write them down. After you have come up with all the ideas you can, select several to develop for the assignment.

**Clustering.** This technique can be useful both to generate ideas and to organize them. In fact, you actually do both at the same time, for as you jot down ideas, you "cluster" the ones that go together.

Begin by putting your main idea—your focused topic—in the center of the page and circling it. As you think of ideas associated with the main idea, write them nearby, circle them, and connect them with a line to the main idea. Then, as you think of ideas related to each of those *subtopics,* attach the ideas to the word they relate to. You can take this process as far as you like. The farther you branch out, the more detailed you get. When you get to the point where you're ready to write your story or your essay, you can use such a diagram as a guide to grouping your ideas. A simple clustering diagram is shown below. The main idea is "symbols in a story."

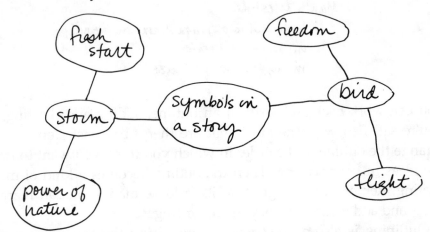

**Outlining.** Outlining is usually thought of as an organizing tool, but it also provides a useful form in which to write down ideas as you think of them. It gives you a way to group ideas, just as clustering does. In addition, it helps you to organize those groups of ideas—to arrange them in the order in which you think you would like to write about them.

Start by writing down some main ideas that you want to include. Leave space after each one for listing related facts or thoughts—details— that you will want to include about the topic. Each idea you list will probably make you think of another idea. Look at the following example. Imagine that your assignment is to write a character sketch. You think you'd like to write about an old man. That's a main idea, so you write it down. One of the aspects of the man you want to talk about is his lifestyle. That, too, is a main idea, so you leave some space after your first idea and write it down. Okay, you ask yourself, what is the old man like? List each specific detail under the first main idea. Go on and do the same with lifestyle, and whatever other main ideas you may have.

*Character Sketch*

Old Man
 about 80 years old
 tall, thin, straight
 athletic
 friendly, outgoing

Man's Lifestyle
 lives in his own apartment in the city
 involved in theater
 many friends of all ages

You can work back and forth in an outline, adding and deleting, until you're satisfied with the ideas that are there. Your last step will be to arrange the outline in the order in which you think you want to present the ideas in your writing. Then the outline becomes a kind of map for writing. Remember, though, that it's a loose map—you can rearrange, drop, and add ideas even as you are writing.

Outlining is also a good way of organizing the ideas you generate through brainstorming and free writing. It helps you place those ideas in some kind of order.

## Stage 2: Writing

The second stage in the writing process is the writing itself. At this stage, you write a first draft of your paper or story, using the notes or outline that you developed in the prewriting stage as a guide. This is the stage at which you turn those loose ideas into sentences and paragraphs that work together.

**Get Your Thoughts on Paper.** When you begin writing, the most important thing to focus on is saying what you want to say—getting all your ideas down on paper in sentences and paragraphs. Some people find it easiest to write their first drafts without worrying if they have chosen exactly the right words and without checking on spelling. Just put a question mark next to anything you aren't sure of and check it later. You can even put a blank in a sentence if you can't think of the right word to put there. Fill it in when you revise.

As you are writing, you may discover that you sometimes have to go back and do some more thinking and planning. You may need to gather more information or think through an idea again. You may also do some rearranging of ideas.

**Develop a Tone.** In the writing stage, you need to begin to develop a tone—an attitude toward your subject. How do you want to *sound* to the reader? What impression do you want the reader to have toward the subject? Do you want to sound authoritative, amusing, sad, pleased?

You'll want to establish your tone right away—in the first paragraph. The first paragraph is important because it must grab your reader's interest and show where you are headed.

**Organize Your Writing.** As you write, you will, of course, be following the basic rules of the language. Sentences should express complete thoughts. They should follow one another in logical order. Each paragraph should focus on one main idea, and it should contain details that support that idea.

As you move from one paragraph to the next, use transition words and phrases to link your ideas. Clearly connect ideas and thoughts that go together so the reader can follow your story, argument, or explanation.

# Stage 3: Revising

The third stage in the writing process is revising. This is the point at which you look for ways to polish your writing. Revising is more than just fixing a few errors. It can involve both major and minor changes.

## Rethink Ideas and Organization

The first goal in revising is to check for clear, logical expression. Does what I have written make sense? Have I clearly said everything I am trying to say? Have I arranged my ideas in the best order?

Reread the entire draft to see if paragraphs and sentences follow in a logical order. You may find that putting paragraphs in a different order makes your points clearer. Remember that each paragraph is part of a whole, and it should relate to your topic. Sometimes you may write an excellent paragraph, only to discover that it has very little to do with the topic. No matter how good you think a sentence or a paragraph is, drop it if it doesn't belong.

As you read what you have written, you may also want to rewrite sentences and paragraphs, or even add new material. At this stage, you may also want to go back to your prewriting notes to see that you included everything you wanted to include.

## Look at Your Language

After you have checked the ideas and organization, review the style and form in which you have written. Think about the language—the words and phrases you have used. Do they say precisely what you mean? Do they create strong images?

If you want your writing to be lively and interesting, write with strong verbs and nouns. They make strong writing. If you find yourself piling on the adjectives and adverbs, you'll know that you're struggling to support weak verbs and nouns. What is a strong verb or noun? It is one that is precise, active, fresh. It paints a clear picture in the mind.

**Use Strong Verbs.** Some verbs, for instance, are tired, overused, dull. The verb *to be*, for example, is about the weakest verb in the language. It doesn't *do* anything. So look at the sentences in which you use the verbs *is, are, am, was, have been,* etc. Are there action words that you can use instead? Instead of saying "Sam was happy," might you describe an action that *shows* that Sam was happy? "Sam smiled shyly and nodded his head," "Sam beamed," "Sam grinned," "Sam jumped into the air, arms raised above his head, and shouted, YES!"

**Use Precise Nouns.** Your nouns too should be precise. Whenever possible, create a strong image for the reader. The word *thing*, for instance, is imprecise and overused. What kind of image does it create in your mind? None. Search for the word that *tells*. If you are describing a street scene, for instance, instead of saying that there is a building on the corner, can you tell what kind of building it is? Is it a bank? A three-story Victorian house? A gothic cathedral? An open-air vegetable market? Draw clear pictures with your nouns.

**Don't Overuse Adjectives and Adverbs.** Adjectives and adverbs have their place, but try not to overdo them. When you do find yourself in need of an adjective, choose one that creates a strong image. Avoid those that are overused and don't really describe. *Beautiful* and *nice*, for instance, are overused adjectives.

**Toss Out Unnecessary Words.** Have you used more words than you need to say something? This is known as being redundant. Saying that someone is "bright and intelligent," for instance, is redundant because the adjectives are synonyms. Use one or the other. Another example is the phrase "crucially important." Why not just say "crucial"?

As you examine your language, throw out any words that don't serve a purpose—that don't give information, paint a clear picture, or create atmosphere. By taking out unnecessary words, you will have "tight writing"—writing that moves along.

**Check the Structure and Rhythm of Your Sentences.** Read your work out loud and listen to the rhythm and sounds of the language. Do the sentences all sound the same? If they do, can you vary the structure of your sentences—making some simple, some complex, some long, some short? Correct any sentence fragments, and divide run-on sentences into two or more sentences.

After you've gone through that kind of thinking a few times at the revision stage, you'll find yourself automatically choosing livelier, clearer language as you write. You'll become a better writer. That, too, is a process.

## Check for Errors

The final step in the revising process is the all-important "housekeeping" review—checking for correct spelling, grammar, and punctuation, and for readable handwriting. You don't, of course, have to wait until the end of the writing process to pay attention to those details. But before you write your final draft, check carefully for errors in those areas.

# *Checklist for the Writing Process*

✓ What is my topic? Is it focused enough? Should I broaden or narrow it?

✓ What do I want to say about the topic? What are my thoughts, feelings, and ideas about it?

✓ Which prewriting activity or activities would most help me to gather ideas?

✓ Do I need to do some research? Some reading? Consult outside sources? What other materials, if any, do I need?

✓ What is the main point or idea that I want to communicate? What ideas are secondary? Which of those ideas are most important?

✓ What details will I include to support and expand on the main ideas?

✓ Should I include examples or anecdotes?

✓ How will I organize my ideas?

✓ What is my purpose for writing? Do I want to entertain? Inform? Explain? Persuade? Perhaps a combination?

✓ Who is my audience?

✓ What kind of language will I use? Will I be formal, informal, or casual? Will I use dialogue? Will I speak directly to the reader?

✓ What tone do I want to take—what feeling do I want to give the reader about the subject? How can I sustain that tone throughout my writing?

✓ How can I effectively begin my first paragraph? Should I use a question? A startling or unusual fact? An amazing statistic? Should I begin with an action or a description? Perhaps a piece of dialogue?

✓ How will I end? If writing nonfiction, should I summarize what I have already said, or should I offer a new thought or argument as my conclusion?

- ✓ Have I developed my ideas in the best order possible? Should I move some paragraphs around?

- ✓ Have I covered my topic adequately? Does the writing fulfill its purpose and get the main point across to my audience?

- ✓ Do I need to rewrite parts? Perhaps some ideas need to be clarified or explained further. Perhaps I could write a better description or account of an event?

- ✓ Do I want to add anything?

- ✓ Are there any unnecessary ideas or details that should be deleted?

- ✓ Is each paragraph well developed—are the facts and ideas presented in a good order?

- ✓ Do all the sentences in each paragraph relate to one idea?

- ✓ Are the ideas between sentences and between paragraphs connected with transition words and phrases that make the connections clear?

- ✓ Is the writing vivid? Have I used active, precise, colorful words that create strong images?

- ✓ Does the final paragraph provide a good ending?

- ✓ Are the sentences well constructed? Are there any run-ons or sentence fragments that need fixing? Do I vary the kinds of sentences—some long, some short, some active, some passive?

- ✓ Is the grammar correct?

- ✓ Are all the words spelled correctly?

- ✓ Is all the punctuation correct?

- ✓ Is the final draft clean and legible?

- ✓ Have I read the final draft over one last time to check for any errors that may have crept in as I was copying?

# Glossary of Literary Terms

This glossary includes definitions for all the important literary terms introduced in this book. The first time they are defined and discussed in the text, the terms are underlined. Following each term in the glossary is a page reference (in parentheses) that tells the page on which the term is introduced.

Many terms are discussed in more than one chapter, especially as they apply to various selections. This glossary provides the fullest definition of each term. Boldfaced words within the definitions are other terms that appear in the glossary.

**act** (page 3) a major section of a play.

**aside** (page 98) a speech in which a character expresses his or her thoughts in words not meant to be heard by other **characters** onstage.

**characterization** (page 37) the methods by which a writer develops a character's personality. Four common methods of characterization are (1) giving a physical description, (2) showing a character's actions, (3) revealing a character's thoughts and words, and (4) showing how one character feels about another.

**characters** (page 7) the people that act and speak in a play. The word *character* also refers to the personalities of those individuals.

**circumlocution** (page 232) an indirect way of saying something. It often involves using many more words than necessary to express an idea. Writers sometimes use circumlocution as a method of adding humor to a work.

**cliché** (page 232) an expression or an idea that has become stale from overuse.

**climax**  (page 40)  the third part of the **plot:** the point of highest tension and greatest interest for the audience. The climax is usually the turning point in the play.

**comedy**  (page 227)  a play that causes laughter and ends happily.

**conflict**  (page 40)  a struggle or tension between opposing forces that is central to the **plot** of the play. *See* **external conflict** and **internal conflict.**

**dialogue**  (page 36)  the actual conversation between the characters.

**drama**  (page 3)  the kind of literature designed for the theater. Actors take the roles of the **characters,** perform the assigned actions, and speak the written words.

**dramatic irony**  (page 98)  the contrast that occurs when the audience has information or an understanding of events that a character or **characters** in a play do not have. Dramatic irony adds **suspense** to a play because the audience wonders when the characters will learn the truth. *See* **irony.**

**exaggeration**  (page 285)  an intentional overstatement of facts or events so that their meanings are intensified. Exaggeration is not meant to deceive the audience but to create humorous results.

**exposition**  (page 40)  the first part of the **plot** in which the playwright introduces the **characters** and **conflicts,** and provides whatever background information is necessary to the story. The exposition often presents information about the **setting.**

**external conflict**  (page 194)  a struggle between a person and an outside force. The four kinds of external conflict are (1) conflict between people, (2) conflict between a person and society, (3) conflict between groups, and (4) conflict between a person and the forces of nature. *See* **conflict.**

**falling action**  (page 40)  the fourth part of the **plot** in which the tension eases and the action begins to slow down. The falling action leads to the **resolution.**

**farce** (page 265) a type of **comedy** designed to provoke the audience to simple, hearty laughter. It contains ridiculous **characters** and improbable situations. A farce often relies on verbal and physical humor.

**foreshadowing** (page 195) the use of hints, clues, or signs to suggest events that are going to happen later on in the play. Foreshadowing is a device used by writers to build **suspense.**

**internal conflict** (page 194) a struggle that takes place entirely within a person's mind. *See* **conflict.**

**irony** (page 98) the contrast between appearance and reality or between what is expected and what actually happens. *See* **dramatic irony, situational irony,** and **verbal irony.**

**monologue** (page 96) an extended speech delivered by one character. A monologue is heard but uninterrupted by the other character or **characters.**

**mood** (page 227) the general feeling or atmosphere of a play.

**narration** (page 257) the kind of writing that gives the events and actions of the story.

**parody** (page 202) a kind of humorous writing in which a writer imitates another, more serious piece of literature.

**plot** (page 7) the sequence of events in a piece of writing. A plot usually has five sections: **exposition, rising action, climax, falling action,** and **resolution.**

**props** (page 257) the movable articles, other than costumes and scenery, used in a play. The word *props* is a shortened version of *properties.*

**pun** (page 233) a play on words that have similar sounds but very different meanings.

**resolution** (page 40) the last part of the **plot:** the conclusion of the play. The resolution contains the outcome of the **conflict.**

**rhetoric** (page 100) the art of using words effectively to sway an audience's opinions.

**rising action** (page 40) the second part of the **plot** in which the tension builds and complications develop. During the rising action, the **conflict** increases and the action moves toward the **climax.**

**satire** (page 285) the kind of writing in which certain aspects of human behavior are ridiculed by the writer. A writer often satirizes foolish ideas, customs, or human weaknesses by using **exaggeration.**

**screenplay** (page 357) the script prepared for a movie production. The screenplay usually includes **technical directions** in addition to the play.

**setting** (page 195) the time and place of the action of a story. Many playwrights establish the setting through **stage directions** in the **exposition.**

**situational irony** (page 259) a type of **irony** in which what happens is different from what the audience expects or what the **characters** expect.

**skit** (page 155) a comic sketch. A skit is often included as part of a longer show or revue.

**slapstick** (page 285) the kind of humor that depends on fast, foolish action to make people laugh.

**soliloquy** (page 96) a speech in which a character speaks his or her thoughts aloud while alone.

**sound effects** (page 321) the sounds called for in the script of a play, radio or television program, or motion picture.

**stage directions** (page 158) any information that is intended for the director, the actors, or the readers of a play. Stage directions are separate from the **dialogue** and are often printed in *italics.*

**stereotype**  (page 228) a stock character who matches a fixed idea held by a number of people. A stereotype conforms to a certain pattern and lacks individuality.

**subplot**  (page 41) the secondary series of events in a story that is woven into the main **plot.**

**suspense**  (page 97) the interest, excitement, and anticipation the reader or the audience feels about what will happen in the play. *See* **fore-shadowing.**

**symbol**  (page 197) an image, an object, or a person that stands for something other or more important than itself.

**technical directions**  (page 329) instructions telling the camera crew, sound crew, and actors how the scenes and sounds should be presented to the viewers.

**theme**  (page 107) the underlying message or central idea of a piece of writing.

**tragedy**  (page 107) a play that involves serious and important actions which turn out disastrously for the main character or **characters.**

**verbal irony**  (page 290) a type of **irony** in which a writer or a character says one thing but means something entirely different.